Service Agreements

Service Agreements

Alan J Julyan

Solicitor, Speechly Bircham

Sixth Edition

LONGMAN

Published by
Longman Law, Tax and Finance
21–27 Lamb's Conduit Street
London WC1N 3NJ

Associated offices
Australia, Hong Kong, Malaysia, Singapore, USA

British Library Cataloguing in Publication Data
Julyan, Alan
Service agreements in employment. – 6th ed.
1. Labor contract – Great Britain
I. Title II. Aldridge, Trevor M.
Service agreements
344.106'24 KD 3096

ISBN 0–85121–699 4

Phototypeset by Input Typesetting Ltd, London
Printed in Great Britain by
Biddles of Guildford Ltd

Contents

Part IV: Safeguards for Employer

Part V: Termination

Part VI: Overseas Employment

Part VII: Precedents of Agreements and Checklists

Preface to Sixth Edition

Written service agreements with some degree of formality can offer considerable advantages to both employers and employees. They both benefit from the advantage of the certainty that a written agreement offers, which is the more important the longer the period of employment lasts. The agreement can be used to define the circumstances and periods of notice that will have to be given to terminate the employment. The agreement will also define the fringe benefits the employee is to receive and to impose restrictions on the employee to protect the employer's goodwill and trade secrets.

This book seeks to take the subject of service agreements beyond the statutory requirements of written particulars, although they are not ignored, into the realms where the agreement offers real benefits. As well as examining the law, there is considerable emphasis on drafting. Many sections end with a summary of the principles to be considered when drafting clauses on that topic, followed by specimen clauses. There are five complete precedent service agreements in the last part of the book, which both illustrate the use of the specimen clauses, and show how they can and need to be adapted to meet individual circumstances. There are also checklists to give guidance on what information needs to be obtained when drafting a service agreement and restraint of trade clauses.

The sixth edition of the book is a complete revision of the fifth edition and incorporates such provisions that have come into force since 1986.

Table of Cases

Table of Statutes

Part I

Written Agreements

Chapter 1

Use of Written Agreements

1.1 When required

There are very few cases in which the law requires an employment contract to be made in writing. These are dealt with below. Sometimes certain provisions only of a service agreement need be in writing. There are other cases in which statutory rules have a similar effect.

Almost every employer must give his employee written particulars of certain of the terms and conditions of his employment. A document which strictly complies with this statutory requirement, but does no more, does not constitute a contract. It gives details of an existing contract, and it can often be used as evidence of the terms of that agreement. Unfortunately, because it causes unnecessary confusion, statutory statements are commonly referred to by employers and employees as contracts. The need for a statement does, however, provide an incentive for drawing up full written service agreements. An agreement which deals with all the terms the Act requires to be mentioned can take the place of a statutory statement, dealing as well with other points the parties wish to record, in a single document.

There are other statutory requirements about employment contracts which can only satisfactorily be complied with if the agreement is in writing, even though that is not an express requirement. The prime example relates to those directors' agreements which have to be available for inspection. A memorandum of the terms of an oral agreement can be used, but again it is simpler to reduce the agreement to writing from the start.

1.1.1 Seamen

An agreement to employ a merchant seaman in a ship registered in the United Kingdom must be in writing. There is a single agreement with the whole crew ('crew agreement'), except in cases where the Department of Trade otherwise permits. That composite document constitutes the separate agreements between the employer and each crew member. The form of agreement must be approved by the Department of Trade, and it signed by each seaman and by or on behalf of the employer (Merchant Shipping Act 1970, s 1). There are exceptions which exempt crews on smaller ships from this requirement, and regulations about displaying the terms of a crew agreement (Merchant Shipping (Crew Agreements, Lists of Crew and Discharge of Seamen) Regulations 1972; Merchant Shipping (Crew Agreements, Lists of Crew and Discharge of Seamen) (Fishing Vessels) Regulations 1972).

1.1.2 Apprentices and trainee solicitors

A contract of apprenticeship must probably be in writing, unless statute otherwise provides (*Kirkby* v *Taylor* [1910] 1 KB 529). The form of apprenticeship deeds and agreements was dealt with by an Act of Elizabeth I (5 Eliz 1, c4), which was partially repealed and amended by the Apprentices Act 1814. The precise effect of this legislation is uncertain. 'The exact extent of the repeal and of the subsequent enactment is not free from obscurity' (*McDonald* v *John Twiname Ltd* [1953] 2 QB 304, 313 per Lord Evershed MR). An agreement which is not executed with due formality may nevertheless be binding. What purported to be an apprenticeship deed was enforced even though the employer 'executed' it merely by applying to the document a rubber stamp bearing its name. ' . . . the [employers] regarded themselves as governed in their relations to the [apprentice] by the terms of the deed, and they took the benefit of it' (ibid, p 314, per Evershed MR).

The regulations as to the contents and registration of the articles of trainee solicitors can only be complied with if the articles are in writing and contain certain specific terms as laid down by the Law Society.

1.1.3 Stoppages

Deductions from wages are governed by the Wages Act 1986, which repealed the Truck Acts. The Wages Act 1986 provides that employers and employees can agree to the payment of wages in any form they wish. Given the imbalance of the negotiating position between an employer and an employee, in practice the employer will stipulate, in the contract of employment, how wages will be paid and what deductions are going to be made from the employee's wages. If the employee wishes to secure employment then he will be bound to accept the conditions being imposed upon him. There are, however, certain specific restrictions giving protection to workers in the retail trades.

Employees have a right to receive an itemised pay Statement (s 8 the Employment Protection Consolidation Act 1978) which he or she must receive 'at or before' every payment of wages or salary. The statement must be in writing and contain certain specified information comprising; gross pay, deductions and net pay.

The Wages Act 1986 provides that an employer is not entitled to make deductions from the wages of any worker unless certain conditions are met. The deductions are authorised if they are required by virtue of any statutory provision or authorised by a specific provision of the worker's contract, or previously agreed to or consented to (in writing) by the worker. In the case of *Pename Ltd* v *Paterson* [1989] IRLR 195, the employee was told at his interview that if he left without giving notice he would forfeit one week's wages. This was repeated in his letter of appointment. However, it was held that, as the employee had never signified his acceptance in writing, the subsequent deduction was unlawful when the employer refused to pay the employee when he left without giving notice.

Workers are defined by s 8 of the Act as individuals working under (a) a contract of service, (b) a contract of apprenticeship, or (c) any other contract whereby the individual undertakes to do or perform personally any work or service or services for another party to the contract whose status is not by virtue of the contract that of a client or customer of any profession or business undertaking carried on by the individual. It is interesting to note the wide definition of 'worker'.

Wages are broadly defined as covering 'any sums payable to the worker by his employer in connection with his employment'. One must presume that this encompasses fees, commissions and payments made under statute, such as statutory sick pay. Excluded from the definition are payments by ways of loans, or advance wages, expenses, pension or allowances or gratuities in connection with retirement, redundancy payment, and any payment to the worker otherwise than in his capacity as a worker (Wages Act 1986 s 7(2)). However, special provision is made for non-contractual bonuses which are for the purposes of the Act deemed to be wages.

1.1.4 London cab drivers

An agreement for a cab driver in London to hand over the takings to his employer must be in writing to be enforceable (London Hackney Carriages Act 1843, s 23). The remainder of his service agreement need not be in writing.

1.1.5 Intellectual property

An employer sometimes wants to use a service agreement to effect the transfer to him from the employee of patents and copyrights. This requires writing. A patent or an application for one is personal property (Patents Act 1977, s 30). A patent must, however, be assigned by an instrument under seal, because it is granted under seal (*Stewart* v *Casey* (1891) 9 RPC 9, 11). An assignment of a copyright must be in writing (Copyright Designs and Patents Act 1988, s 90 (3)).

1.1.6 Covenants in restraint of trade

Where an employer wishes to impose restrictions on an employee's activities following the termination of his employment, it is necessary that the terms of such restrictions be recorded in writing. As the courts will construe the terms restrictively, precise drafting is essential to ensure the best chance of them being enforced.

1.1.7 Excluding statutory rights

The statutory rights to compensation for unfair dismissal and to redundancy payments can, in one type of case, be excluded by agreement between the employer and the employee, so long as the agreement is in writing. The employee must be employed for a fixed term of one year or more. This period remains valid despite the extension of the qualification period for protection from unfair dismissal from one year to two years for employees employed after 1 June 1985 (Unfair Dismissal (Variation of Qualifying Period) Order 1985 (SI 1985/782)). The rights can only be excluded to the extent that they arise as a result of the fixed term expiring and not being renewed (Employment Protection (Consolidation) Act 1978, s 142 as amended by the Employment Act 1980).

A suitable clause would be:

Exclusion of statutory rights

Pursuant to s 142(1) and (2) of the Employment Protection (Consolidation) Act 1978, the Executive hereby agrees that no rights shall rise under ss 54 and 81 respectively of that Act in relation to this Agreement if the term of the Executive's employment under it expires without being renewed.

1.2 When desirable

The possible advantages of a written service agreement, in cases in which one is not strictly required, may be summarised:

1.2.1 Certainty of terms

Whenever it is necessary to reply upon an oral contract, success in enforcing it always depends on the recollections of the parties. Written agreements in a standard form ensure uniformity of terms for all employees of one employer, or all the employees in a particular category.

Also, should the employee bring a claim for wrongful dismissal against the employer, it will be necessary for him or her to establish the losses suffered. The employee will only be able to claim the loss of contractual benefits and therefore it is important that the benefits the employee enjoys as of right are stated clearly in the service agreement.

1.2.2 Employee reference

Fewer disputes between employer and employee are likely if the employee knows and understands precisely the terms on which he is employed, and can refresh his memory of them when necessary. This is not only a reason for having a written agreement, but also for including in it expressly some of the terms which would otherwise be implied, eg the employee's obligation of fidelity.

1.2.3 Confidential information

Where an employee is engaged in work which affords him access to trade secrets and confidential information equivalent to trade secrets, it is important that the employee understands his obligation to preserve the confidentiality of that information and that the nature of the information is clearly defined.

1.2.4 Third party rights

When a service agreement confers rights on a third party, eg on the employee's widow, it should be in writing for his or her benefit. The third party, unless present when the bargain was struck, will necessarily never be able to give evidence as to the terms agreed orally.

1.2.5 Long term agreements

A contract for long term employment will increase the difficulties for the employer of providing evidence of its terms. The employee will be available, to give evidence of terms orally agreed, throughout the period of employment. The employer, or the relevant officer of the employing company, may well change.

1.2.6 Superseding statutory statement

The need to give almost every employee a written statement of particulars of his contract of employment can be seen as an argument against a full, formal, written service agreement. However, any employer who wants to make and record terms outside the statutory minimum list of matters to be included can avoid the need for two documents, by making a full written agreement which can take the place of the statutory statement.

1.2.7 Inventions

Although the Patents Act 1977 governs the ownership of inventions, and it is not possible to deprive the employee of his rights under that Act, it can be helpful to have a clear job description which reflects the employee's normal duties where he is likely to invent or improve products within the scope of his employment.

1.3 Formalities

1.3.1 Deed

It is not generally necessary for a service agreement to be executed as a deed. If it is, the normal limitation period for enforcing the covenants under it is extended from six years to twelve (Limitation Act 1980, s 8).

A company need not execute a service agreement under its common seal. As individuals can contract in writing, a company can validly be committed to a binding written service agreement by a person acting under its authority, express or implied (Companies Act 1985, s 36). The same rule applies to other corporations (Corporate Bodies Contracts Act 1960, s 1(1)).

A deed is necessary or desirable in these cases:

(i) *A director's service agreement.* Because of a director's close involvement with the management of a company, it is advisable for the agreement between the two to be evidenced with formality to ensure its validity.

(ii) An agreement which assigns a patent (*Stewart* v *Casey* (1891) 9 RPC 9, 11).

By s 130 of the Companies Act 1989, there are now two alternative ways in which a company can execute a document as a deed. It can either affix its common seal; which in most cases can only be used by the authority of the directors or, where the company has no seal, the document can be validly executed if signed by a director and the secretary of the company, or by two directors, and is expressed to be executed by the company. It must be made clear on the face of the document that it is intended to be a deed. In the former case, the testimonium and attestation clause would read as follows:

IN WITNESS whereof the parties hereto have executed this Agreement as a Deed the day and year first above written.

Signed.
Director.
Company Secretary.

1.3.2 Stamp duty

A service agreement is not as such liable to stamp duty (Finance Act 1964, s 23). This also applies to statutory statements of terms of employment.

It is possible for a service agreement also to fall into some other category for stamp duty purposes, eg it may also constitute a tenancy agreement of accommodation let to the employee. The general rule is that a document is to be stamped 'for its leading and principal object', and that stamp duty covers everything ancillary (*Limmer Asphalte Paving Co* v *IRC* (1872) LR 7 Exch 211). A single instrument may fall to be stamped under either of two heads, in which case the Crown is entitled to opt for the higher duty (*Speyer Brothers* v *IRC* [1908] AC 92).

Chapter 2

Capacity of Parties

2.1 Corporations

2.1.1 Limited companies

The powers of a company are defined by the objects clause of its memorandum of association. The former strict rule was that unless a contract related to the carrying on of an activity expressly mentioned in the clause, or necessarily incidental to it, it was void (*Ashbury Railway Carriage Co* v *Riche* (1875) LR 7 HL 653). Service agreements employing people for unauthorised activities were therefore void. The harshness of this rule has now been mitigated in favour of a person dealing with a company in good faith. In such a case, any transaction decided on by the directors is deemed to be one which the company has the capacity to enter into. The employee is not bound to enquire as to the company's capacity or any limitation on the directors' powers to bind the company. He is presumed to have acted in good faith unless the contrary is proved (Companies Act 1985 s 35(2)).

Wide though that exception is, it stops short of abolishing the ultra vires rule. Presumably, anybody who happens to have actual notice of the limits on the company's powers, even if for some other purpose, cannot purport in good faith to contract in ignorance of them. Similarly, it is likely that a director will be assumed to know both the extent of his company's objects and details of any restrictions on the directors' powers. When acting for a company employer it is essential that the memorandum and articles of association are checked to ensure that the company has the power to enter into the contract, and whether or not the matter requires the approval of the shareholders.

A person who purports to make on a company's behalf a service agreement which it is not entitled to enter into may become personally liable to the employee, for breach of warranty of authority. 'If a person requests, and by asserting that he is clothed with the necessary authority, induces another to enter into a negotiation with himself in a transaction with the person whose authority he represents that he has, in that case there is a contract by him that he has the authority of the person with whom he requests the other to enter into the transaction' (*Dickson* v *Reuter's Telegram Co* (1877) 3 CPD 1, 5 per Bramwell LJ). Table A of the Companies Act 1985 provides that the board of directors will be empowered to authorise the execution of the agreement on behalf of the company (art 70 of Table A in the Companies (tables A–F) Regulations 1985). Ideally, the employee director concerned should not form part of the quorum or vote when the board of directors meets to approve the terms of his own service agreement.

2.1.2 Other corporations

A body incorporated by royal charter has the unrestricted powers of an individual, unless its charter imposes some limitation. Corporations set up by special Act of Parliament and foreign corporations will normally have their powers defined. The ultra vires rule continues to apply to these bodies. The Companies Act, s 35, applies to companies formed under that Act or companies existing at that date.

2 Unincorporated bodies

2.2.1 Partnerships

One partner can make a service agreement on behalf of his firm, so long as it is in the usual way of the firm's business. The only exception is where the partner actually has no authority from his partners to enter into that contract—because their agreement restricts it—and the prospective employee knows of his lack of authority (Partnership Act 1890, s 5).

It is generally convenient to make the agreement in the firm's name. That makes it binding on the firm and all the partners (s 6). The liability of the partners is joint (s 9).

A firm cannot employ one of its partners. It is normally legally impossible for a person, even jointly with others, to employ himself (*Ellis* v *Joseph Ellis & Co* [1905] 1 KB 324). There is a limited exception: a personal representative can, in his representative capacity, employ himself as an individual (*Rowley, Holmes & Co* v *Barber* [1977] 1 WLR 371). A partnership can employ the wife of one of its partners (*Bernstein* v *Bernstein Brothers* [1969] ITR 106).

The effect of a change in the constitution of the firm upon their employees' service agreements can lead to doubts. When the partnership is dissolved, at least in the form in which it previously carried on business, service agreements are terminated. This was the effect of two solicitors, who practised in partnership from two offices, deciding to end the partnership so that each practised in future from one of the offices (*Tunstall* v *Condon* [1980] ICR 786). In that case, the Employment Appeal Tribunal suggested that a lesser upheaval with one of a number of partners leaving or dying would not necessarily have the effect of dismissing employees.

Formerly, a stricter view was taken, and it may not have been totally abandoned. The death of a partner dissolves the partnership, unless there is a term to the contrary in the partnership agreement (Partnership Act 1890, s 33(1)). That was held to terminate a service agreement (*Tasker* v *Shepherd* (1861) 6 H&N 575). It was suggested, nevertheless, that that would not be the case if the personality of the deceased partner had no bearing on the employment contract, as where the employee did not even know the identity of the partners. '. . . it must be determined in each case whether the obligations which it is sought to enforce depended upon the personal conduct of the deceased party' (*Phillips* v *Alhambra Palace Co* [1901] 1 KB 59, 62–3 per Lord Alverstone CJ). The retirement of a partner has also been held to end a service agreement and constitute wrongful dismissal (*Brace* v *Calder* [1895] 2 QB 253).

These doubts may not make a great deal of practical difference to where the business of the partnership continues and where it may be that a 'transfer of an undertaking' has occurred within the meaning of the Transfer of Undertakings (Protection of Employment) Regulations 1981 (SI 1981/1794). The employee who stays in his job, under the newly constituted firm, exonerates the old firm from any penalty for the notional wrongful dismissal (*Hobson* v *Cowley* (1858) 27 LJ Ex 205). An offer of employment on the same terms by the new firm will normally reduce any damages payable to a nominal amount or eliminate them (*Brace* v *Calder* [1895] 2 QB 253). A change in the composition of the employing partnership does not break the continuity of an employee's employment for the purposes of the statutory rights (Employment Protection (Consolidation) Act 1978, Sched 13, para 17(5)).

It may be that a partnership can enter into a service agreement as employees, rather than as employer. This point has been left open (*E Rennison & Son* v *Minister of Social Security* (1970) 10 KIR 65).

2.2.2 Clubs

An unincorporated body, such as a club, which is not carrying on a business with a view to profit cannot be a partnership within the statutory definition (Partnership Act 1890, s 1). The rules relating to a partnership's contracts do not therefore apply to it. Such a body has no power to enter into an agreement, except as one entered into by or on behalf of its constituent members. On the facts, a contract may only bind the members of the committee managing the club (*Bradley Egg Farm Ltd* v *Clifford* [1943] 2 All ER 378). The rules of a club could give the authority of each member of the committee to contract on his or her behalf, in which case a contract would bind all members.

Where one of the individuals who together constitute the employer changes, this would normally discharge the contract in the same way as on a change of partners: one of the contracting parties is disclaiming further liability, which on the face of it must be a repudiation of the contract. This conclusion is scarcely practical where the employer is a club with a large membership. It may be that an employee knowingly taking a job with a club of that size waives his right to treat every change in membership as a discharge of his contract.

These and any other difficulties stemming from lack of incorporation may be solved, without the club itself becoming a corporate body, by the incorporation of a service company to take over the administration of the club including the employment of staff.

2.2.3 Trade unions

A trade union is in an anomalous position, because it is not a corporate body, and yet it is capable of making contracts. It can sue and be sued in its own name (Trade Union and Labour Relations Act 1974, s 2(1) (*a*), (*c*)).

When a union's rules contain appropriate provisions relating to the employment of its employees, those employees can be bound by those terms which are implied into their service agreements (*Taylor* v *National Union of Seamen* [1967] I WLR 532). This may require the union's executive committee, or whatever other body exercises disciplinary powers as employer, to abide by the rules of natural justice (*Stevenson* v *United Road Transport Union* [1977] ICR 893).

2.3 Governments

2.3.1 The Crown

There is no limit on the Crown's capacity to enter into service agreements, but, having done so, it enjoys certain anomalous privileges. Without a statutory provision to the contrary—as in the case of High Court judges—no contract can curb the Crown's prerogative to dismiss an employee at will (*Terrell* v *Secretary of State for the Colonies* [1953] 2 QB 482). A Crown employee cannot successfully sue for his pay (*Lucas* v *Lucas* [1943] P68; *Kodeeswaran* v *Attorney General of Ceylon* [1970] AC 1111), nor for superannuation (*Nixon* v *Attorney General* (1930) 47 TLR 95), and he is not entitled to a statutory redundancy payment. He can, however, claim compensation for unfair dismissal, unless employed in the armed forces, or in a job specified by a Minister of the Crown as excluded to safeguard national security (Employment Protection (Consolidation) Act 1978, s 138(1), (3), (4)).

A Crown employee is fully bound by his contract of employment (*Hearson* v *Churchill* [1892] 2 QB 144).

2.3.2 Foreign governments

The traditional rule that no legal action could be taken against a foreign government unless it voluntarily submitted to the jurisdiction of our courts (*Taylor* v *Best* (1854) 14 CB 487) has been substantially modified by statute in relation to employment contracts. The general rule now is that a foreign state enjoys no immunity in respect of a contract of employment which it makes in the United Kingdom or under which the employee is to perform his work wholly or partly in the United Kingdom (State Immunity Act 1978, s 4(1)).

To this general rule, there are three possible exceptions (s 4(2)):

(i) When the proceedings are brought, the employee is a national of the employer state.

(ii) When the contract was made the employee was neither habitually resident in the United Kingdom nor a citizen of the United Kingdom and colonies, nor in one of certain categories of British citizen (from 1 January 1983, under the British Nationality Act 1981, a British citizen, a British dependent territories citizen, a British overseas citizen, a British subject under that Act or a British protected person within the meaning of it: Sched 7).

Neither of these two exceptions applies to work for an office, agency or establishment maintained in the United Kingdom for commercial purposes, unless when the service agreement was made the employee was habitually resident in the foreign state (s 4(3)).

(iii) When the parties so agree in writing. This exception does not apply to a case in which United Kingdom law requires the proceedings to be brought before a United Kingdom court, including any tribunal exercising judicial functions (ss 4(4), 22(1)).

2.3.3 Diplomats

Diplomats have full capacity to enter into contracts, but they may enjoy immunity from legal process which prevents contracts being enforced against them. That immunity can be waived. Social security provisions do not affect a diplomat in his capacity as employer, except in the case of private employees who are either foreign nationals or not permanently resident in the United Kingdom and, in either case, are covered by the social security provisions of another country (Diplomatic Privileges Act 1964). The privilege extends to sovereigns and heads of state, the members of their families forming part of their households and their private servants (State Immunity Act 1978, s 20).

2.4 Minors

A person under the age of eighteen can validly enter into a service agreement. On his attaining the age of majority it is voidable if, but only if, it was not for the minor's benefit. '. . . the question has always been . . . whether the contract, when carefully examined in all its terms, is for the benefit of the infant. If it is so, the court before which the question comes will not allow the infant to repudiate it' (*Clements* v *London and North Western Railway Co* [1894] 2 QB 482, 491 per Kay LJ). This does not mean that each and every term of the contract must positively benefit the minor. '. . . it is no objection that the contract contains stipulations and provisions usual in the particular trade, and such as a master may reasonably impose as protection to himself' (*Young* v *Hoffmann Manufacturing Co Ltd* [1907] 2 KB 646, 650 per Cozens-Hardy MR). Whether or not a contact is beneficial to a minor is a question of law (*Flower* v *London and North West Railway Co* [1894] 2 QB 65). If it is not, it is voidable at the instance of the minor, before or immediately after he comes of age.

There are various statutory provisions forbidding or restricting the employment of minors, carrying criminal penalties. These are outside the scope of this book.

A minor can also enter into a service agreement as employer, rather than as employee. Such an agreement can also be voidable when he attains the age of eighteen. The same test applies, whether the contract as a whole is beneficial from his point of view (*Thomas* v *Waldo* (1858) 1 F&F 173).

Chapter 3

Variation of Agreements

3.1 Introduction

The terms of a service agreement cannot be varied without consent. However, service agreements are frequently varied in minor ways, or where some flexibility can be found within a contract term, so that a change can be imposed without a breach of contract, as in the case of *Cresswell* v *The Board of Inland Revenue* [1984] IRLR 190. In this case the employers wished to impose a change in working practice on the employees. The employees refused to accept that change, arguing that it was outside the scope of their original terms of employment. The court held against the employees, stating that employees were expected to adapt themselves to new methods and techniques introduced in the course of their employment. Although it was accepted that the jobs had been altered to some extent by computerisation, the degree of alteration was not sufficient to fall outside the terms of their contract. However, where the changes that are required are more substantial, then certain formalities will have to be complied with.

3.2 Consent

In many cases, when a service agreement is varied, the employee may happily accept the variation even though his consent has not been sought. For instance, every increase in pay is an alteration of the terms of the contract. However, generally to be effective a variation must have the agreement of both parties and be supported by consideration—it cannot be imposed unilaterally. An employer circulating a memorandum stating that all employee's agreements will be subject to termination on one month's notice did not effectively change the conditions of employment of an employee who had been entitled to three months' notice and did not respond. He remained entitled to the longer period (*Cowey* v *Liberian Operations Limited* [1966] 2 Lloyds REP 45 (*Mayors and City of London CT*)). An employer who seeks unilaterally to change employment terms and does not obtain the employee's consent, eg by requiring him to take a cut in wages, repudiates the contract and dismisses the employee (*Marriott* v *Oxford and District Cooperative Society Limited* (No 2) [1970] 1QB 186). When it may be necessary to vary the terms of a contract, it would be advisable to include in the contract an express term to allow certain changes to be made, eg to hours of work, or to the location of the workplace. However, there may be limits to such clauses. In the case of *United Association for the Protection of Trade Limited* v *Kilburn* (17 September 1985 EAT 787/84) a clause was incorporated into the employees contract which read:

> This Handbook constitutes your contract of employment. The Association reserves the right to make alterations to the contract of employment. Such changes will be notified to you . . .

The EAT held that it did not give the employer the freedom to rewrite the contract and their power to unilaterally vary the contract was limited to changes of a minor and non fundamental nature.

Faced with an attempt by his employer to change the contract terms in a non-acceptable way, an employee has several options. He can accept the change, he can treat the contract as at an end, which he is entitled to do because the employer has repudiated it, and finally he can treat it as continuing. If he does adopt the latter option, the terms remain in force unaltered (*WPM Retail Limited* v *Laing* [1978] ICR 787). The significance of this is that the employee who continues to work after a demand for a change in the contract terms cannot automatically be taken to have agreed to the alteration, particularly when the employee has protested about the change.

It becomes a question of fact whether he has agreed to the variation, in which case the contract takes effect in its new form or whether he has not, when it continues unaltered. The continued employment by the employee will not be deemed to be implied consent to the change where the employee has clearly protested against the variation. The Courts will be reluctant to hold that an employee in such a case has given consent. In the case of *Sheet Metal Components Limited* v *Plumridge* [1974] ICR 373, it was said:

the Courts have rightly been slow to find there has been a consensual variation where an employee has been faced with the alternative of dismissal and where the variation has been adverse to his interests.

It was said that it was believed necessary to determine whether the employer and employee had freely and voluntarily agreed to vary their contract.

It is also necessary for some consideration to pass between the parties. Clearly it is insufficient that the variation simply benefits one of the parties to the contract. This can cause particular difficulties when the variation that is at issue is the incorporation of a restraint of trade provision. Quite often it is difficult to establish what consideration passes from the employer to the employee for such a change. In the case of *Norbrook Laboratories Limited* v *J Smith* (*High Court of Justice in Northern Ireland*, 30 September 1986) the Court held that the employer's statement that they would not have continued to employ the employee if he had refused to sign the confidentiality undertaking in issue, was sufficient consideration to support the change. I would suggest a readiness to find consideration in such a situation, may not be accompanied by an equal readiness to find the parties were in some form of equal bargaining position when the clause was imposed. Accordingly, if such changes are contemplated it would be better to link them to other changes which are clearly to the benefit of the employee, eg improved contract benefits. However, where it is thought the consent will not be forthcoming for the variation, an alternative method to secure the change will have to be contemplated.

3.3 Varying contracts without consent

Where it is clear from the outset that it will not be possible to achieve a consensual variation of the terms of the contract, then an alternative method will have to be adopted. The employer has the option of terminating the current contract on giving proper contractual notice and offering the employee a new contract incorporating the desired changes, to operate immediately after the termination of the notice period. To be successful it is important that the termination is unequivocal and that it should not be possible to construe it simply as an attempt to unilaterally vary the original contract (*Burdette-Coutts* v *Hertfordshire County Council* [1984] IRLR 91). In the case of *Rigby* v *Ferodo Limited* [1987] IRLR 61 the employer argued that the notice given to vary the contract terms was a repudiatory breach, which was not accepted on the employee's behalf, but nevertheless ought to be construed as a notice to determine the contract of employment because it was an unequivocal statement that the employers would not continue with the contract under which the employee had been employed. The effect of that argument would be that words which constitute a repudiatory breach if accepted, had to be treated as a lawful determination of the contract on due notice if not accepted. That amounted to saying that the Court should seek to construe an unlawful notice as a lawful one. The Court was not prepared to accept the argument and as the employee had not accepted the breach of his contract, the contract continued on the original terms.

However the consequence of taking such action is that the employer may face claims for unfair dismissal or redundancy. To defend such claims, the employer must establish that the reason for the dismissal is one which falls within the permitted categories of reasons set out in s 57(i)(b) and s 57(ii) of the Employment Protection (Consolidation) Act 1978. It is then necessary for them to show that they have acted fairly and reasonably in treating that reason as a sufficient one for the decision to terminate the contract. The relevant reasons are redundancy or 'some other substantial reason of a kind so as to justify the dismissal of an employee holding the position which the employee held'. This has been given wide interpretation by the Courts. The leading case in this area is that of *Hollister* v *The National Farmers Union* [1979] IRLR 238. Lord Denning MR said that he considered that, provided there was 'some sound, good business reason for the re-organisation' a failure to go along with the new arrangements might constitute some other 'substantial reason'. He added 'it must depend in all the circumstances whether the re-organisation was such that the only sensible thing to do was to terminate the employee's contract unless he would agree to a new arrangement'. For the dismissal to be fair, it is also necessary to show that the employer has sought to consult with the employee about the variation, and has taken his comments into account, before insisting on the change. A failure to consult may not be fatal if the employer can show that it was simply not practical for such consultation to take place. However, if the employer has cogent reasons for implementing the change the Courts are likely to accept the employer's reasons for implementing the change and that the requirements of the business are given greater importance than the interest of the employee.

The employer has greater difficulty in making changes in this way when the changes follow a transfer of a business which has been subject to the Transfer of Undertakings (Protection of Employment) Regulations 1981, when the changes sought are simply to harmonise the terms of employment, unless there is to be a reduction in the numbers in the workforce (*Delabole Slate Limited* v *Berryman* [1985] IRLR 305).

3.4 Duration

A variation to a service agreement which is agreed between the parties can be either temporary or permanent. If it is intended to be permanent, it is in effect an agreement to rescind one contract and substitute another on the varied terms. It makes no difference whether it is looked at as a single contract continuing with altered terms, or a new one being substituted, as the statutory rights which depend on a qualifying period of continuous employment are not prejudiced by a variation in the course of employment by one employer.

There can be confusion of nomenclature when there is a temporary variation. In one case, employers changed from single shift working on Saturdays to double shifts, and later a group of the employees insisted on reverting to single shift working without giving the notice which would have been required to end the contract. The position was summed up: 'that scheme was not intended by the parties to be one which effected a variation of the contractual terms, nor was it intended by the parties to operate so long as the contract of employment operated, or until some new arrangement was mutually arrived at' (*Dorman Long & Co Ltd* v *Carroll* [1945] 2 All ER 567, 569 per Croom-Johnson J). It would be better to say that there was a variation, but that the new term was subject to the condition that it could be cancelled unilaterally on short notice.

Once there is a permanent variation, both parties are bound to observe the contract in that varied form. So, a toolmaker engaged to do day shift work whose contract was subsequently varied to provide that he was permanently employed on night shift, which carried a higher wage, was entitled to insist on continuing to work at night. The employer could not require him to revert to day work (*Simmonds* v *Dowty Seals Ltd* [1978] IRLR 211).

3.5 Formalities

3.5.1 Employees

An agreement generally executed as a deed can only be varied by another deed or by an agreement in writing. Any other service agreement, whether written or oral, can be varied verbally, although it is generally desirable for written agreements to be amended in writing. In the absence of a written agreement setting out the variation, its terms are to be deduced from evidence of any oral arrangement which was made (*Simmonds* v *Dowty Seals Ltd* [1978] IRLR 211).

Any change in the terms of employment of which particulars have to be given in the statutory statement must be notified to the employee, within a month of the change, unless an alternative arrangement complying with the Act has been made (Employment Protection (Consolidation) Act 1978, s 4). Failure to notify an alteration does not prejudice its effectiveness. '. . . there is nothing in section 4 to provide that a change in the contractual terms shall be ineffective between the parties merely because the employer failed to give written notice of the change' (*Parkes Classic Confectionery Ltd* v *Ashcroft* [1973] ITR 43, 46 per Lord Widgery CJ). Equally, as the statement is not in itself a contract, but merely evidence of one, the service of an amended statement is not evidence that the employee has consented to the change, even if the employee does not protest (*Jones* v *Associated Tunnelling Co Ltd* [1981] IRLR 477).

3.5.2 Directors

When the service agreement is to be varied to that of a director of the employer, then the same rules set out in 1.3 and 2.1.1 will apply. The problems of the City Code on takeovers and mergers may also be relevant as the reason prompting the variation in terms is the possibility of an offer being made for the company. Any attempt to improve pay or benefits significantly is likely to be considered 'otherwise than in the ordinary course of business' for the purposes of Rule 21.

3.6 Remedies

3.6.1 Termination of the contract

If the employee chooses to treat the contract as having been repudiated by the employer's attempt to vary the contract, then the employee may have claims for wrongful or unfair dismissal on redundancy depending on the surrounding facts.

3.6.2 The contract continues

Where the employee does not accept the employer's action as repudiating the contract then the employee may bring a claim for damages for breach of contract. If the breach of contract complained of is not capable of being assessed in financial terms, the employee can seek an injunction to prevent the employer bringing the changes into effect, and an order for specific performance requiring the employer to comply with the original terms of the contract or finally an application for a declaration, declaring the parties' legal rights. The best course of action may be to apply for a declaration.

Chapter 4

Statements of Terms: General

4.1 General

4.1.1 Statutory requirements

The Employment Protection (Consolidation) Act 1978 requires that an employer shall, with some exceptions, give every employee a written statement of certain of the terms of his employment (s 1). It must be given not less than thirteen weeks after the employment begins. This does not have to be a continuous period of thirteen weeks. It can be made up by ignoring intervening weeks when the employee was engaged for less than sixteen hours (s 3(1)). Suggestions that it can be accumulated from an aggregate of separate periods of employment are doubted. The thirteen weeks are counted from 'the beginning of an employee's period of employment with an employer'. Dismissal and re-employment, if genuine, seem to start the period running afresh.

There is no prescribed form which the statutory statement must take. The Act simply provides that it shall contain details of any contractual terms on certain specified points. These particulars should therefore relate not only to terms expressly agreed between the parties, but also to any implied by custom, a course of dealing, another document incorporated by reference, or any other source. If the contract contains no terms relating to the matters which have to be mentioned, the document must say so (s 2(1)). In addition, the statement must contain a note concerning disciplinary and grievance procedures.

As an alternative to setting out in detail the particulars required, the statement may refer the employee, in respect of any or all of them, to another document which the employee has reasonable opportunities to read in the course of his employment or which is made reasonably accessible to him in some other way (s 2(3)).

This is particularly useful in respect of complicated matters dealt with in bulky documents, eg pension schemes. There is the additional advantage that if there are changes to information separately recorded, the employer does not have to notify his employees individually, but can merely amend the document to which they were originally referred (s 4(3)). It should be noted that the provision can never relieve the employer of the duty to give every employee a statutory statement. Even if all the details were recorded elsewhere with adequate access for the employee, he would still be entitled to a statement referring him to those details. If the service agreement seeks to refer to or incorporate terms from other documents it is important for the draftsman to have copies of the documents and to ensure that it is intended that the employee should benefit fully under the accepted terms.

Neither party need sign a statutory statement. Some employers ask their employees to sign a duplicate to confirm that they have received a statement. That gives useful evidence that the employer has complied with his statutory duty. The effect of the signature may not be limited to constituting a receipt. Should it be stated to be, or if it can be implied as being, agreement to the terms set out, the nature of the statement may be changed from being evidence of the terms of agreement into being a contract on those terms. In such a case, a statement which inaccurately represents the terms of the original agreement may serve to vary the contract.

An acknowledgment signed by the employee saying, 'I confirm receipt of a new contract of employment dated . . . , which sets out, as required under the Industrial Relations Act 1971 [the terms of which were consolidated by the present Act], the terms and conditions of my employment', made it a binding contract (*Gascol Conversions Ltd* v *Mercer* [1974] ICR 420). In another case, in contrast, '. . . all that the employee did was to sign an acknowledgment that he had received the statement. In no sense did he sign it as a contract or acknowledge the accuracy of the terms of it' (*System Floors (UK) Ltd* v *Domal* [1982] ICR 54, 58 per Browne-Wilkinson J). The statement remained persuasive but not conclusive evidence of the disputed commencement date of the contract.

4.1.2 Effect

Merely to comply with the statute, the statement does itself not have to constitute the contract. For one thing, it does not have to be given to the employee until thirteen weeks after the employment starts. For another, some essential terms of the employment—eg the employee's duties—do not have to be included in it. 'It is, of course, quite clear that the statement . . . is not the contract: it is not even conclusive evidence of the terms of a contract' (*Turriff Construction Ltd* v *Bryant* [1967] ITR 292, 294 per Lord Parker CJ). On the other hand, a full service agreement containing, inter alia, what the Act requires is a substitute for a statement, and renders a separate one unnecessary (Employment Protection (Consolidation) Act 1978, s 5).

It has been suggested that terms referred to in a statement become contractual. 'A notice was issued . . . [as a statutory statement] . . . saying to every man: "Your rate of wages, hours of work, holidays and holiday pay are in accordance with the provisions of the constitution and working rule agreement issued by and under the authority of the National Joint Council". In view of that notice those working rules are not only a collective agreement between the unions and the employers. They are incorporated into the contract of employment of each man' (*Camden Exhibition & Display Ltd* v *Lynott* [1966] 1 QB 555, 563 per Lord Denning MR). That view was not confirmed by the other members of the court of appeal, and it is submitted that it is wrong to the extent that it states that the terms of the collective agreement became terms of the individual employment contracts merely by reason of the statutory statement. They may well already have been terms of the individual contracts, in which case they were properly referred to in the statement. They were in the statement because they were contractual terms, not vice versa, as decided in *Robertson* v *British Gas Corporation* [1983] ICR 351.

4.1.3 Additional contents

Provided a statement of terms of employment deals with the minimum requirements of the Act, there is no restriction on the employer adding other matters. *The Industrial Relations Code of Practice* recommends that employers should give employees information on other matters (para 62). This can conveniently be done in the statutory statement, although other means can be equally appropriate. The additional headings are:

(i) the requirements of the employee's job and to whom he is directly responsible;

(ii) disciplinary rules and procedures and the type of circumstances which can lead to suspension or dismissal. This overlaps the statutory requirement;

(iii) trade union arrangements;
(iv) opportunities for promotion and any training necessary to achieve it;
(v) social or welfare facilities;
(vi) fire prevention and safety and health rules;
(vii) any suggestions schemes.

This guidance does not have the backing of any statutory sanctions. The special jurisdiction for challenging the contents of statutory statements extends only to the items which the Act requires employers to include.

4.1.4 Contracting out

A contractual term, whether in a service agreement or elsewhere, which purports to exclude the employee's right to a statement of the terms of his employment is void (Employment (Consolidation) Act 1978, s 140(1)). The same applies to a term which seeks to preclude an employee from complaining to an industrial tribunal about the absence or inadequacy of a statement.

4.1.5 Variation

In most cases, once a statutory statement has been given, the employer must give the employee written notice of any changes in particulars which have to be included—but not in any which the employer adds voluntarily—within one month. The notice of change is either to be left with the employee, or the employer must ensure that he has reasonable opportunities to read it in the course of his employment, or that it is otherwise reasonably accessible to him (Employment Protection (Consolidation) Act 1978, s 4(1)). As in the case of an original statement, a notice of change may refer to another document to which the employee has reasonable access (s 4(2)). Failure to give the employee notice of variation does not render ineffective the change in the contract terms (*Parkes Classic Confectionery Ltd* v *Ashcroft* [1973] ITR 43).

In two cases in which there is or appears to be a change in the identity of the employer, and no other alteration in employment terms, a notice of change can be given rather than a complete new statutory statement (s 4(4)). This applies first where the employer changes his name but not his identity. Secondly, a notice can be used where a change of employer does not involve a break in the continuity of the employee's employment for statutory purposes, eg on the takeover of a business, a change of partners or the death of an employer whose personal representatives continue the employment (Sched 13, para 7). In that second type of case, the notice of change must give the date on which the employee's continuous period of employment started (s 4(8)).

The cases in which no notice of variation need be given are:

(i) where the original statement referred the employee to another document and said that changes would be made to that document or recorded in some way for those referring to that document, and the variation is made or recorded in that way within one month (s 4(3));

(ii) presumably, if a reduction in the employee's hours of work has made him cease to qualify for a statutory statement.

4.2 Exceptions

An employer is not required to give an employee a statutory statement of terms of employment in a number of cases.

4.2.1 Part time employment

No statutory statement of terms of employment need be given to an employee normally working less than sixteen hours a week. Any such period of part time work does not have to be taken into account when calculating the first thirteen weeks of a job at the end of which the employer must give the statement to the employee (Employment Protection (Consolidation) Act 1978, s 3(1)).

To this, there are two artificial exceptions. After an employee has been continuously employed for five years under a contract normally involving employment for between eight and sixteen hours a week, he is treated as employed full time (s 3(4)). He therefore becomes entitled to a statement after being employed for five years and thirteen weeks. The other exception relates to an employee whose hours of work are cut. If they are reduced to between eight and sixteen hours a week, he counts as employed full time for a further twenty-six weeks. The period is extended by: any weeks during which he is actually employed for at least sixteen hours; weeks of strikes, lockouts and layoffs; and weeks when there is no contract of employment but the employee could not work because of sickness, injury, pregnancy or confinement, or by arrangement or custom he is treated as continuing in employment (s 3(2), (3)).

4.2.2 Alternative documents

The need for a statutory statement is normally obviated when an employee is given a formal service agreement. Certain terms have to be observed if the exemption is to apply. This is one of the benefits to be gained from having a formal service agreement. To avoid duplication and unnecessary trouble, care should be taken to ensure that any agreement fulfils the conditions. They are (Employment Protection (Consolidation) Act 1978, s 5):

(i) The contract of employment has been reduced to writing in one or more documents. The service agreement should therefore include or supersede any implied terms which might apply to the employment. This could be an extremely onerous requirement if interpreted literally to mean, eg that the employee's duty of fidelity must be spelled out.

(ii) The agreement contains express terms giving the particulars which a statutory statement must give as to remuneration, hours of work, holidays, holiday pay, sickness and injury, sick pay, pensions and pension schemes, notice and job title.

(iii) A copy of the agreement, and any variation of it, is given to the employee. Alternatively, he has reasonable opportunities to read a copy in the course of his employment, or a copy is made reasonably accessible to him in some other way.

(iv) A note about disciplinary and grievance procedures must also be given to him or made available in the same way.

If at any time these conditions cease to be fulfilled—which in practice must mean that a variation of the contract is not notified to the employee, or the employer ceases to afford him access to a copy of the agreement or note—the duty to give the employee a statutory statement applies within one month.

The other case in which an employee need not be given a statutory statement within thirteen weeks of the start of his employment is where he was employed by the same employer during the previous six months, and the terms are the same (s 2(4)).

4.2.3 Public employment

Employees of the Crown, including members of the armed forces, do not have a right to a statement, because these provisions of the Act are not extended to them (Employment Protection

(Consolidation) Act 1978, s 138(1)). Employment by the national health service is Crown employment for this purpose (*Wood* v *United Leeds Hospitals* [1974] IRLR 204).

Members of the staff of the House of Commons, including the Speaker's personal staff, have no right to a statement (s 139(1)).

4.2.4 Foreign employment

An employee engaged in work wholly or mainly outside Great Britain is not entitled to a statutory statement, unless he ordinarily works in Great Britain and the work outside is for the same employer (Employment Protection (Consolidation) Act 1978, s 141(1)).

The interpretation of this provision has caused difficulty, and early cases have been overruled. The test is not a comparison of the total time the employee spends in Great Britain with the total time spent outside (*Todd* v *British Midland Airways Ltd* [1978] ICR 959). The vital question to answer is: where is the employee based? '. . . the correct approach is to look at the terms of the contract, express and implied, . . . in order to ascertain where, looking at the whole period contemplated by the contract, the employee's base is to be. It is, in the absence of special factors leading to a contrary conclusion, the country where his base is to be which is likely to be the place where he is to be treated as ordinarily working under his contract of employment' (*Wilson* v *Maynard Shipbuilding Consultants AB* [1978] 1 QB 665, 677 per Megaw LJ).

These have been suggested as possible factors in determining from the contract where the employee's base is: the situation of his headquarters; where the employee's travels in his employment begin and end; where his home will be; where and in what currency he is paid; and whether he has to pay national insurance contributions in Great Britain. As far as the travel is concerned, it is suggested that there is an important distinction to be made between travel 'in' the job and travel to it. The fact that an employer undertakes to pay an expatriate's fare to his place of employment abroad and his fare back on repatriation, and even on periodic leaves during his employment, will not of itself make Great Britain his base. On the contrary, it almost emphasises that the base of the employment is overseas, although doubts have been expressed as to the importance to be attached to the base test (*Janata Bank* v *Ahmed* [1981] IRLR 457).

4.2.5 Husbands and wives

No statement need be given to an employee who is the wife or husband of the employer (Employment Protection (Consolidation) Act 1978, s 146(1)). This can only apply where the employer is a single individual. A partnership which employs the wife or husband of one of the partners must comply with the general requirements (*Bernstein* v *Bernstein Brothers* [1969] ITR 106). Similarly, a 'one man company' which employs the controlling shareholder's spouse must give the employee a statement.

4.2.6 Seamen

The right to a statutory statement of terms of employment does not apply to the following (Employment Protection (Consolidation) Act 1978, s 144(1)):

(i) a master of, or seamen on, a sea-going British ship with gross registered tonnage of eighty tons or more. This includes a person ordinarily employed as a seaman engaged to do work on a ship in port of a kind which seamen usually do;

(ii) a skipper of, or seaman on, a fishing boat required to be registered under the Merchant Shipping Act 1894, s 373.

4.2.7 Dock workers

A registered dock worker is not entitled to a statutory statement of terms of employment unless he is engaged on work which is not dock work (Employment Protection (Consolidation) Act 1978, s 145(1), (5)).

4.2.8 Small employers

Employers with less than 20 employees do not have to give particulars of disciplinary rules and procedures (The Employment Protection Act, 1989).

4.3 Contents

4.3.1 Parties

The statutory statement must identify the parties to the employment contract (Employment Protection (Consolidation) Act 1978, s 1(2)(*a*)). Presumably, firm names, business names, pen names and stage names are acceptable if regularly used and readily identifying the person in question. It is convenient to use the collective name of an unincorporated body which is the employer, eg a club, as there is no other reasonable way to comply with the terms of the Act when the membership changes frequently.

4.3.2 Dates

The date the employment began must be given on the statutory statement (Employment Protection (Consolidation) Act 1978, s 1(2)(b)). It must also say whether any employment with a previous employer counts as part of the employee's continuous period of employment. If it does, the date of the beginning of that period is to be given (s 1(2)(*c*)). This is important in the calculation of the entitlement to a number of statutory benefits. An employer stating that earlier employment counts towards the continuous period is bound by that statement (*Evenden* v *Guildford City Association Football Club Ltd* [1975] ICR 367).

The particulars of the employment terms which the statement sets out must apply on a date not earlier than week before the statement is given. That date has to be specified (s 1(3)). There is no requirement to date the statement itself, but this can usefully be done, to show that the time limit was not exceeded.

4.3.3 Remuneration

A statutory statement must give the employee's scale or rate of remuneration, or the method of calculating it, and the intervals at which the money is paid (Employment Protection (Consolidation) Act 1978, s 1(3)(*a*), (*b*)).

There is no definition of 'remuneration'. Details should be given under this head of any sum, in addition to salary or wages, which the employer agrees to pay, eg £5 a week for car expenses (*S & U Stores Ltd* v *Lee* [1969] 1 WLR 626). The expression may include a share of tips even though paid by customers, rather than by the employer (*Palmanor Ltd* v *Cedron* [1978] ICR 1008). For another purpose, a very wide definition was adopted. It was to include 'any benefit, facility or advantage, whether in money or otherwise, provided by the employer or by some other person under an arrangement with the employer, whether for the employee or otherwise, by reason of the fact that the employer employs him' (Prices and Charges (Notification of Increases and Information) Order 1977, Sched 4, para 16(2)). There seems little justification for applying this definition here, although the suggestion has been made. To do so would render much of the other requirements as to the contents of statutory statements otiose, which indicates that such a wide interpretation was not Parliament's intention.

4.3.4 Hours of work

A statutory statement must give any terms and conditions relating to the employee's hours of work and normal working hours (Employment Protection (Consolidation) Act 1978, s 1(3)(*c*)). Normal working hours are the number of hours in a week, or other period, after which the employee is entitled to overtime pay or, if greater, the number or minimum number of working hours fixed by the contract of employment (s 152, Sched 14, paras 1, 2).

4.3.5 Holidays

The details which a statutory statement gives about holidays include both the employee's entitlement to holidays and to holiday pay (Employment Protection (Consolidation) Act 1978, s 1(3)(*d*)(i)).

Holiday entitlement should specify the length of holiday in a given year or other period, how the dates are fixed and whether the holiday entitlement can be carried forward into subsequent years. The Act expressly requires mention of the entitlement to public holidays (not defined, but presumably bank holidays prescribed by or under the Banking and Financial Dealings Act 1971, s 1, and other days which may be specified as Public Holidays by Royal Proclamation), which will include details of any arrangements for time off in lieu for those who do or may work on those days.

The details about holiday pay must be sufficient to allow a precise calculation of the employee's entitlement. That includes anything due on termination of the employment such as accrued holiday pay.

4.3.6 Sickness

Terms and conditions relating to incapacity for work due to sickness or injury, and to sick pay, must be included in a statutory statement (Employment Protection (Consolidation) Act 1978, s 1(3)(*d*)(ii)). These should include requirements for self-certification, the delivery of medical certificates, inspection by the employer's doctor and deductions from pay to balance statutory sick pay and social security sickness benefits. It is not clear whether this heading extends to medical matters designed to avoid absence from work, eg regular medical inspections and inoculations for employees going abroad.

4.3.7 Pensions

Although details of pensions and pension schemes are to be included in a statutory statement (Employment Protection (Consolidation) Act 1978, s 1(3)(*d*)(iii)), it will generally be convenient to refer the employee to a rule book or some other document kept separately by the employer which can be updated as necessary. If benefits other than pensions are included in the pension scheme—eg a commutation option, death in service benefits for widows—particulars should be included under this heading. Where they are provided separately, there is no obligation to give details.

Pension details do not have to be given to an employee whose rights depend on a statutory pension scheme, when the employer is required by the provision establishing it to give new employees information about their pension rights or about determining questions concerning them (s 1(3) proviso).

In any case, the statutory statement must contain a note stating whether a contracting out certificate, for the purpose of social security pensions, is in force in relation to that employment (s 1(4)(*d*)).

4.3.8 Termination of employment

The length of notice which the employee is both obliged to give and entitled to receive to end the employment must be stated in the statutory statement (Employment Protection (Consolidation) Act 1978, s 1(3)(*e*)). In the case of a fixed term contract, it gives the expiry date (s 2(2)). It is possible to have a fixed term contract without an expiry date determinable in advance, eg where a part time teacher's employment ended on the date her course happened to finish at the end of the academic year (*Wiltshire County Council* v *Guy* [1978] IRLR 301).

Apparently, it would suffice to state that the employee was entitled to 'reasonable notice' if that was the term of his agreement (*Cuthbertson* v *AML Distributors* [1975] IRLR 228 (*IT*)). The statutory minimum notice to which an employee is entitled varies with the period for which he has been continuously employed (s 49(1)). Although this is a statutory right which cannot be ousted by contract, the duty to give the notice period requires that it be expressly stated in the contract. To avoid the need for amendment when an employee entitled to the minimum notice qualifies for a longer period, the statement can include a table showing the qualification periods and the appropriate notice. It may be that a note that the employee is entitled to the statutory minimum notice suffices, although this is not as informative as the statutory statement is intended to be.

4.3.9 Job title

The statutory statement has to include the title of the job which the employee is employed to do (Employment Protection (Consolidation) Act 1978, s 1(3)(*f*)). A job description, or a list of duties, is not required. Only in cases where the employer has adopted a rigid employment structure, with named grades of employee each with carefully defined duties and entitled to specified benefits, is the title likely to be significant, although it can be used as the basis for an argument on the scope of the employee's duties.

An industrial tribunal has suggested that neither employer nor employee should regard a short title as rigidly defining the employee's duties, so that when naming one 'planning engineer' it was unnecessary to add 'and associated duties' (*Churcher* v *Weyside Engineering (1926) Ltd* [1976] IRLR 402 (*IT*)). However, the Employment Appeal Tribunal took the view that when a title is to be interpreted widely, that should be made clear. '. . . where one is dealing with a small unit . . . where the job description tends to be wide precisely because to run a small unit one has to have flexibility, that should be pointed out to employees' (*Glitz* v *Watford Electric Co Ltd* [1979] IRLR 89, 91 per Arnold J).

4.3.10 Disciplinary and grievance procedure

The statutory statement which the employer gives an employee must include a note dealing with discipline and grievances, except so far as they relate to health or safety at work (Employment Protection (Consolidation) Act 1978, s 1(4)(*a*)-(*c*), (5)).

As far as discipline is concerned, the statement must contain the rules which apply to the employee, or refer him to a reasonably accessible document setting them out. The note must name or identify, eg 'personnel manager', 'works foreman', a person to whom the employee can appeal if dissatisfied with a disciplinary decision. It must detail the appeals procedure. That procedure can be in a separate accessible document to which the note refers.

Someone to whom the employee can apply to seek redress of any grievance relating to his employment must be named or identified in the statement. Again, a procedure should be laid down, and explained in the statement or in an accessible document to which the statement refers the employee. In drafting such procedures, account should be taken of the ACAS guidance document entitled, '*Disciplinary Procedures*'.

Although small employers do not need to have a formal disciplinary and grievance procedure such employers must still follow the principles of the ACAS guide and should also follow the guidance given in the ACAS booklet '*Discipline at Work.*' Also, there is nothing to prevent such employers from drafting and issuing procedures if they wish.

When drafting a service agreement for a senior executive, it may be inappropriate to adopt the standard form disciplinary and grievance procedure prepared for the employees at large. As a failure to follow the procedure may constitute a breach of contract, it is advisable to prepare a disciplinary procedure which reflects the senior executive's position and which permits a degree of flexibility in its operation.

4.4 Enforcement

An employee whose employer either does not give him a statutory statement or notice of change in particulars, as he is required to do or gives an incomplete statement of particulars may refer the matter to an industrial tribunal to determine what ought to have been included in the statement or notice (Employment Protection (Consolidation) Act 1978, s 11(1)). Where an employer gives the employee a complete but incorrect statement, which contains all the required particulars, but where some of them are wrong in that they do not accurately reflect what was agreed between the employer and employee, the matter can be referred to the tribunal by either party (s 11(2)). The only matter excluded from this jurisdiction is whether the employment is contracted out for the purpose of the Social Security Pensions Act 1975, Pt III (s 11(4)(*b*)). The criminal sanction which was originally applied in cases of failure to supply particulars was repealed.

The reference to a tribunal must be made while the employment continues, or within thirteen weeks after it ceases (s 11(9)). This settles a difference of opinion which arose between English and Scottish tribunals, as to whether there was any jurisdiction once the employment had come to an end. English tribunals would only hear a reference made while the job lasted (*Fountain* v

Simmons [1968] ITR 343 (*IT*)), but that restriction no longer applies. Although there is no statutory provision for extending the period, even where the reason for the employee's failure to apply is fraud on the employer's part (cf Limitation Act 1980, s 32), the courts may be persuaded to allow a late application by giving equitable relief. 'In a suitable case it may well be that the courts will be prepared to develop this equitable doctrine and to apply it to postpone the operation of a time limit in a statute where otherwise a plaintiff might suffer a real injustice by reason of the unconscionable behaviour of the defendant' (*Grimes* v *Sutton LBC* [1973] ICR 240, 244–5 per Sir Hugh Griffiths, giving the judgment of the National Industrial Relations Court: time was not extended in that case).

How far industrial tribunals should and will go when exercising this jurisdiction, in redefining contract terms as given in statutory statements, is a matter of some doubt. When no statement has been given, the tribunal is to determine what ought to have been included or referred to (s 11(5)), and given the necessary evidence this seems straightforward. On the other hand, when a statement has been given and the employee disagrees with its contents, there seems to be some conflict of authority. The Act says the tribunal 'may either confirm the particulars as included or referred to in the statement given by the employer, or may amend those particulars, or may substitute particulars for them, as the tribunal may determine to be appropriate' (s 11(6)).

Two cases illustrate the contrasting approaches.In *Owens* v *Multilux Ltd* [1974] IRLR 113, the National Industrial Relations Court considered an agreement to pay the managing director of a company £2,500 'net of deductions', which was said to be intended to mean net of tax. As that would be illegal under the then Companies Act 1948, s 189 (now the Companies Act 1985, s 311), the court declared that the statutory statement should refer to a salary of £2,500 gross. In *Construction Industry Training Board* v *Leighton* [1978] IRLR 60, the Employment Appeal Tribunal was faced with a dispute as to whether an annual salary of £3,150 stated in a letter of appointment was inclusive or exclusive of a bonus of £104. They declined to alter the statement. 'An industrial tribunal can only embark upon an exercise of amendment or substitution of particulars where there is an omission to include or refer to a statutory requirement when setting out the terms of a contract of employment . . . the words of the statute do not mean and were not intended to mean that an industrial tribunal could rewrite or amend a binding contract which had one small area of misunderstanding between the parties' (ibid, p61, per Kilner Brown J).

It is suggested that three conclusions may be drawn. First, if one of the statutory particulars is not included, the tribunal will make a declaration as to what this should have been. This is an exercise in deciding on the evidence what was the agreement between the parties, not imposing what the tribunal considers would have been the appropriate term (*Cuthbertson* v *AML Distributors* [1975] IRLR 228 (*IT*)). That evidence can extend to the conduct of the parties since the contract was made (*Mears* v *Safecar Security Ltd* [1982] 2 All ER 865, 877). Secondly, where the parties were in agreement on a term, which was reproduced in the statement either inaccurately or ambiguously, the tribunal will make a declaration as to its meaning. Thirdly, if it proves that the parties were never in fact in agreement, by reason of mistake or from some other cause, the tribunal will not declare what the disputed term was. This is a jurisdiction to ensure that agreed terms are accurately recorded, not to determine what the terms should have been in the absence of agreement.

Chapter 5

Statements of Terms: Special Cases

5.1 Directors

A company has to keep a copy of its directors' written service agreements, or a written memorandum of the terms of the contract of any directors whose agreement is not in writing, at an appropriate place so that shareholders may inspect them (Companies Act 1985, s 318). This applies equally to any variation of such a contract. The only exception is a contract which will expire within twelve months, or which the company can end during that period without paying compensation. The contracts of shadow directors, as defined in s 251 of the Insolvency Act 1986 would also be covered by this provision. Formerly, contracts requiring a director to work wholly or mainly outside the United Kingdom were not covered by this requirement, but that exemption has been cancelled (Companies Act 1980, Sched 4).

The company must keep all the copy contracts or memoranda in the same place, which must be one of three possibilities. They may be kept at the company's registered office, where it keeps its register of members if that is different, or at its principal place of business provided that is in England for a company with a registered office in England, or in Scotland for a company with a registered office there. Unless the company has always kept them at its registered office, it must notify the registrar of companies on the prescribed form of the place where they are kept.

Members of the company may inspect the copies and memoranda free during usual business hours, or any restricted period which still allows at least two hours a day for inspection.

If inspection is refused, the court may compel production. Failure to keep the copies and memoranda as required is an offence for which the company and every officer in default maybe fined.

The fines on summary conviction are: up to £200, and up to £20 per day for further default. The figures are fractions ($1/5^{th}$ and $1/50^{th}$) of the 'statutory maximum' of £1,000, which can be altered (Companies Act 1985 s 730, Sched 24; Magistrates' Court Act 1980 s 32).

Where the employing company is listed on the Stock Exchange, further provisions which must be complied with are set out in 'The Yellow Book' (Admission of Securities to Listing). These rules provide that any service agreement of over a years' duration must be available for inspection for a specified period prior to the company's annual general meeting.

5.2 Temporary workers

5.2.1 Statutory duty

An employer who is engaging an employee who is to be supplied to another person ('hirer'), to act for and under the control of the hirer, has a special duty to supply a written statement of the employee's terms and conditions of employment. This arises under the Employment Agencies Act 1973 (SI 1976 715 reg 9. Failure to comply is an offence, carrying a maximum fine of £400 (s 5(2)).

One familiar example of the arrangement to which this applies is the supply of temporary office staff who remain in the employ of the supplying agency. But, subject to specific exceptions, it applies to all types of worker, and there is no limit on the time for which the worker is supplied to the hirer. The major exceptions are: nurses; seamen; services supplied ancillary to hiring out aircraft, vessels, vehicles, plant or equipment; services supplied by local authorities, employers' or employees' organisations working for their members; and university appointments boards (s 13(7)).

5.2.2 Statement

Unlike the statutory statement to which most workers are entitled, the contents of the statement for temporary workers are not limited. It must contain 'full details of the terms and conditions of employment' (Conduct of Employment Agencies and Employment Business Regulations 1976, reg 9(6)). It specifically must set out the kind of work which the employee may be supplied to a hirer to do, the minimum rate of pay for that work, and details of any expenses payable. Highlighting those matters, however, does not limit the comprehensive nature of the employer's duty.

The statement must be given to the employee 'on entering into a contract'. Although the regulations do not contemplate that the statement will itself be the contract, it is best to have a service agreement and treat it as the statement. This follows from the requirements that the statement be comprehensive and be given at once. The consensual nature of the arrangement is emphasised by the provision about variations. If the employee agrees to changes, a new statement—not simply a notice of the changes—must be given to him without delay.

The employer has to keep copies of these statements readily available at his place of business for at least a year, presumably for checking on the enforcement of the regulations. To provide evidence of compliance, it will be useful to retain copies signed by the employees.

Part II

The Job

Chapter 6

Defining the Job

6.1 Qualifications

Particular qualifications may be a prerequisite for a certain job, either in the sense of the experience and skill of the employee, or of legal authority to do the work. In such a case it is good practice for the employer to enquire in advance from the employee as to his qualification, and it is appropriate to include in the service agreement what amounts to a warranty of the accuracy of the information which induced the employer to take on the employee.

In practice, where an employee fails satisfactorily to do his job, it will be difficult to distinguish between laziness, inefficiency, negligence and lack of experience which qualifies him for the job. A warranty in the service agreement can still strengthen the employer's hand.

6.1.1 Legal qualifications

When some form of licence or authority is required by law before undertaking particular work, a contract to employ an unqualified person for that work is illegal and void, and there may be other consequences for the employer. To employ an unlicensed driver is a criminal offence on the part of the employer (Road Traffic Act 1972, s 84(2)). It is for the employer to prove that the driver is licensed (*Griffiths* v *Studebakers Ltd* [1924] 1 KB 102). It is likely that an employer who held out an employee as qualified when he was not would be liable to third parties for any resulting loss or damage. A disqualification will not always give grounds to terminate employment, even where the employee is expected to drive in the course of his work. A three months' disqualification did not affect a commercial traveller's employment, because he could have arranged for someone else to drive him (*Hands* v *Simpson, Fawcett & Co Ltd* (1928) 44 TLR 295). An employer is well advised to have an express term dealing with the point, to avoid misunderstanding.

Apart from the very common case of a driving licence, there are many others in which an employer may wish to insist on a professional qualification. There are acts which by law can only be done by qualified doctors, pharmacists and solicitors. A contract to employ a psychiatrist part time automatically came to an end when his suspension from registration for twelve months made it illegal under the Medical Act 1956, s 28(1), to continue to employ him (*Tarnesby* v *Kensington, Chelsea and Westminster Area Health Authority (Teaching)* [1980] ICR 475). Again, the employer's business may require that an employee obtains and keeps a licence, eg for the sale of alcoholic liquor. Or, the employer may wish to advertise his employees' qualifications, as in the case of a school staffed with qualified teachers. The last example overlaps with legal requirements, because state schools must employ qualified teachers, so that a teacher declared unsuitable by the Department of Education and Science will face dismissal (*Sandhu* v *Department of Education and Science and Hillingdon London Borough* [1978] IRLR 208).

Rather than relying on implied terms, and the possibility that an agreement may become illegal, it is better that a service agreement should spell out the requirement that the employee has and keeps the necessary qualification.

6.1.2 Convictions

For some jobs it is reasonable for the employer to require that the employee has no record of criminal convictions. The prospective employee need not volunteer information about this, even if he has a conviction directly relevant to the duties he will be taking on (*Hands* v *Simpson, Fawcett & Co Ltd* (1928) 44 TLR 295). Nevertheless, subject to statutory intervention, he must truthfully reply to any enquiries put to him. 'It is of the utmost importance that an employer seeking an employee to hold a position of responsibility and trust should be able to select for employment a candidate in whom he can have confidence. It is fundamental to the confidence that the employee should truthfully disclose his history so far as it is sought by the intending employer' (*Torr* v *British Railways Board* [1977] ICR 785, 789–90, per Cumming-Bruce J: a railway guard was fairly dismissed having refused employment in a lower grade, after it became known that he had concealed convictions when applying for employment).

The Rehabilitation of Offenders Act 1974 allows convictions which carried all but the severest penalties to be considered 'spent' after a rehabilitation period if the offender is not convicted again during that period. Once a conviction is spent, an employee or a prospective employee does not have to disclose it, and neither the spent conviction nor the failure to disclose it is a proper ground for an employee's dismissal or for prejudicing him in his occupation or employment (s 4(3)). This even applies to jobs where an employer might reasonably be concerned with convictions, eg a security guard (*Property Guards Ltd* v *Taylor* [1982] IRLR 175). Exceptionally, this does not apply to teachers in schools and establishments for further education and other employment there bringing the employee into contact with pupils under the age of eighteen, employment in connection with the provision of social services, of health services, or the promotion of leisure activities for those under the age of eighteen, and certain public employment mostly connected with the administration of justice (Rehabilitation of Offenders Act 1974 (Exceptions) Order 1975).

Every conviction becomes spent, unless the sentence awarded is life imprisonment, imprisonment or corrective training for more than thirty months, preventative detention, or, under Acts applying to juveniles, detention during Her Majesty's pleasure, for life or for more than thirty months. The length of rehabilitation period depends on the sentence. For imprisonment for over six months and up to thirty months, it is ten years; imprisonment for six months or less, seven years; a fine or any other sentence, five years. For those under the age of seventeen when convicted those periods are halved, but there are special periods relating to sentences confined to young offenders. For borstal training the rehabilitation period is seven years; detention for more than six months and up to thirty months, five years; detention for six months or less and detention in a detention centre, three years.

6.1.3 Precedents

General qualification warranty

The Company has agreed to employ the employee on the understanding that he is as he warrants himself to be a fully experienced [ ] with [15] years' experience in that trade and competent to undertake the work normally entrusted to a craftsman in that trade without supervision or instruction

Statutory qualification

The employee is a registered medical practitioner/holds a practising certificate as a solicitor and it is a condition of his employment under this agreement that he continues at all times to be so registered/to hold such a practising certificate

Driving licence

(i) The employee holds a valid licence to drive motor cycles/private motor cars/heavy goods vehicles and shall take all steps and make all payments necessary to renew the same and shall ensure that he holds a current licence at all times

(ii) The employee shall immediately report to the Company any order of any court to endorse his driving licence or to disqualify him from holding a driving licence

(iii) The employee shall produce his driving licence to the Company for inspection on demand at any time

(iv) The employee shall not drive any motor vehicle in the course of his employment by the Company at any time when he does not hold a valid driving licence relating to that class of vehicle

(v) The Company shall be at liberty to terminate the employee's employment under this agreement without notice if at any time he ceases to hold or to be qualified to hold a valid licence to drive motor cycles/private motor cars/heavy goods vehicles

6.2 Period of employment

If no time limit is placed on employment it will normally be terminable at common law on reasonable notice given by either party. An exception to this would be employment specifically for a particular project, which will last as long as necessary to fulfil its purpose. An express term in a service agreement can make the employment last for a predetermined period, or can require a certain length of notice. These arrangements can also be combined, eg by a term giving the employee an initial probationary period during which he is liable to be dismissed on short notice, followed by a fixed period or a requirement for longer notice.

In every case, an employer can instantly dismiss the employee, or the employee can leave his job without notice, if the other party's conduct justifies it by amounting to a repudiation of the contract.

Some employment is referred to as 'permanent'. Obviously, that cannot be taken literally. It must be construed in accordance with the course of dealings between the parties, and particularly the framework of employment rules operated by the employer. Permanent or established employment will normally carry with it an expectation of a job until a predetermined retirement age, but unless there is a definite arrangement to the contrary, it will still be terminable on notice. It is also possible to have a service agreement lasting for the life of the employee, but this will only be appropriate in special cases.

The statutory employment protection rules have an important effect on the period of employment. First, after a short period of employment, there are minimum periods of notice required to end a contract. These minimum periods supersede any shorter periods laid down by the agreement, but do not alter any longer contractual requirements. Secondly, there is an incentive for employers to make fixed term contracts, because that can exclude the employee's rights to compensation for unfair dismissal or a redundancy payment if the term is not renewed.

6.2.1 Fixed term

There are two principal reasons for having a fixed term contract: first to provide the parties with security, and secondly to remove the employee's statutory rights.

A fixed term contract is appropriate where the employer wants to ensure that a particular job will be finished by the employee whom he recruits for the purpose. Both parties will welcome it for employment abroad. It gives the employee the assurance that the upheaval involved in moving abroad will be justified, and that he will be able to stay there long enough to reap the tax benefits. For the employer, it should ensure that the expensive initial costs of recruiting and transporting a new employee, with his family and goods, are not repeated too frequently. However, it is usually advisable to place the financial burden of travelling home on the employee, should he break the contract and return before the expiry date.

The reason why a fixed term contract provides an employee with security is that if the employer prematurely and without justification dismisses an employee the damages to which the employee is entitled will be to compensate him for the lost period of employment (*Re English Joint Stock Bank, Yelland's Case* (1867) LR 4 Eq 350), and for further benefits that employment for the full period would have gained him, eg an increased pension payable at the end of it (*Bold* v *Brough, Nicholson & Hall Ltd* [1964] 1 WLR 201). Such a contract is therefore excellent insurance for managers against adverse effects of the business being taken over. Compensation for loss of salary does not extend to loss of benefits to which the employee is not contractually entitled, such as bonuses or prospective salary increases (*Lavarack* v *Woods of Colchester Ltd* [1967] 1 QB 278). So any contract entered into with this object in mind should concentrate on cash salary rather than bonuses or commission. A fixed term contract cannot in practice prevent the employee being discharged, but it guarantees him considerable compensation should he not secure comparable employment during the unexpired term of the contract. This is at least one of the reasons why there are provisions for disclosing details of directors' service agreements which will not expire, or which the company cannot bring to an end without paying compensation, within twelve months (Companies Act 1985, s 318).

In contrast a fixed term contract does not necessarily provide an employer with similar security. An employer cannot seek an order for specific performance to enforce the employee's compliance as the court will not enforce a contract for personal service. In any event in practice an employee who has expressed the wish to leave the employer's employment, because of his personal dissatisfaction with the work or the terms of employment, may be of dubious value to the employer. The employer in such circumstances may be prepared to allow the employee to leave, regardless of the strict terms of the contract. However, the employer may also send the employee on 'garden leave' (*see Chapter 11 below*).

If the employee prematurely breaks the contract, the measure of damage was thought to be the cost of obtaining a substitute employee and no more (*National Coal Board* v *Galley* [1958] 1 All ER 91). However, it has now been stated that 'although the damages due to an employer for a wrongful termination of the contract by an employee in certain circumstances may be the cost of hiring a substitute that will be so, not because there is any legal rule to that effect but because that may turn out to be the proper method of calculating the loss which the employee has suffered by the breach'. (*Strathclyde Regional Council* (pursuers) v *Neil* (defender) [1984] IRLR).

A contract of employment for a fixed term of one year or more may provide that, if it is not renewed, the employee will not be entitled either to compensation for unfair dismissal or, when the employment is for two years or more, to a statutory redundancy payment. Only the result of deemed dismissal by non-renewal is affected; the employee remains fully entitled to his statutory rights if the contract is brought to an end at any other time. The agreement excluding the rights can be separate from the service agreement (Employment Protection (Consolidation) Act 1978, s 142). However, it should be noted that where an employer has a specific reason for seeking a fixed term contract and has explained the reason to the employee before he takes up employment, its expiry without it being renewed may constitute a fair dismissal despite the lack of the incorporation of the exclusion permitted by the Employment Protection (Consolidation) Act 1978 (*North Yorkshire County Council* v *Fay* [1985] IRLR 247).

This right for employers naturally raises the question, what amounts to a fixed term contract? 'A "fixed term" in my judgment means a term which has a defined beginning and a defined end' (*Wiltshire County Council* v *National Association of Teachers in Further and Higher Education* [1980] ICR 455, 462 per Lawton LJ). This generalisation must be qualified. An agreement for a definite period which is nevertheless subject to earlier termination on notice is a fixed term contract for this purpose (*Dixon* v *British Broadcasting Corporation* [1979] QB 546). However, the statutory rights are only excluded if it runs its full course and the option to end it earlier is not exercised. Also in the fixed term category is a contract to teach for an academic session provided sufficient students enrol for the class, although one terminable on the happening of a specified event at an uncertain time in the future is not (*Wiltshire County Council* v *National Association of Teachers in Further and Higher Education*, supra). Employment for a certain job of work, but without the period of time being specified, is not a fixed term contract (*Ryan* v *Shipboard Maintenance Ltd* [1980] ICR 88).

Care is needed where the original fixed term is extended for a further period. If the original contract contains an express waiver of rights and it is extended or renewed, then the courts will treat it as one continuous fixed-term contract. However, if fresh terms are agreed so that it is essentially a reengagement under a new contract, the waiver would have to be reincorporated and the second contract term would have to be sufficient to fall within the terms of s 142 (*British Broadcasting Corporation Ltd* v *Ioannou* [1975] IRLR 184).

A fixed-term agreement for all but the shortest periods needs to make provision for adjusting the employee's salary periodically. Without that, it will remain fixed at the initial figure, in the absence of changes by agreement.

Quite often contracts are drafted which incorporate provisions for fixed-term contracts automatically to be extended on the happening of a predetermined event. This is known as a 'roll over' provision. It is particularly prevalent where employees who are directors consider the company employing them to be vulnerable to a take-over bid or a change in management control, which would (if it happened) lead to their dismissal from the Company. In such a case they wish to secure for themselves the maximum protection and to negotiate a 'golden handshake'. The 'roll over' provision gives the director a fixed-term contract which constantly renews itself.

6.2.2 Employment for life

A service agreement for the whole of the employee's lifetime will not normally be appropriate.

6.2.3 Retirement date

The contractual significance of a retirement date is that it is the date beyond which an indefinite service agreement will not extend, even though no notice is given to end it. Retirement dates are normally fixed in relation to the employee's age, and they are a matter of contract. There is no universally accepted retirement age, although those when the national insurance retirement pension first becomes payable—sixty for women and sixty-five for men—was often adopted, but this changed following the decision of the European Court of Justice in *Marshall* v *Southampton and South West Hampshire Area Health Authority (Teaching*) (case 152/84) [1986] QB 401, which held that compulsory retirement of men and women at different ages contravened the EEC Equal Treatment Directive. The Sex Discrimination Act 1986 (s 311) prohibited different contractual retirement ages for men and women and the maximum age limit for making unfair dismissal applications was amended so that both men and women could make applications up to 65 years of age.

An employee is not entitled to compensation for unfair dismissal if on or before the effective date of termination of his employment he had attained 'the normal retiring age for an employee holding the position he held'. The 'normal retirement age' will not always be the contractual retirement date specified by the contract. In the case of *Waite* v *Government Communications Headquarters* [1983] IRLR 161 it was stated that the concept was not a purely contractual one; but the contractual age was not irrelevant and it is often the best evidence of the normal retirement age. Lord Fraser said:

I therefore reject the view that the contractual retiring age conclusively fixes the normal retiring age. I accept that where there is a contractual retiring age, applicable to all, or nearly all, the employees holding the position which the appellant employee held, there is a presumption that the contractual retiring age is the normal retiring for the group. But it is a presumption which, in my opinion, can be rebutted by evidence that there is in practice some higher age at which employees holding a position have regularly retired, which they have reasonably come to regard as their normal retiring age . . . the contractual retiring age will *prima facie* be the normal, but it may be displaced by evidence that it has regularly departed from in practice.

That evidence will have to be significant before the presumption is rebutted. Changes in practice and policy could conceivably introduce a normal retirement age below the contractual retirement age. However the circumstances would have to be unusual for this to occur.

6.2.4 Directors

A long term service agreement for a company director must be approved by a resolution of the company in general meeting, after observing certain formalities. In default, the agreement is deemed to contain a term entitling the company to terminate it at any time on giving reasonable notice. Any provision to the contrary in the agreement is void. This applies to any service agreement, including a contract to employ a director of a holding company within the group consisting of that company and its subsidiaries, for over five years on terms that the company cannot end the employment by notice, or can only do so in specified circumstances. To prevent evasion, if a service agreement is renewed or extended more than six months before it expires, the period of the new agreement counts for this purpose as extended by the unexpired portion of the original term. So if, eg, a five year agreement is extended after running for four years by a further five years, the extension counts as an agreement for six years (the new five years plus the final year of the old agreement), and it becomes one to which this provision applies. Before a resolution can be passed in general meeting approving an agreement for this purpose, a written memorandum setting out the proposed agreement must be made available for inspection by members of the company at its registered office for at least fifteen days prior to the date of the meeting (Companies Act 1985, s 319).

Even if an agreement is duly approved in this way, it does not override the power of the company to remove a director from office by ordinary resolution (Companies Act 1985, s 303))

6.2.5 Precedents

Fixed term contract.

The Executive's employment under this agreement shall commence on the [*specify date*] and shall (subject as hereinafter provided) continue for a fixed period of [*specify number*] [months/years] until the [ ] day of [ ] 199[ ] and thereafter until terminated by either party giving to the other not less than [*specify number*] [weeks/months] written notice expiring on or at any time after the said fixed period.

Contract for a particular project.

The Executive is engaged to supervise the installation and commissioning of [ ] at [ ] in accordance with the contract between the company and its customer and the Executive's employment under this agreement shall continue until that work is completed and the customer signs a certificate of satisfaction in accordance with the terms of the said contract.

Probationary period.

The Executive's employment shall begin on [ ] 199[ ]. During the first six months of the employment either party shall be entitled to terminate it on giving to the other one month's written notice. If no notice is given on the expiry of the probationary period, the employment shall continue until terminated by either party giving to the other not less than six months written notice.

Indefinite employment until retirement.

The Executive's employment shall begin on [ ] 199[ ] and shall continue until ended by not less than [three months] written notice given by either party to the other or if no notice expiring earlier is given until the end of the month in which the Executive attains the age of [65] years of age.

Rolling appointment.

The Executive's employment under this agreement is for a fixed period of four years from the [ ] day of [ ] 199[ ] ('the Commencement Date') subject to termination by the Executive during the fixed period by not less than six months prior written notice to the Company, such notice to expire on any anniversary of the Commencement Date provided that the period of fixed term shall be extended automatically on each anniversary date of the Commencement Date for a further period of one year unless either party shall have given written notice to the other not less than six months before any anniversary date of its or his desire to terminate the further extension of the fixed term in which event the period of employment shall (subject to prior termination by the Executive as above mentioned) be the expiration of four years from the anniversary date immediately preceding the giving of such written notice.

6.3 Place of work

6.3.1 Introduction

Stating where the employee is to perform his duties is an essential part of the full definition of his job. It is also necessary to be able to decide whether the employer is entitled to order the employee to work in a particular place, or to require him to transfer to another. Similarly, an employee will wish to know whether he is obliged to work in a different place, or whether he has the opportunity to negotiate additional payment as a condition of doing so. An employer who purports to require his employee to move his place of work when he has no power to do so repudiates the contract and renders the employee free to end it (*Maher* v *Fram Gerrard Ltd* [1974] ICR 31).

6.3.2 Implied terms to vary the place of work

Whether a term is to be implied into a service agreement as to the place where the employee's duties are to be performed, and if so what term, is a matter of law (*O'Brien* v *Associated Fire Alarms Ltd* [1968] 1 WLR 1916). The point must be determined on the evidence, (*Robottom* v *Arthur Lee and Sons Ltd* [1975] 1CR 109). In the case of *Courtaulds Northern Spinning Ltd* v (1) *Sibson* and (2) *Transport and General Workers Union* [1988] IRLR 305, it was held that where there is no express term in a contract of employment as to the employee's place of work or the employer's right to transfer. In order to give the contract business efficacy, it is essential to imply into it that term which the parties, if acting reasonably, would probably have agreed to upon entering into the contract, if they had directed their minds to the problem. This case involved an employee, who was a heavy goods vehicle driver. His contract was silent as to his place of work or any right on the employer's part to transfer him. The employer, due to a dispute between the employee and his union, sought to move the employee's place of work to a depot one mile away from the one at which he normally worked. The Court considered that if the parties had directed their minds to the question of mobility at the outset, they would have agreed that the employer had a power to direct the employee to work at any place within a reasonable distance of his home, for any reason. Further, the Court decided that there was no need or justification to import a requirement into the implied term that the employer's request that the employee work at another place must itself be reasonable, or that a request could be reasonable only if made 'for genuine operational reasons'. The Court also approved the guidelines given by Browne-Wilkinson J in *Jones* v *Associated Tunnelling Co Ltd* [1981] IRLR 477. In that case Browne-Wilkinson J said:

> the term to be implied must depend on the circumstances of each case. The authorities show that it may be relevant to consider the nature of the employer's business, whether or not the employee has in fact been moved during the employment, what the employee was told when he was employed, and whether there was any provision made to cover the employee's expenses when working away from daily reach of his home. These are only examples; all the circumstances of each case have to be considered.

The following are examples of how these factors have been taken into account by Courts in determining whether a contractual term is to be implied allowing the employer to direct the employee to change the location of his job:

(i) Nature of the job. Some types of work naturally require workers to move from place to place. This applied to a steel erector, whose work on a particular construction site was naturally limited to the period during the building that his trade was required, and whose employers needed to use him successively on sites on which they were engaged in different parts of the country (*Stevenson* v *Tess-side Bridge and Engineering Ltd* [1971] 1AII ER 296). In other jobs, it is accepted that employees are directed from one of the employer's branches to another, eg banking. '. . . the evidence shows that transfer is one of the ordi-

nary incidents of the bank's employment' (*Bouzourou* v *Ottoman Bank* [1930] AC 271).

(ii) Contract terms. Other terms of a contract may demonstrate the parties' intention that the employee should work at different locations, eg provision as to travelling expenses and subsistence allowances (*Stevenson* v *Tees-side Bridge and Engineering Ltd*, supra).

(iii) Residence. The fact that a change in the place of work would require the employee to move house may be a factor in showing that that was not a term of the agreement. An apprentice was not required to go to work in Derby instead of London, although in that case the position was complicated by the apprentice's father being a party to the deed and covenanting to provide board and lodging, which he did by having his son live at home. 'I do not say that a removal of the business to a small distance would be material, but when the removal necessitates a change in the place of residence of the apprentice I think it is contrary to the intention of the parties, and cannot be enforced against the apprentice' (*Eaton* v *Western* (1882) 9 QBD 636, 642 per Lindley LJ). Something less than a need to move may be material. The fact that if the employees went to work where the employers wanted them to they would no longer be able to return home daily, but only at weekends, was a factor in deciding that there was no implied contractual term that they would elsewhere (*O'Brien* v *Associated Fire Alarms Ltd* [1968] 1WLR 1916).

There is probably an overriding qualification to any implied terms imposing mobility on an employee. The employer cannot require him to move to or remain in a place in which his life is in danger (*Ottoman Bank* v *Chakarian* [1930] AC 277). That proviso must presumably must be qualified if the nature of the job involves danger, eg a war correspondent.

6.3.3 Express terms to vary place of work

A service agreement can give the employer the right to vary the place where the employee works. Such a term may be interpreted in the light of the circumstances surrounding the making of the contract, and the wider the power is intended to be, the more important it is to make its scope clear. In one case, a term incorporated into the agreement read, 'at the discretion of the employer, an operative may be transferred at any time during the period of his employment from one job to another'. This was held to allow the employer to require the employee to transfer from

South Wales to Somerset, but Parker C J expressly left undecided whether it was enough to justify a relocation to anywhere in the United Kingdom (*Parry* v *Holston and Co Ltd* [1968] ITR 317). However, two recent cases demonstrate the Court's readiness to imply into such an express term an obligation on the part of the employer not to enforce the term unreasonably.

In *United Bank Ltd* v *Akhetar* [1989] IRLR 507, the employee's contract of employment contained a mobility clause in the following terms:

> The Bank may from time to time require an employee to be transferred temporarily or permanently to any place of business which the Bank may have in the UK for which relocation or other allowance may be payable at the discretion of the Bank.

The employee was given seven days notice of his employer's wish for him to move from Leeds to Birmingham. The employee was of a junior rank in the Bank, and he also had personal difficulties relating to his wife's ill health and the impending sale of his house which he suggested should justify the employer postponing the transfer request. However, his request was turned down, and as his employers continued to take an intransigent line as to his personal position he resigned and claimed constructive dismissal. On appeal to the Employment Appeal Tribunal, the EAT held that there should be implied into the contract the requirement that reasonable notice should be given in the exercise of the employer's power to require mobility of its employees. Further, unless the employer exercised discretion under the mobility clause by implementing relocation or other allowances, their actions would make the employee attempt to perform something which in practical terms, was impossible. It therefore suggested that it was possible to imply a term that the employer's discretion under the mobility clause was one which they were bound to exercise in such a way as not to render it impossible for an employee to comply with his contractual obligation to move. It was necessary to imply this requirement into the contract in order to avoid impossibility of performance. It was not accepted that the implied requirement relating to the exercise of the employer's discretion to give relocation or other allowances was inconsistent with the expressed terms of the contract and that, by accepting employment on terms which included the grant of a discretion to the employer to make those allowances, the employee had thereby agreed that he would be under an obligation to live without any financial assistance if the employer thought fit to require such a move. There was a clear distinction between implying a term which negates a provision which is expressly stated in the contract and implying a term which controls the exercise of discretion which is expressly confirmed in the contract. The first is not permissible but the second is, as there may well be circumstances where discretions are conferred but which nevertheless are not unfettered discretions which can be exercised in a capricious way.

Further limitations on the employer's right to rely on an expressed term were imposed in the case of *Woods* v *W M Car Services (Peterborough) Ltd* [1981] IRLR 347. In that case it was said that employers will not, without reasonable and proper cause, conduct themselves in a manner calculated or likely to destroy or seriously damage the relationship of confidence and trust between employer and employee. It was considered that in the field of employment law, it is proper to imply an overriding obligation in these terms which is independent of and in addition to the literal interpretation of the actions which are permitted to the employer under the terms of the contract, since there may well be conduct which is calculated or likely to destroy or seriously damage the relationship of confidence and trust between employer and employee, which a literal interpretation of the written words of the contract might appear to justify.

Accordingly, incorporation of an express term requiring mobility is important where this is an essential part of the job, but the employer will not be able to exercise that right in an unfettered way.

6.3.4 Work abroad

If a contract is intended to allow the employer to require the employee to work abroad for limited periods, it should state this expressly. Even the broadest general clause as to location of a job is likely, without more, to be interpreted only to give the employer the power to direct the employee within the United Kingdom. This is because the conditions of employment—physical conditions, social security, statutory employment protection, taxation—are likely to be radically different abroad. It cannot be assumed that they would be within the parties' contemplation when the agreement is made. On the other hand, there is no restriction on the employer being given power to send the employee abroad. If this is likely to be for more than temporary trips, the points dealt with below under employment abroad on a permanent basis should be considered.

An employee who works abroad for at least thirty days during any year of assessment is entitled to a twenty-five per cent reduction in his income tax on the proportion of his income attributable to that period (Finance Act 1977, Sched 7, para 2). To be counted, a day has to be one on which the employee was absent from the United Kingdom at the end of it (para 6), ie at midnight (*Hoye* v *Forsdyke* [1981] 1 WLR 1442). It must come into one of three classes. The day must be substantially devoted to performing the employee's duties outside the United Kingdom; or, it must be one of at least seven consecutive days of absence from the United Kingdom, which taken as a whole were substantially devoted to those duties; or, it must be spent travelling outside the United Kingdom in or for the purpose of those duties.

The amount of the employee's emoluments on which the tax is reduced under this provision is that fraction of the year's total which represents the proportion that the number of qualifying days abroad bears to 365, or any lesser number of days during which he held the job. This amount can be increased if it is reasonable having regard to the nature of and time devoted to duties performed in and outside the United Kingdom respectively, and to all other relevant circumstances (para 4). If in substance a job is to be performed in the United Kingdom, duties undertaken abroad which are merely incidental to those performed in the United Kingdom are treated for this purpose as performed in the United Kingdom (para 8).

It may be part of the understanding on which a job is offered and accepted that the employee will spend a sufficient part of his time working abroad to allow him regularly to qualify for this income tax reduction. If so, it is desirable from the employee's point of view that this should be made a term of his service agreement. In the event of any change of circumstances which deprives him of the benefit, he will then have recourse against the employer for a compensating payment. This could cover such contingencies as changes in methods of work or the reallocation of responsibilities, which reduce the need for the employee to work abroad, or even variations in the nature of the employer's business. The employer is unlikely to be prepared to guarantee the employee's income against changes in the tax system, so the precise terms of any clause must be carefully considered.

6.3.5 Consequences

An employee with the prescribed qualifications is entitled to a statutory redundancy payment if dismissed by reason of redundancy. That means (inter alia) if the dismissal is attributable wholly or mainly to the fact that his employer ceases to carry on business, or that the requirements of the business for employees to carry out work of a particular kind have diminished, 'in the place' where the employee was employed (Employment Protection (Consolidation) Act 1978, s 81). This has been interpreted to mean where he could be required to work under his contract.

The extent of the area in which the employee is to work is a matter of interpretation of his contract. A process worker employed in one works was held not to be confined to that plant, when the employer wanted to move him to another on the same industrial site (*Briggs* v *Imperial Chemical Industries Ltd* [1968] ITR 276). In another case, the area of employment of an employee engaged in laying gas pipes was not a single place but the county of Sussex (*R H McCulloch Ltd* v *Moore* [1968] 1 QB 360). The manageress of a particular office in London was employed to work anywhere in central London, different parts of which were equally accessible to her by public transport (*Managers (Holborn) Ltd* v *Hohne* [1977] IRLR 230).

To avoid liability for redundancy payments, an employer must be careful to draw a distinction between two possible situations. On the one hand, if he offers alternative employment in another area that demonstrates that there is redundancy (*John Laing and Son Ltd* v *Best* [1967] ITR 3), although the new job offer may avoid the need to make a payment if it is accepted or the employee's refusal is unreasonable (Employment Protection (Consolidation) Act 1978, s 82(5)). On the other hand, if the employment continues with its terms unaltered, but the employer directs the employee to undertake work elsewhere in accordance with the original contractual terms, there is no redundancy (*Parry* v *Holst and Co Ltd* [1968] ITR 317).

Another point to be taken into account in implementing a mobility provision is that of sex discrimination. This discrimination could either be direct or indirect.

An employer to whom a service agreement gives the power to require the employee to change his place or work must make it clear when he is exercising that compulsory requirement. He must do so on reasonable notice and in a way which is not designed to destroy the trust and confidence between employer and employee. If an employer merely requests the employee to consider moving, a refusal on the employee's part will not be construed as a breach of contract. 'If the contract of employment enables an employer to transfer an employee from a place where there is no work to some other place where there is work, the employer should first seek to persuade the employee to transfer voluntarily. If this is unsuccessful he should require the employee to transfer' (*United Kingdom Atomic Energy Authority* v *Claydon* [1974] ICR 128, 133 per Sir John Donaldson P). The same must apply where the transfer is for some other reason other than a lack of work at the first location, eg simply a transfer from one branch to another. If the employee refuses to move then before dismissing the employee it is important that the refusal is treated as a disciplinary offence within the employer's normal disciplinary procedure as a refusal to obey a lawful order. Dismissal should not occur until the full procedural requirements of the contract of employment have been completed with regard to such a disciplinary offence.

6.3.6 Drafting

A clause enabling the employer to direct the employee to work at a different place should be explicit. If the intention is that the employee should be compensated for any inconvenience, the terms should be set out as precisely as possible. Even when a term gives an employer complete discretion to direct the employee to a different location, there is a chance that it could be interpreted in relation to surrounding circumstances, eg that a change would only be required if the employer's business ceased at one site, or on the employee's promotion. Express words to negative such implications may be desirable.

6.3.7 Precedents

Mobility provision.

(i) The Executive shall initially carry out his duties at [*specify place*].

(ii) Relocation expenses. The Company shall at any time and from time to time be at liberty on giving reasonable notice to the Executive to require the Executive to carry out his duties at such other place in the United Kingdom as the Company shall specify notwithstanding that the work until then performed by the Executive at the place from which he is required to move continues to be required to be done and notwithstanding that there is no other change in the terms of the Executive's employment.

(iii) If any such change in place of work shall reasonably require the Executive to change his place of residence the Company shall pay the following expenses necessarily incurred by the Executive as a consequence in accordance with the terms of the Company's Employee Relocation Plan: hotel charges while working at the new location and before moving house (for a maximum of ten weeks), furniture removal, estate agents' selling commission, solicitors' fees on sale and purchase, stamp duty, land registry fees and other incidental expenses of the sale and purchase transactions, bridging loan financing charges (where necessary and for a maximum period of six months) and a contribution to miscellaneous expenses.

Guaranteed employment abroad

(i) The Executive agrees to perform outside the United Kingdom such part of his duties under this agreement as their efficient discharge shall require provided that he shall not be required to spend more than ninety days in any calendar year outside the United Kingdom for that purpose.

(ii) The Company agrees that the duties allocated to the Executive shall require him to devote at least thirty/the minimum number of qualifying days in every year of assessment outside the United Kingdom to performing the duties of his employment or travelling in or for the purpose of such performance. Terms in this subclause shall be interpreted in the same way as the like terms in Schedule 7 to the Finance Act 1977 or any statutory amendment or re-enactment of it. [The minimum number of qualifying days shall be the number stated in paragraph 2 of that Schedule and any number from time to time substituted for it.]

6.4 Hours of work

6.4.1 Duties

If an employee's hours of work are precisely agreed they will be an important term of the employment contract. Not only do they define the extent of the employee's job, they may also be used to calculate his pay. The hours of work may nevertheless be indeterminate, the employee being expected to put in as much time as the satisfactory performance of his duties requires. An agreement may oblige an employee to work overtime, but if it does not the employer cannot insist on his doing so (*Evans* v *Elemeta Holdings Ltd* [1982] IRLR 143) unless a term to that effect can be imputed by custom or practice.

An agreement may stipulate not only how many hours the employee is to work, but also which hours, or at least at what time of day. If the bargain is that the employee is to do night work exclusively, the employer cannot insist, in defiance of the contract, the he work by day (*Simmonds* v *Dowty Seals Ltd* [1978] IRLR 211). On the other hand, the contract may provide that the employer decides when work is to be done. An agreement to work on such days or part days as the employer reasonably required was held to be enforceable. It allowed the employer to insist on Saturday morning working when that was specified by a collective agreement to which the service agreement referred (*National Coal Board* v *Galley* [1958] 1 WLR 16).

The total of an employee's actual or normal working hours in a week is important for his entitlement to statutory benefits. Any week for which he works for less than sixteen hours, or sometimes eight hours, or in which his relations with his employer are governed by a contract to work for less, is excluded when calculating his period of continuous employment (Employment Protection (Consolidation) Act 1978, Sched 13, paras 3–6). A period of continuous employment is a qualification for compensation for unfair dismissal and for a redundancy payment (ss 64(1)(*a*), 81(1), (4)). A similar calculation applies to qualify for a statement of particulars of employment terms (s 3). Employment which is normally for less than sixteen hours a week gives no right to an itemised pay statement, or time off for trade union duties or activities or for public duties (s 146(4)).

A term of an agreement stating that the employee's hours are under the limit may not be conclusive. At a time when the limit was twenty-one hours a week, rather than sixteen, an agreement stating that the employee's normal hours of work were twenty per week did not prevent his obtaining compensation for unfair dismissal when the evidence was that in fact he worked an average of twenty-three hours a week (*ITT Components (Europe) Ltd* v *Kolah* [1977] IRLR 53). On the other hand, work done voluntarily cannot be used to increase the total. A part time teacher argued that a term must be implied into her contract that she do extra work outside school, which would have taken the total over the qualifying limit. The court of appeal rejected the suggestion, on the ground that such extra work could not be controlled by the employer so that it was not reasonable to assume that it would have agreed to the proposition (*Lake* v *Essex County Council* [1979] ICR 577).

To calculate a week's pay for statutory purposes, there is a definition of 'normal working hours'. This is the number of hours after which the employee is entitled to overtime pay, or, when a contract provides for compulsory overtime, the number or minimum number of hours the employee agrees to work (Employment Protection (Consolidation) Act 1978, Sched 14, paras 1, 2).

6.4.2 Spare time

There is no implied term in employment contracts that an employee will not work in his spare time, nor even that he will not work for one of the employer's rivals (*Nova Plastics Ltd* v *Froggatt* [1982] IRLR 146). If, however, it is inevitable that that spare time employment will lead to a disclosure of the employer's trade secrets, then the employee will be restrained from doing that work (*Hivac Ltd* v *Park Royal Scientific Instruments Ltd* [1946] Ch 169). There is no reason why a term of a service agreement should not restrict an employee to working only for that employer while the job lasts.

6.4.3 Precedents

Regular hours

The Executive shall attend the offices of the Company to carry out his duties from 9.30 am to 5.30 pm on Mondays to Fridays inclusive (other than days on which he is entitled to a holiday) and one hour each day being allowed for lunch his normal working hours are accordingly thirty-five hours per week.

Shift work

In each week the employee shall work five shifts each of nine hours during which there will be a meal break of one hour and two fifteen minute refreshment breaks. The Company shall decide which shifts the employee is to work but he shall not be required to start any shift earlier than sixteen hours after finishing the previous one. The employee's normal working hours are thirty-eight-and-a-half hours per week.

No precise hours

The Executive is required to work at such times and for such periods as the efficient and conscientious discharge of his duties requires. There are no normal working hours for his employment

No spare time work

The Executive's employment under this agreement is a full time appointment and while he is employed by the Company he shall not undertake any other paid work whatsoever whether as an employee of any other person firm or corporation or on his own account or in partnership.

6.5 Duties

6.5.1 Introduction

When drafting a service agreement, the employee's duties should be carefully considered and defined as clearly as possible. It may be best for the employer to use a wide generic term describing the job, but the circumstances of the negotiation of the contract or the practice of the parties may restrict it. All the same, the fact that an employee is asked to do something he has not done before does not necessarily mean that it is outside the scope of his duties. An employee engaged as a 'copy typist/general clerical duties clerk' was bound to operate a duplicating machine, even though she was only asked to do so three years after she was first employed, when its former operator was made redundant. That job fell within 'general clerical duties' (*Glitz* v *Watford Electric Co Ltd* [1979] IRLR 89). Further in the case of *Cresswell* v *Inland Revenue Board* [1984] IRLR 190 the court held that 'employees were expected to adapt to new methods which were reasonably introduced provided that in introducing them the employer gave appropriate training'.

6.5.2 Unlawful discrimination

It is unlawful to discriminate in offering terms of employment on the grounds of sex or marital status (Sex Discrimination Act 1975, ss 1–3, 6), or on the grounds of colour, race, nationality or ethnic or national origins (Race Relations Act 1976, ss 1, 3, 4). There are various exceptions. The most general is genuine occupational qualification (1975 Act, s 7; 1976 Act, s 5). This allows, eg, actors to play parts when authenticity requires a male performer, and vice versa, and waiters of appropriate origin to serve in Indian and Chinese restaurants. Discrimination is also lawful to comply with statutory requirements, in small firms, in households and certain other cases.

Discrimination normally manifests itself in recruitment, but can extend to the definition of the employee's duties. For example, it was discrimination to exclude women examiners from a rota to do a particularly dirty job done by men of the same grade, even though the men were paid more as a consequence (*Ministry of Defence* v *Jeremiah* [1980] QB 87). Discrimination can be indirect, when it is known that applying a rule which has no apparent connection will have that effect. This happened when postmen's rounds were allocated on seniority, and the rules operated with a bias against women (*Steel* v *Union of Post Office Workers* [1978] ICR 181).

6.5.3 Illegality

An employment contract which is illegal in its purpose, or in its intended method of execution, is unenforceable by either party. To this, there are some exceptions dealt with below. The most common examples of illegal contracts are those intended to mislead the Inland Revenue and evade tax (*Napier* v *National Business Agency Ltd* [1951] 2 All ER 264: the employee was allowed an excessive amount for expenses; *Corby* v *Morrison* [1980] ICR 564; in addition to his ordinary wage, the employee received £5 a week free of tax; *Tomlinson* v *Dick Evans 'U' Drive Ltd* [1978] ICR 639; part of the employee's pay was taken out of the petty cash). Another example would be an agreement to drive without third party insurance (*Gregory* v *Ford* [1951] 1 All ER 121).

If only one party to the contract knows of the illegality, the other can enforce the contract (*Burrows* v *Rhodes* [1899] 1 QB 816: Cecil Rhodes wrongly represented to the plaintiff when employing him to go on the Jameson raid that the Queen had given a licence which enabled him to be recruited without contravening the Foreign Enlistment Act 1870. Rhodes could not set up the illegality when sued for breach of contract). The effect of illegality can be avoided by the employer indemnifying the employee against the consequences of committing a criminal offence. The indemnity may be implied (*Gregory* v *Ford*, supra).

6.6 Directors

6.6.1 Status

The position of a director opposite his company is sui generis, and in considering whether or not the rules relating to service agreements apply to that relationship, it is necessary to decide in each case whether the director is employed by the company. At one extreme, it has been said that 'A director is not a servant. He is a person who is doing business for the company, but not upon ordinary terms' (*Hutton* v *West Cork Railway Co* (1883) 23 Ch D 654, 672 per Bowen LJ). As a result, it was held that the managing director of a company was not entitled to the preference on a winding up for outstanding salary, which he would have had if 'a clerk or servant' (*Re Newspaper Proprietary Syndicate Ltd, Hopkinson* v *Newspaper Proprietary Syndicate Ltd* [1900] 2 Ch 349). On the other hand, there have been plenty of modern instances in which director's service agreements have been treated in the same way as other employees' are.

It is suggested that executive directors should now be treated as employees. Non-executive directors with service agreements requiring them to perform certain duties should be in the same category. Non-executive directors performing no other functions are better regarded as holding an appointment. In every case, the director's position is subject to special provisions implied by reason of company law.

The mere fact that a director effectively has total control over a company does not prevent his entering into a service agreement to become its employee (*Lee* v *Lee's Air Farming Ltd* [1961] AC 12). The courts have been insistent that controlling directors must observe the distinction between their own interests and those of the company. Even if they use their votes as shareholders to procure the company to pass a resolution in general meeting ratifying their improper acts they do not escape liability to account to the company. '. . . men who assume the complete control of a company's business must remember that they are not at liberty to sacrifice the interest which they are bound to protect and, while ostensibly acting for the company, divert in their own favour business which should properly belong to the company they represent' (*Cook* v *Deeks* [1916] 1 AC 554, 563 per Lord Buckmaster).

A person may have three distinct positions in relation to a company: shareholder, director and employee. An employee who is also a director may have to observe even higher standards in dealing with the company's affairs and property than other employees. It may prove important to make it clear just what position the director does occupy. An employed chief metallurgist who was subsequently appointed technical director claimed, when dismissed, compensation both for loss of office as director and as chief metallurgist. It was held, on the facts, that he only held a single post (*Wellman Alloys Ltd* v *Russell* [1973] ICR 616). Presumably, the express terms of a service agreement could adopt either alternative.

Other difficulties can arise in relation to the controlling director of a 'one man company'. One was refused a redundancy payment because he failed to prove that he was an employee (*Howarth* v *Howarth (Garments) Ltd* [1968] ITR 288 (*IT*)). When the same question arose in determining whether industrial training levy, a percentage of emoluments of 'any persons employed by the employer', should be paid on a controlling director's salary, it had to be decided by ascertaining whether the facts demonstrated that there was a contract of service (*Road Transport Industry Training Board* v *Readers Garage Ltd* [1969] ITR 195). In those circumstances, a formal service agreement could well be conclusive in favour of the status of employee.

Whether a director is entitled to compensation for unfair dismissal also depends on whether he is an employee. In a case where a director was held not to be an employee the factors leading to the conclusion were: there was no service agreement; remuneration was voted annually, and was shown in the accounts as 'fees and emoluments' and separately from the item for 'wages'; he paid national insurance contributions as a self-employed person (*Parsons* v *Albert J Parsons & Sons Ltd* [1979] ICR 271). But the managing director of an English subsidiary of a Nigerian company was held to be employed by the English company as, although he had no written agreement, he performed the duties of chief executive of it. '. . . where a managing director has no separate contract of service, the terms and conditions of his contract are to be deduced from the terms of the resolution under which he is appointed and the terms of the articles under which the resolution is authorised' (*Folami* v *Nigerline (UK) Ltd* [1978] ICR 277, 282 per Phillips J). Again, there is an argument for a formal service agreement to put the position beyond doubt.

6.6.2 Companies Acts

Certain provisions of the Companies Acts apply automatically to a director, whatever the terms of his agreement with the company:

(i) if a director is required to have a share qualification, he has two months from the date of his appointment to obtain it. In default, the office is vacated (Companies Act 1985. s 291);

(ii) a provision exempting a director from liability for negligence, default, breach of duty or breach of trust is void (s 310);

(iii) a company can always, subject to complying with certain formalities, remove a director from office by ordinary resolution (ss 303, 304).

6.6.3 Articles of association

The terms of a director's appointment will always be subject to the company's articles of association. The same applies to the memorandum of association, although it is rare for them to contain relevant provisions. The articles may subordinate themselves to any agreement between the company and the director, so they must be carefully construed.

The appointment of a managing director under article 72 of the Companies Table A Regulations 1985 is revocable by the directors at will. Accordingly, in the absence of any agreement, a resolution gives rises to no action for damages (*Read* v *Astoria Garage (Streatham) Ltd* [1952] Ch 637). That case in fact arose under article 68 of Table A in the Companies Act 1929, which made no reference to the possibility of an agreement between the company and the managing director. Article 72 in the 1985 Act Table A makes the power of revocation 'subject to any conditions the directors may impose.'

A company is always at liberty to alter its articles (Companies Act 1985, s 9). If in doing so it abrogates an agreement with a director, it will be liable for breach of contract. The position is the same if the new articles merely give power to end an agreement which would not otherwise have been terminable, and it is then brought to an end (*Southern Foundries (1926) Ltd* v *Shirlaw* [1940] AC 701).

Chapter 7

Performing the Duties

7.1 The employee's duties

7.1.1 Competence

Every employee has a duty to perform the duties which he agrees to undertake efficiently, conscientiously and to the best of his ability. This fundamental term is implied into all service agreements. It is rarely necessary, or even desirable, to repeat it expressly. The danger in doing so is that any explicit formulation of the obligation might be interpreted as reducing its scope. Breach of the implied term may give rise to a claim for damages against the employee (*Janata Bank* v *Ahmed Qutubuddan, Same* v *Same* (1981) 1 CR 791). Unusual circumstances should nevertheless be mentioned, eg if the employer delegates his right to give orders and directions to someone whom the employee would not normally have to obey, but it is as well to make it clear that that is in addition to the employee's general duties.

Negligence may not justify an employee's dismissal, unless it is repeated. In contrast, a single act of neglect of duty can be enough to allow the employer to end a contract. It was on this ground that a supervisor employed to oversee croupiers in a casino was sacked for overlooking a croupier's misconduct at a time when there was nothing else which should have been claiming the supervisor's attention (*Turner* v *Pleasurama Casinos Ltd* [1976] IRLR 151). If the employee is employed on the basis that he has some special skills, and is capable of undertaking some special kind of work, then the employee's failure amounts to a fundamental breach of contract (*Harmer* v *Cornelius* (1858) 5 CB(N5)).

Serious incompetence can also be a ground for dismissal. This applied to a pilot who landed his plane so badly that it was seriously damaged. 'The reason for the dismissal was because of the way Captain Taylor handled the aircraft on this day—his lack of skill, his error of judgment, in coming down heavily and putting passengers and crew in peril . . . if the company honestly believed on reasonable grounds that this pilot was lacking in proper capability to fly aircraft on behalf of the company, there was good and sufficient reason for the company to determine the employment there and then' (*Taylor* v *Alidair Ltd* [1978] IRLR 82).

7.1.2 Lawful orders

Part of the employee's duty is to obey the employer's lawful orders. This involves the employee's co-operating in the way the employer decides to organise his business. A lecturer who declined to teach when reasonably required to do so, because he disagreed with the college's reorganisation, was fairly dismissed. His conduct justified the employer in bringing his contract to an end. '. . . an educated man in a responsible academic position must, or at least certainly ought to, have appreciated . . . that his failure to co-operate in the work of the department as directed by the head of the department must put his employment at risk' (*Farnborough* v *Governors of Edinburgh College of Art* [1974] IRLR 245 per Lord Thomson). However, an employee is not obliged to carry out orders which are outside the contractual duties he has agreed to perform (*O'Brien* v *Associated Fire Alarms* [1969] 1 All ER 93). This can often cause problems where there is a dispute as to what the terms encompass (*Cresswell* v *Board of Inland Revenue* [1984] ICR 508).

An order may be unlawful because it would result in an employee committing a crime, or because it is unreasonable. An employee does not have to obey an order to stay at his post when his life would be threatened if he did so (*Ottoman Bank* v *Chakarian* [1930] AC 277). In an old case concerning a domestic servant, circumstances were suggested that might justify wilful disobedience of a similar order: '. . . where the servant apprehends danger to her life, or violence to her person, from the master; or where, from an infectious disorder raging in the house, she must go out for the preservation of her life' (*Turner* v *Mason* (1845) 14 M&W 112, 117–18 per Alderson B).

The fact that an order inconveniences the employee, eg by increasing the amount of his own time spent in travelling to work, does not necessarily make it unreasonable and unlawful (*Beale* v *Great Western Railway Co* (1901) 17 TLR 450).

There are cases in which an employer loans an employee to

someone else, frequently in connection with hiring out a machine, but some temporary clerical workers are in the same position. While the loan continues, the power to give orders may be, wholly or partly, with the 'temporary employer'. There has been litigation about which employee in those circumstances is liable for the employee's negligence, and this suggests the principles to be followed in determining the orders the employee is bound to obey. When a crane and driver were hired out, the owners and not the hirers were responsible (*Mersey Docks and Harbour Board* v *Coggins and Griffith (Liverpool)* [1947] AC 1). But an electrician who was loaned sued for negligence following an injury, and recovered against the temporary employer (*Garrard* v *AE Southey & Co and Standard Telephones and Cables Ltd* [1952] 2 QB 174). The court distinguished between the loan of complex technical machinery and its skilled operator, and the temporary transfer of a worker in a routine trade. It is suggested that the temporary employer should only give orders, and therefore the employee only need obey them, to the limit of his technical competence and of the responsibility which he is undertaking.

7.1.3 Loyalty

An employee has a fundamental duty of fidelity to his employer. It is probably impossible to define all the circumstances in which this applies, so it may well be better for an agreement, if it mentions the point at all, to confine itself to such general and traditional words as 'the employee shall well and faithfully serve the employer'.

One aspect of this is that the employee must not turn his position as employee to his private profit. He must account to the employer for any private profit which he makes. The reason for this is that, 'He puts himself in such a position that he has a temptation not faithfully to perform his duty to his employer' (*Boston Deep Sea Fishing and Ice Co Ltd* v *Ansell* (1888) 39 Ch D 339, 357 per Cotton LJ). This applies to an employee who accepts commission from a third party, even though there is no evidence of corrupt influence or improper advice tendered to the employer (*Harrington* v *Victoria Graving Dock Co* (1878) 3 QBD 549). Similarly, the directors of a company having entered into a number of contracts in the company's name could not later contract in their own names for their own profit, even though they used their votes as holders of seventy-five per cent of the company's shares to pass a resolution approving the position (*Cook* v *Deeks* [1916] 1 AC 554).

An employee is not entitled to benefit from corrupt behaviour, even though he would not be doing so at the expense of his employer. A soldier who wore his uniform to prevent illicit goods being seized by the police, and was paid £20,000 for his services, could not recover the money taken from him when he was arrested, even though that was money which would never have gone to his employer, the Crown (*Reading* v *Attorney General* [1951] AC 507).

The requirement of loyalty also imposes a duty on an employee to report to his employer dishonest or improper conduct on the part of a fellow employee. This not only applies to an employee whose job is one of supervision (*Turner* v *Pleasurama Casinos Ltd* [1967] IRLR 151), but also generally (*Swain* v *West (Butchers) Ltd* [1936] 3 All ER 261: the general manager was properly dismissed because he did not report the misdeeds of the managing director).

However, in the case of *Ladbroke Racing Ltd* v *King* [1989] EAT 794 where an employer's own rules did not include an express duty to report malpractices, the implied obligation involved leaving a discretion to the employee as to whether or not the employee should report such malpractices. So in this case the employees were not unreasonable in failing to report the misdeeds and management of the man to whom they reported. However, the employee is not under a duty to disclose his own misconduct (*Bell* v *Lever Brothers Ltd* [1932] AC 161). But his obligation to disclose the misconduct of others subsists even if by doing so he incriminates himself (*Sybron Corporation* v *Rochem Ltd* [1983] 2 All ER 707).

Other aspects of this duty are considered elsewhere in this book as follows:

(i) the duty not to solicit customers (chapter 11),
(ii) the duty not to disclose trade secrets or equivalent confidential information (chapter 12),
(iii) the duty not to solicit other employees (chapter 11),
(iv) the duty not to compete during employment (chapter 11),
(v) the springboard principle (chapter 12).

7.1.4 Disobedience and impudence

Although obedience to lawful orders is of the essence of an employee's duty, not every act of disobedience is a sufficient ground for the employer to dismiss the employee. '. . . one act of disobedience or misconduct can justify dismissal only if it is of a nature which goes to show (in effect) that the servant is repudiating the contract, or one of its essential conditions' (*Laws* v *London Chronicle (Indicator Newspapers) Ltd* [1959] WLR 698, 701 per Lord Evershed MR).

Wilful disobedience in a matter of that kind gives the employer the option to treat the contract as repudiated by the employee. If, on the other hand, he elects to allow the employment to continue, the contract remains in full force and the employee is even entitled to payment of wages for any period of suspension on account of the disobedience (*Gorse* v *Durham County Council* [1971] 1 WLR 775).

The position is similar in a case of impudence or insubordination. Even where the incident is grave, as where an apprentice was very rude to the managing director of the employing company in front of other apprentices, a single act may be insufficient to justify dismissal (*Shortland* v *Chantrill* [1975] IRLR 208).

7.1.5 Honesty

Honesty in performing his duties is a fundamental obligation of an employee, which need not be expressly stated in his contract. 'There must be in such relation an implied contract on the part of the servant to do the work of his office honestly' (*Boston Deep Sea Fishing and Ice Co Ltd* v *Ansell* (1888) 39 Ch D 339, 347 per Kekewich J). The standard required of an employee can be such that conduct is unacceptable even though it is not criminal. A betting shop manager was properly dismissed for taking money out of the till, when he knew his employer would disapprove, even though his motive may not have been dishonest to the extent of making it an offence (*Sinclair* v *Neighbour* [1967] 2 QB 279).

An employee who steals his employer's goods is liable to instant dismissal. There can be difficulties in justifying dismissal while a case is under investigation or while a trial is pending. Although suspension will sometimes be appropriate at that stage, dismissal before the charges have been proved can, on the facts, be fair, a standard which is generally more favourable to the employee (*Scottish Special Housing Association* v *Linnen* [1979] IRLR 265).

In order to determine whether dismissal is the appropriate action where an employer suspects an employee of dishonesty, the employer should be able to establish:

(i) that he believed the employee to be guilty of the offence,
(ii) that he had reasonable grounds to sustain that belief, and

(iii) that he had carried out all reasonable investigations given the circumstances of the case (*British Home Stores Ltd* v *Burchell* [1978] IRLR 379).

This applies particularly when there may be appreciable delay before the outcome of the case is known (*Carr* v *Alexander Russell Ltd* [1976] IRLR 220 (*Ct of Sess*)).

Dishonesty in connection with clock cards, recording hours of work, is a particularly sensitive issue, generally justifying instant dismissal. '. . . false clocking in or false claims in respect of hours done can be matters which justify instant dismissal. In the industrial scene these are serious offences of dishonesty' (*Stewart* v *Western SMT Co Ltd* [1978] IRLR 553, 555 per Slynn J). The sanction can also apply to an employee who falsifies a fellow employee's clocking card (*Dalton* v *Burton's Gold Medal Biscuits Ltd* [1974] IRLR 45).

7.1.6 Spare time

In some jobs honesty and integrity are justifiably considered prerequisites, even if the conduct which falls below the standard demanded occurs outside working hours and is not connected with the employment. Trustworthiness is not a 'qualification' for the purpose of justifying the fairness of a dismissal in answer to a claim for compensation (*Singh* v *London Country Bus Services Ltd* [1976] IRLR 176). All the same, it is considered that a dismissal would not be wrongful in a case where the employee's job involved handling the employer's money and the employee was convicted of an offence involving dishonesty.

7.2 Director's duties

7.2.1 Introduction

The appointment of the employee as a director carries with it additional general responsibilities and duties to those already owed by the employee. It is important for the employee to understand the nature of the appointment but there is no readily available summary of the duties owed as a director to which an employee can be referred. In Re *City Equitable Fire Insurance Co Ltd* [1925] Ch 407 Romer J observed that 'it is indeed impossible to describe the duty of directors in general terms, whether by way of analogy or otherwise'.

The company director is an agent of the company. It is now

common for the director to be an employee of the company. However, the director's status as employee is quite distinct from his status as director (*Lee* v *Lee's Air Farming* [1961] AC12). A director owes two main duties, a fiduciary duty and a duty to exercise skill and care in carrying out his office.

7.2.2 Fiduciary duty

The fiduciary duty owed requires the director to act in good faith in his dealings with or on behalf of the company and exercise the powers and fulfill the duties of his office honestly (Re *Smith* v *Fawcett Ltd* [1942] Ch 304 CA). The duty is owed to shareholders primarily (*Percival* v *Wright* [1902] 2 Ch 421) and it may include the company's creditors where the company has become insolvent and the interest of employees.

The director must not put himself in a position where there is an actual or potential conflict between his personal interest and his duty to the company. The fiduciary duty owed by the director would prevent him from making a personal profit from any opportunities which result from his position and of course this would particularly apply to price sensitive information which he gained and used to secure a profit (Percival v *Wright* [1902] 2 Ch 421). In the case of *Regal (Hastings) Ltd* v *Gulliver* [1942] 1 AER 378 Lord Porter said

> Directors, no doubt, are not trustees, but they occupy a fiduciary position towards the company whose board they form. Their liability in this respect does not depend upon a breach of duty but upon the proposition that a Director does not make a profit out of property acquired by reason of his relationship to the Company of which he is a Director. The matter is not that he could not have acquired the property with the Company itself—the profit which he makes is the company's even though the property by means of which he has made it was not or could not have been acquired on its behalf.

7.2.3 Duty of care

Generally the duty of care is the same for both executives and non-executive directors. But executive director's who are employee's, will normally have service agreements which contain a clear statement of what is required of them. Whether the duty has been discharged will be judged subjectively, save where the duties have been set out in the service agreement, where it will be judged objectively. In Re *City Equitable Fire Insurance Co Ltd* [1925] Ch 407 Romer J expressed three basic principles:

(1) A director need not exhibit in the performance of his duties a greater degree of skill than may be reasonably required of a man whose knowledge and experience . . . is perhaps only another way of stating the same proposition to say the directors are not liable for mere errors of judgement.
(2) A director is not bound to give continuous attention to the affairs of his company. His duties are of an intermittent nature to be performed at periodical board meetings, and at meetings of any committee of the board upon which he happens to be placed. He is not, however, bound to attend all such meetings although he ought to attend whenever, in the circumstances, he is reasonably able to do so.
(3) In respect of all duties that, having regard to the exigencies of business, in the articles of association, may properly be left to some other official a director is in the absence of grounds for suspicion, justified in trusting that official to perform such duties honestly.

As a statement of principle this is still valid, but it should be noted that the judgement reflects attitudes current at that time and due account must be taken of the fact that many directors are now executive directors whose obligations are specified in their contracts of employment, and accordingly the standard of skill they are expected to demonstrate will be higher than before.

7.2.4 Liability for breach of duty

Liability for breaches of duty can result in significant claims being brought against the director. These claims can be made even if the director has not made any personal gain from the breach. Generally claims against a director are brought by the company itself, although shareholders can, in exceptional cases, bring claims. Any attempt to exclude the director's liability for negligence, default, breach of duty, or breach of trust is void (s 310 of the Companies Act 1985) but it is now possible and indeed not uncommon for the company to provide professional liability insurance to indemnify the director against such claims (s 137 of the Companies Act 1989). It is also common practice for executive directors to be indemnified against the cost of a successful criminal action. The court also has a power to exempt a director from liability if he has acted honestly and reasonably and having regard to all the circumstances all fairly to be excused (s 727 of the Companies Act 1985).

7.3 The employer's duties

7.3.1 Good faith

An employer now has a statutory duty not to dismiss an employee unfairly (Employment Protection (Consolidation) Act 1978, s 54). This concept of general fairness was a major extension of the law's traditional insistence on contractual rights. It now forms a separate topic, outside the scope of this book. It has been said, and it seems likely that it was under the influence of this change in the emphasis in the role of employment law, that there is an implied term in service agreements that there should be mutual trust and confidence (*Post Office* v *Roberts* [1980] IRLR 347: the employer was in breach in not telling the employee of a poor assessment made of her performance). This concept is still in a state of flux. There does not seem to be anything that can usefully be added to service agreements on the point.

7.3.2 Remuneration

The employer undertakes to pay his employees in return for the provision of their services. This is fully discussed in chapter 8.

7.3.3 Indemnity

The employer is obliged to indemnify his employees regarding all expenses which are incurred during the proper performance of their duties under their contracts.

7.3.4 Safety of employees

The employer has a duty to take all reasonable care for the safety of his employees in the course of their work (*Mathews* v *Kuwait Bechtel Corporation* [1959] 2 QB 57). The employers also has statutory duties under the Health and Safety at Work Act 1974. This act imposes commercial sanctions in respect of an employer's breach of the duties created by it. Claims for injuries sustained in the course of employment are generally formulated as breaches of contract or statutory duty.

7.3.5 Provision of work

The employer is not generally under any obligation to supply his employee with work to do, although he is not absolved from paying the agreed remuneration merely because there is no work (*Turner* v *Sawdon & Co* [1901] 2 KB 653). That decision has been criticised, but it appears correctly to state the general rule. To this, there are exceptions, where the employee stands directly to gain from doing the work, in addition to his remuneration from the employer. The following are entitled to insist on work, or to treat the contract as repudiated if there is none:

(i) Entertainers who stand to benefit in public reputation and prestige by appearing (*Marbé* v *George Edwardes (Daly's Theatre) Ltd* [1928] 1 KB 269). On the breach of such a contract, there can be an award of damages for the loss of publicity, in addition to loss of wages (*Herbert Clayton and Jack Waller Ltd* v *Oliver* [1930] AC 209).

(ii) Employees whose remuneration, or part of it, depends on doing work, eg a salesman working on commission (*Re an Arbitration between Rubel Bronze and Metal Co Ltd and Vos* [1918] 1 KB 315). Another example was a press photographer paid a retainer for the first option on all his ideas, who was held to have a contract of service with an implied term that the employee would be given sufficient commissions to allow him to earn reasonable renumeration (*Bauman* v *Hulton Press Ltd* [1952] 2 All ER 1121).

(iii) Possibly, a person entering employment at a low wage to gain business experience or mechanical skill (*Re an Arbitration between Rubel Bronze and Metal Co Ltd and Vos*, supra, p324). Apprentices and articled clerks would come into this category.

(iv) An employee whose contract contains a term, whether express or implied, that he be provided with suitable work (*Breach* v *Epsylon Industries Ltd* [1976] ICR 316).

A similar type of case is where the employer puts it beyond his power to continue the employment, where again he is liable for breach of contract in not providing the work. '. . . it would be implied that the council, having employed the plaintiff to build their town hall, agreed with him that they would not prevent him from doing the work, and so prevent him from earning his remuneration' (*Thomas* v *Hammersmith Borough Council* [1938] 3 All ER 203, 208 per Slesser LJ, obiter). This will apply where the employee's appointment was to a unique post. A man was employed as a chief sub-editor of a particular Sunday newspaper. When the employer sold the newspaper he broke his contract, because he could not continue to employ the employee in that capacity and although other journalistic work could be similar it could not be equivalent (*Collier* v *Sunday Referee Publishing Co Ltd* [1940] 2 KB 647).

An employer's failure to provide work can lead to a liability to make a statutory redundancy payment. One of the definitions of redundancy for this purpose is: 'the fact that the requirements of that business for employees to carry out work of a particular kind, or for employees to carry out work of a particular kind in the place where he was so employed, have ceased or diminished or are expected to cease or diminish' (Employment Protection (Consolidation) Act 1978, s 81(2)(*b*)). The employer must dismiss the employee for liability to arise; failure to provide work, while still employing the employee, does not without more trigger off the duty to make a payment. An employer who cannot provide work in one place, although he can in another, can avoid the need to make a redundancy payment, by a provision in the employee's service agreement reserving the right to require him to change his place of employment.

7.3.6 Drafting

An employer's undertaking to provide work is a useful safeguard for an employee whose remuneration depends on the opportunities it gives him. However, it is difficult to draft a satisfactory clause where pay is linked to performance as an incentive to the employee to work hard. The result the employee would like to achieve—a guarantee of income—depends not only on the provision of work, but also on the employee's own subsequent efforts. The best that can often be achieved is a reference to a reasonable income.

7.3.7 Precedents

Provision of work to earn selling commission

THE Company shall at all times allocate to the Executive a sufficiently wide area as his exclusive selling territory to enable him to earn a reasonable sum in commission

As an employer's liability for additional damages, for lack of the chance of publicity, on the cancellation of an entertainment contract depends on the breach of an implied contract term, it can be negatived by a clause in a service agreement.

Damages restricted to loss of earnings

IN the event that the Company for any reason whatsoever is not able or decides not to stage or continue to stage the production for which the Executive has been employed the Company shall not be liable to compensate him for any loss he may suffer as a result except by reason of the fact that he is not paid the salary due under this agreement

Part III

Pay and Benefits

Chapter 8

Pay

8.1 Amount

8.1.1 Contract terms

A wage or salary paid by the employer is normally the central benefit which the employee receives under a service agreement, as consideration for the work he undertakes to do. It is possible to have a contract where this is not so. The whole of an employee's pay may come from third parties. '. . . a person may be none the less a servant by reason of the fact that his remuneration consists solely of tips' (*Pauley* v *Kenaldo* [1953] 1 WLR 187, 191 per Birkett LJ). Or again, an employee may work exclusively for some benefit in kind, eg for free accommodation.

A service agreement should state with certainty the amount of the employee's pay, or, on the principle *id certum est quod certum reddi potest*, should give the terms from which it can be calculated, eg £*x* per hour up to thirty-nine hours a week, and thereafter £*x* × 1½ per hour. This amount is also one of the statutory particulars which the employer is required to give to the employee under s 1 of the Employment Protection (Consolidation) Act 1978. The assumption is that sums stated are in sterling.

A service agreement may stipulate that the wage to be paid under it is to be as fixed by collective agreement between the employer and trade unions. That incorporates the collective agreement terms into the service agreement (*National Coal Board* v *Galley* [1958] 1 WLR 16).

8.1.2 Quantum meruit

The fact that a person agrees to do work does not automatically give rise to an obligation to pay him (*Loftus* v *Roberts* (1902) 18 TLR 532). But if there is an agreement to pay a wage, although the amount of it is not fixed, then the employer has a duty to pay. The employee can recover a reasonable sum, assessed quantum meruit (*Way* v *Latilla* [1937] 3 All ER 759). '. . . if no trade usage assists the court as to the amount of the commission [which was there the relevant form of remuneration], it appears to me clear that the court may take into account the bargainings between the parties, not with a view to completing their bargain for them, but as evidence of the value which each of them puts upon the services' (ibid, p. 764, per Lord Atkin). The quantum meruit principle can be used to assess and enforce payment of a reasonable sum to represent an unquantified bonus payable in addition to a fixed salary (*Powell* v *Braun* [1954] 1 WLR 401).

The question whether any payment is due must be considered in two stages. First, is there any enforceable contract that some payment, albeit unspecified, will be made? Were a salary figure to be omitted from a formal service agreement, it would take a great deal to negative the assumption that there was an intention to pay. Secondly, what is a reasonable sum?

A director of a company has no automatic right to payment by reason of his appointment. 'It is not implied from the mere fact that he is a director that he is to have a right to be paid for it' (*Hutton* v *West Cork Railway Co* (1883) 23 Ch D 654). A director who is to be paid, but who loses office because he does not acquire a qualifying shareholding in the company within the time limit, can make a quantum meruit claim (*Craven-Ellis* v *Canons Ltd* [1936] 2 KB 403).

8.1.3 Equal pay

A service agreement to employ a woman incorporates, by statutory implication, 'an equality clause'. The effect that this has is that, where the woman is employed on like work with a man, or work rated equivalent to that of a man, the terms of the woman's contract may not be or become less favourable than the man's. If necessary, the agreement is treated as modified to make it equivalent to the man's. The only case where the woman's contract is not varied is where the reason for the disparity is a material difference, other than the difference of sex, and this is for the employer to prove (Equal Pay Act 1970, s 1(1)-(3); Sex Discrimination Act 1975, s 8(1)).

The Act is worded on the assumption that a woman is unjustly paid less than a man. Nevertheless, it expressly declares that it is to be read in the reverse sense as well (1970 Act, s 1(13); 1975

Act, Sched 1, para 1(4)). This explanation of the provisions is also framed from the woman's point of view, but must similarly be read in reverse as well.

A woman seeking to enforce a claim for higher wages under an equality clause can do so by way of complaint to an industrial tribunal not later than six months after the end of her employment, and subject to a limitation period of two years (1970 Act, s 2). It may, however, be that a claim can be made for a full six years (Limitation Act 1980, s 5) if action is taken in the courts under art 119 of the Treaty of Rome, which also guarantees equal pay for equal work (*Charles Early & Marriott (Witney) Ltd* v *Smith; Snoxell* v *Vauxhall Motors Ltd* [1978] QB 11, 33–4). That article of the treaty is directly enforceable in domestic courts (*Defrenne* v *Sabena* [1976] ICR 547 (*ECJ*)).

No express term in a service agreement can exclude or limit the provisions of the Equal Pay Act 1970. One which purports to do so is void (Sex Discrimination Act 1975, s 77(3)). All that the draftsman can do to try to avoid its application is so to define the duties of the employee in question that there is a material difference which gives rise to and justifies any wage differential or any other material factor apart from sex. '. . . the burden of proof upon the employer is not a very heavy burden of proof. . . . It is on the balance of probabilities' (*National Vulcan Engineering Insurance Group Ltd* v *Wade* [1979] QB 132, 140 per Lord Denning MR).

8.1.4 Minimum wages

In a number of trades, statutory minimum rates of pay are laid down. These only rarely affect cases where formal service agreements are used. An agreement which specifies less than the minimum remuneration has effect as if that minimum were substituted (Wages Councils Act 1979). Orders made by wages councils for the industries affected may fix not only pay, but also holidays and holiday pay, and other terms and conditions of employment (s 11; Employment Protection Act 1975, Sched 7, Pt I). Few wages councils remain in existence following the repeal of the Wages Councils Act 1979.

8.1.5 Directors

The articles of association of a company may require that the directors' remuneration be determined by the company in general meeting (as does art 82 of Table A of the Companies (Tables A-

F) Regulations 1985). If the only shareholders entitled to vote at general meetings are the only directors, their approval of the accounts showing the remuneration is equivalent to a resolution approving it, and nothing more is needed (*Re Duomatic Ltd* [1969] 2 Ch 365).

A company is forbidden to pay a director remuneration, whether or not in his capacity as director, free of income tax. This prohibition does not apply to a contract in force on 18 July 1945 which expressly provides for such a payment. A service agreement which purports to provide for a tax free sum takes effect as if the payment specified were a gross sum, subject to tax (Companies Act 1985, s 311). This statutory interpretation of the figure will apply when the proper contents of a statutory statement of particulars of employment are being considered (*Owens* v *Multilux Ltd* [1974] IRLR 113). The fact that the Act imposes on the contract, rather than merely declaring it to be illegal, saves it from becoming totally unenforceable.

Where the director is an executive director of the company it is normal to state clearly in the service agreement that the remuneration paid to the employee director includes directors' fees in respect of all directorships he holds solely by virtue of his employment with the company.

8.2 Variation

8.2.1 Subsequent agreement

All terms of a service agreement continue unaltered and enforceable until varied by agreement, even if the parties contemplate, as is likely with terms about pay, that there will be an alteration. When the employer proposes to increase the employee's wage, there will normally be ready agreement. However, if there is no agreement, as is likely if the proposal is to reduce the salary, the original sum remains payable (*WPM Retail Ltd* v *Lang* [1978] ICR 787). An employer who requires an employee to accept a reduction in wages repudiates the contract, and the employee can treat himself as having been dismissed (*Marriott* v *Oxford & District Co-operative Society Ltd (No 2)* [1970] 1 QB 186).

Because neither party to a service agreement can oblige the other to agree to a later variation in the terms, every long term agreement should contain some provision for varying the salary payable under it. There are a number of ways in which this can be done. If the particular employment is covered by a collective agreement, the wage level agreed from time to time by the collective bargaining procedure can be adopted by reference. Another way is to link pay levels to some outside index, such as the index of retail prices. A default possibility is to give the employee the option to leave the job before the end of the fixed term if no satisfactory rise is given.

If the parties rely on subsequent negotiation to agree upon salary increases, it is arguable that the increases are not enforceable, because they are not supported by consideration, the employee having a continuing obligation to perform his duties under the agreement. For this reason, the cautiously correct way to record such a salary increase is by an agreement as a deed. It can be endorsed on the service agreement. An agreement by deed requires no consideration to make it enforceable.

8.2.2 Index linking

The most common form of index linking for salary, although the practice itself is not common, is a tie to the index of retail prices (commonly called the cost of living index). This is not wholly appropriate, because it probably will not maintain the comparability of the employee's salary with that earned by others in equivalent jobs and it bears no relation to the value of the employee's contribution to the employer's business nor to the profitability of that business. More important, it must be appreciated that at high income levels, to increase an employee's gross salary by the average inflationary rise may well not increase his net spending power after tax by the same proportion.

Other indices could be used, eg the average industrial wage, but none is wholly appropriate. The attraction to a link to the index of retail prices is that the employee's salary can be seen roughly to maintain its purchasing power, subject always to the point just made about the effect of taxation. Further, the validity of that appearance of maintaining comparability depends on whether or not the employee spends his money on the items which go to make up the index.

In selecting an index for this purpose, it is suggested that the criteria should be: that it is prepared by an independent body of accepted objectivity, that it is recalculated fairly frequently, and that it is published in a reasonably accessible manner. Any clause referring to the index should make provision for any temporary suspension of publication, perhaps because of industrial action, for its ceasing to be published and for its basis of calculation being altered.

8.2.3 Precedents

Supplementary deed recording pay increase

BY this deed dated . . . 19 . . which is supplemental to the within written agreement the parties to that agreement now agree that from . . . 19 . . the salary payable to the Executive under that agreement shall be £ . . . a year but that all other terms of the agreement shall remain unaltered.

Option to determine in default of pay increase

THE parties intend that the salary payable by the Company to the Executive shall from time to time be increased. For [three] months following every [second] anniversary of the start of the Executive's employment he shall have the option to end this agreement by giving at least [one month's] written notice to the Company unless on that anniversary his salary is at least [eighteen] per cent greater than it was [two years] previously.

Index linked salary

(i) ON every [second] anniversary of the start of the Executive's employment his salary shall be reviewed and the annual amount of it payable immediately before that review date shall be increased as from that date by such percentage (if any) as the last figure of the Index of Retail Prices ('index') published by the Department of Employment prior to that date shall have increased over the figure of the index current [two years] previously.

(ii) If during the [two years] immediately prior to any review date the basis of computation of the index shall have changed any official reconciliation between the two bases of computation published by the Department of Employment shall be binding on the Executive and the Company.

(iii) In the absence of such official reconciliation adjustments shall be applied to the latest index figure to make it as nearly as practicably fairly comparable with the figure with which it is being compared.

(iv) If the index is no longer published an alternative method of periodically adjusting the Executive's salary shall be adopted either by reference to other published statistics or otherwise.

(v) If the parties are unable to agree on any question arising under paragraphs (iii) or (iv) it shall be referred for decision to an independent Fellow of the Institute of Chartered Accountants of England and Wales nominated and paid by the Company whose decision shall be final and binding on the parties.

(vi) In this clause any reference to the Department of Employment includes the body for the time being officially responsible for publication of the index and any reference to the index includes any index expressly published to replace the Index of Retail Prices.

8.3 Performance linked

8.3.1 Commission

A clause which entitles the employee to commission payments should make clear: on what commission is to be paid (eg in the case of a salesman, is it on orders placed with the employer, orders which the employer actually executes or orders for which the employer is paid?), at what rate, when it becomes due and how frequently it is paid. An employee who receives commission in advance normally has to repay any part of it which has not been earned when his employment comes to an end (*Rivoli Hats Ltd* v *Gooch* [1953] 1 WLR 1190), although a service agreement can be so worded as to allow him to retain whatever he has been paid (*Clayton Newbury Ltd* v *Findlay* [1953] 1 WLR 1194*n*).

8.3.2 Bonus on profits

An incentive appropriate for managers is a bonus linked to the employer's profit, which is the ultimate test of management, and may not be directly linked to expanding sales or turnover. There are two problems in drafting such a clause.

First, care must be taken to define the meaning of profit for this purpose. While defining what is to be taken into account, it is generally best to have the final figure certified by the employer's auditors. They should be consulted at the drafting stage to make sure that they accept that the proposed formula is workable. It may also be advisable to express the employee's entitlement as a percentage of net profits in excess of a base figure.

Secondly, provision needs to be made for the result of the introduction of more equity capital into the business. This capital may be raised to finance the takeover of another business, which will increase the profit earned. That capital will be serviced by the payment of dividend, which, without more, will not be a charge against the company's earnings before arriving at the profit figure. This brings the danger that the profit figure on which the bonus is calculated is unduly high, being inflated simply because of the decision to finance an acquisition out of equity capital rather than borrowings. Apart from the unfairness of paying a bonus on what is not, from the shareholders' point of view, true profit, this involves the disadvantage that the executive with such an agreement might be influenced in deciding or recommending how an acquisition should be financed by the impact of the alternatives on his own earnings. The point can be met by a notional charge of interest on any new capital against profit before the bonus is calculated or simply fixing a ceiling figure for the bonus.

8.3.3 Precedents

Commission on sales

IN addition to his monthly salary the Company shall pay to the Executive a commission of . . . per cent of the retail price (excluding value added tax) of the goods sold by him/of the orders taken by him and executed by the Company. Commission shall be earned on the date of the sale/of the execution of the order by the Company but shall be paid on the last day of the month following the month during which it was earned.

Bonus on profits

(i) IN addition to his monthly salary the Company shall pay to the Executive a bonus of . . . per cent of the Company's net profit throughout the period of his employment to be paid to him within one month of the adoption of the Company's accounts by its annual general meeting in each year.

(ii) For this purpose the Company's net profit means profit after paying or making adequate reserve in respect of:

(*a*) the Company's liability to corporation tax
(*b*) depreciation of the Company's plant and equipment
(*c*) directors' fees and salaries of working directors [including the salary of the Executive] and
(*d*) the Company's future requirements of working capital or for such other purposes as its board of directors considers it desirable to create reserves

and after deducting notional interest in accordance with paragraph (iii) if applicable but before payment of the bonus payable under this clause or the payment of any bonus calculated as a percentage of the net profit of the Company now or at any time payable to any other director or employee of the Company.

(iii) If the Company has issued shares for cash or other valuable consideration after the date of this agreement notional interest shall be charged in respect of the net proceeds of every such issue of shares at the rate of One and a half per cent above the base rate for the time being of . . . Bank plc (or if that rate shall no longer be published at such other rate as the Company's auditors shall determine).

(iv) The Company shall cause its auditors to act as experts and to certify on or before the date of each annual general meeting of the Company the amount of the net profit of the Company for the purpose of this clause for the period covered by the accounts presented to that meeting and such certificate shall be conclusive and binding on the parties.

(v) For the purposes of calculating the Executive's bonus the net profit of the Company shall be deemed to accrue without fluctuation from day to day and shall be apportioned on a daily basis.

[(vi) The Company shall make payments on account of bonus to the Executive on the last day of every month of one-eighteenth of the sum which was or (had this agreement then been in force) would have been due in respect of the profit shown in the Company's last audited accounts PROVIDED THAT if the aggregate of the monthly sums paid to the Executive exceeds the amount due in any year under paragraph (i) the excess shall be repaid by the Executive to the Company as soon as the amount of it is ascertained.]

(vii) Payments to the Executive under this bonus clause shall not exceed £ . . . in respect of the said financial period.

8.4 Payment

The Wages Act 1986 makes specific provisions as to the deductions that can be made from 'workers' wages but makes no provision as to the way in which the wages are paid, although certain provisions will still be found in certain industries where Wages Councils retain some measure of control, particularly with regard to the wages of low paid employees.

When an employee to whom wages must normally be paid in cash is absent from his proper or usual place of employment at the time for payment, those wages can normally be paid to him by postal order or money order. This applies in the case of absence on duty or by reason of illness or personal injury. The employee can cancel the effect of this provision by giving notice to the employer to that effect (Payment of Wages Act 1960, s 4). The limits of this rule should be noted. It does not apply to cases of absence on holiday or by reason of temporary layoff. The authorised methods of payment do not include cheque or transfer to a bank account. There is no express mention of sending the payment to the employee by post, although this must presumably be the intention.

Most employees have a right to a written itemised pay statement at or before the time of payment, and, if the employer wishes, a standing statement of fixed deductions (Employment Protection (Consolidation) Act 1978, ss 8, 9). This right cannot be excluded or limited by a service agreement. Any provision purporting to do so is void (s 140(1)).

8.4.1 Non cash payments

An employee whose wages would otherwise have to be paid in cash may request his employer to pay in another, specified way, and if the employer agrees, payment in that way is lawful. The methods of payment which can be requested are: direct to a bank account in the employee's sole name, or a joint account with one or more other people; by postal order; by money order; or by cheque. The employee's request must be in writing, can only specify one of the payment methods and may be withdrawn on four weeks' notice (Payment of Wages Act 1960, ss 1, 3).

A service agreement can contain a clause which constitutes an employee's request for payment in some way other than cash, and the employer's agreement to it. Although the Act envisages the procedure starting with an employee's request, there is nothing to prevent the employer initiating the process and providing the documentation. Incorporating the request into a service agreement will not prevent either party's being able to cancel the arrangement.

8.4.2 Seamen

A seaman's wages under a crew agreement must be paid to him in full on discharge from his ship, and he is entitled to an account showing how they are made up. If the amount due exceeds £50, and it is not practicable to pay it all at once, a quarter of the sum due (or £50 if greater) must be paid at once and the remainder within seven days. The penalties for late payment are stringent. For the first fifty-six days of delay, full wages continue to become due. Then, anything outstanding carries interest at the rate of twenty per cent a year. Failure without reasonable cause to render an account is an offence punishable on summary conviction by a fine of up to £20 (Merchant Shipping Act 1970, ss 7, 8). Sums may be deducted from the wages due in respect of canteen bills, goods supplied, radio or telephone calls, postage expenses, cash advances and allotments, and also for any actual losses to the employer by reason of the seaman's absence without leave (maximum £50) and of breaches of the seaman's obligations under the crew agreement (maximum £50) (Merchant Shipping (Seamen's Wages and Accounts) Regulations 1972, regs 4–6; Merchant Shipping (Seamen's Wages and Accounts) (Fishing Vessels) Regulations 1972, regs 6–8).

Chapter 9

Other Payments

9.1 Sick pay

9.1.1 When payable

Every employer is obliged by statute to pay statutory sick pay ('SSP') for the first eight weeks of any absence on account of sickness during each tax year (the Social Security and Housing Benefits Act 1982). Payment or SSP is separate and distinct from any contractual right that an employee may have to be paid sick pay.

There is a presumption, rebuttable by agreement between the parties, that the employer's obligation to pay an employee's salary continues unabated notwithstanding the employee's absence as a result of illness or injury. It was said that the remedy of the employer who wished to cease to pay was to dismiss the employee. Sick pay schemes and terms in service agreements were therefore introduced not so much as additional cash benefits for employees, but rather to modify the employer's liability in the interests of achieving a reasonable balance. With arrangements to pay sick pay at a rate less than full wages, an employer can be persuaded to enter into a long term service agreement, and does not need to dismiss an absent employee whose employment contract was subject to notice. '. . . under a contract of service, irrespective of the question of the length of notice provided by that contract, wages continue through sickness and incapacity from sickness to do the work contracted for until the contract is terminated by notice by the employer in accordance with the terms of the contract' (*Marrison* v *Bell* [1939] 2 KB 187, 198 per Scott LJ). This approach was adopted when a production manager was held to be entitled to a production bonus geared to output despite his absence on account of sickness (*Orman* v *Saville Sportswear Ltd*

[1960] 1 WLR 1055). Employers' rights to determine employees' contracts in the event of the employees' illness have also been modified by the unfair dismissal provisions.

The presumption that pay continues during absence through sickness can be reversed even by an informal oral agreement between the parties. In one case, a written statement of terms of employment made no mention of sick pay, but a term excluding it was implied from evidence that that was the employer's general practice and that the employee had not claimed sick pay for seven months' absence (*Mears* v *Safecar Security Ltd* [1982] 2 All ER 865). It seems that the strength of evidence of an agreement to reverse the presumption need not be great.

That reliance on a contractual term is consistent with another older formulation of the rule: 'If you have a weekly hiring of a servant without more, and with nothing in the terms of it, whether they are express or implied, to suggest that during temporary absence through illness he is not to be paid, then you may assume that he is to be paid, and that it was the intention of the parties that he should be paid' (*Petrie* v *MacFisheries Ltd* [1940] 1 KB 258, 265 per du Parcq LJ). When sick pay is payable under the contract, but no term has been agreed as to the period during which sick pay will be paid, then the courts may imply a term that the sick pay should be paid for a reasonable period (*Howman & Son* v *Blythe* [1983] IRLR 139).

When payment is made during sickness, the question also arises whether the employer is liable for the full salary, with the employee keeping any social security sickness benefit that may be paid, or whether the employer can deduct the amount of any benefit. It has been held, obiter because the decision was that no sick pay at all need be paid, that when the employer pays he may deduct the amount of the benefit (*Mears* v *Safecar Security Ltd* [1981] 1 WLR 1214 (*EAT*), the point was not decided on appeal, but Stephenson LJ indicated agreement: [1982] 2 All ER 865, 881).

9.1.2 Funded schemes

Some employers fund sick pay by contributing to insurance policies which pay out when employees fall ill. Any payment to or for an employee, or a member of his household, by reason of sickness or disability, received under such a scheme is subject to income tax in the hands of the employee as if it was part of his emoluments. If the employee contributes to the premiums to provide this cover, only that part of the benefits attributable to the employer's part of the premium is taxable (Finance Act 1981, s 20).

In the case of a scheme which was set up before 5 June 1981, this tax charge on benefits only operates from 6 April 1983. Until then, benefits are covered by an extra statutory concession (A26).

9.1.3 Accident claims

A separate problem arises where an employee is absent from work by reason of injury in an accident which is the fault of a third party. If the result of the accident is that the employee loses pay, that will be a good head for the recovery of damages, but if in fact the employee continues to be paid, the damages will be that much less. For the employer, this means that if he is generous to the employee, and continues to pay him, he is merely subsidising the person who is responsible for the accident. On the other hand, to suspend payment may seriously embarrass the employee, and the outcome of personal injury litigation can never be certain.

The solution is to treat the employer's payments to an employee absent through an injury of this sort as a loan, repayable if and when recovered from the third party. The obligation to repay the debt should be sufficient to entitle the employee to recover damages, but the employer can still let the employee have the money he needs in the meantime (*Dennis* v *London Passenger Transport Board* [1948] 1 All ER 779).

There will be difficulty in dealing with the taxation of the employer's interim payments to the employee, because until the outcome of the claim is known it is not clear how much will be a loan. It is suggested that the employer should continue to deduct PAYE tax, adjusting the position when the final outcome is known. The service agreement can usefully make clear that this is without prejudice to the employee's obligation to repay.

9.1.4 Access to medical reports

The Access to Medical Reports Act 1988 gives certain rights to individuals in relation to any reports concerning their state of health which are obtained for employment or insurance purposes from a medical practitioner who is, or has been, responsible for treating that individual. For example, when an employer who is seeking a medical report on an employee prior to confirming the appointment, the Act provides that the employer must first seek the consent of the employee to him obtaining such a report from that person's doctor. The individual is entitled to withhold his consent if he so wishes. Further if the individual consents to the report being obtained, he has the right to see the report before it is sent to the employer. If there are any parts of the report which the individual feels are inaccurate or misleading, he may request the doctor to amend it. The Act also specifies certain procedures which must be followed before the report is obtained and sent to the employer. However, the Act would only appear to deal with the reports obtained from the employee's own doctor, so if the employer seeks a report from a doctor who has not treated the employee during the past, the Act does not apply. Accordingly, a doctor appointed by the employer can deliver a report to the employer without the employee's involvement.

9.1.5 Drafting

Because of the uncertainty surrounding the entitlement to sick pay, and the complication of social security benefits, a service agreement should make express provision as to the rules and regulations governing the payment of sick pay. Among the points to be dealt with are:

(i) *Reason for absence.* The scope of any sick pay scheme should be defined. It can relate merely to accidents incurred at work. Normally, all disability as a result of accident or illness is covered, but the result of accidents not in the course of work is sometimes excluded. Limits may be strictly interpreted. In one case, absence from work as a result of complications in pregnancy was covered, although absence during or after confinement would not have been (*Roberts* v *BICC Ltd* [1976] IRLR 404).

(ii) *Self certificates and Medical certificates.* As doctors no longer provide sick notes for periods of absence of less than one week, a clause should require the employee to complete and submit a self certificate. The clause should also require the employee to deliver medical certificates when the absence exceeds one week. It is also important to give the employer the power to require the employee to attend a medical examination. The employee should tell his employer about his progress, but without express rules the employer will probably not receive adequate information. '. . . it is an employee's duty, when he is away sick, to keep his employer fully informed as to the progress he is making towards recovery, in order that the employer may know that his employee intends to return for further work' (*Harrison* v

George Wimpey & Co Ltd [1972] ITR 188, 190 per Sir John Donaldson P).

(iii) *Periods of absence*. Entitlement to sick pay often drops after a stated period of absence. It is suggested that such periods should not be defined as continuous periods, lest the employee be tempted to return briefly to work although unfit to do so, merely to start the period of higher sick pay running again. The more satisfactory alternative is to provide for specified periods of absence in a floating twelve month period.

(iv) *Notice*. If a long term service agreement provides for a low salary, or none at all, to be paid after a protracted period of absence, the parties may consider it fair that they should at that stage have the right to be released. The agreement can give an option to terminate by notice in those circumstances, but the period of notice must not be shorter than the statutory minimum (Employment Protection (Consolidation) Act 1978, s 49(1)). The statutory provision for long notice, intended to benefit long serving employees, can work against their interests here. Although there is also a guarantee of payment during the period of notice, it is calculated by reference to the average remuneration of the twelve weeks immediately prior to the notice period (Sched 14, paras 3–6, 7(1)(*e*)). An employer who waited long enough to give notice, therefore, might give as much as twelve weeks' notice, the effect of which was to bind the employee to him for that period at very low sick pay. Parties may like to consider whether an employer who gives notice, thereby putting an end to his long term obligation, should not expressly agree to pay more during the period of notice.

(v) *Medical Reports Act 1988*. To avoid the consequences of this Act, it may be appropriate to reserve the right to send the employee to a doctor appointed by the company if a medical report as to the employee's fitness for duty is required.

9.1.6 Precedents

Sick pay

(i) IF and whenever the Executive is incapacitated through illness or accident from performing his duties, he shall telephone, or cause to be telephoned, his immediate superior on the first day of the absence to inform him of the reason for his absence. He will also, where the absence is due to illness and is likely to be for a period of longer than three days need to complete a certification of absence form within four days from the commencement of the period of absence. The form will be sent to the Executive by the Company.

If the Executive's absence is for a period of eight days or more, then he must send to the Company a certificate of his disability signed by a registered medical practitioner and during his continued absence the Executive shall send a further certificate each week.

(ii) During the first [3] months' absence in any period of 12 months the Company shall pay to the Executive his normal basic salary less any benefit from the Department of Health and Social Security or other statutory sick pay payable to him. The Executive must notify the Company of the benefits payable by the Department of Health and Social Security and any other benefits receivable by him.

(iii) During the next [6] months' absence in any period of 12 months, the Company shall pay to the Executive sick pay instead of his salary an amount equal to one half of his full salary.

(iv) Thereafter and until either party ends this agreement by giving notice under paragraph (v) the Company shall pay to the Executive sick pay instead of his salary an amount equal to 10 per cent of his full salary during his continued absence.

(v) At any time when the Executive is entitled under this clause to sick pay at the rate of 10 per cent of his full salary his employment may be brought to an end:

(*a*) by the Executive giving at least four weeks' written notice to the Company or

(*b*) by the Company giving to the Executive at least 12 weeks' written notice in which case the Company shall from the date of giving notice until the notice expires pay to the Executive as sick pay an amount equal to one half of his full salary instead of 10 per cent of it.

Loan following accident.

IN the event that the Executive is incapable of performing his duties by reason of injuries sustained wholly or partly as a result of actionable negligence nuisance or breach of any statutory duty on the part of any third party all payments made to the Executive by the Company whether of salary or sick pay shall to the extent that compensation is recoverable from that third party constitute loans by the Company to the Executive (notwithstanding that as an interim measure income tax has been deducted from payments as if they were emoluments of employment) and shall be repaid when and to the extent that the Executive recovers compensation for loss of earnings from that third party by action or otherwise.

Medical Reports

The Executive agrees that at the request of the Company he shall submit himself to a medical examination by a registered medical practitioner nominated by the Company. The purpose of such medical examination shall be to determine whether, there are any matters which might impair the Executive's ability to perform the duties under this agreement and accordingly the Executive will give such authority as is required for the Company's nominated doctor to disclose to the Company his findings. All expenses associated with obtaining the report will be borne by the Company.

9.2 Holiday Pay

9.2.1 Introduction

There is no statutory obligation on employers to provide holidays other than those described as public or bank holidays. However, an employer is required to provide the employee as part of the statutory particulars under s 1(3) of the Employment Protection (Consolidation) Act 1978 what holidays the employee will be entitled to (including public holidays) and any entitlement to holiday pay (with sufficient details to enable the employee to calculate how much accrued holiday pay he can claim if he leaves his job). The United Kingdom has also accepted the principles of the European Civil Charter which requires the contracting parties to provide a minimum of two weeks annual holiday with pay, additional paid holidays for those employed in certain dangerous or unhealthy occupations, and a weekly rest period. No legislation has yet been enacted to secure these standards. In drafting service agreements employers usually grant to employees longer periods of holiday than these minimum obligations. What one is more concerned with, is to ensure that the taking of holidays is regulated, so that work is not interrupted by unauthorised absences and to encourage employees to take their allotted holiday within the year in which it accrues, to prevent them carrying their annual holiday entitlement into a subsequent holiday year and then seeking to take a long single period of absence from the workplace.

9.2.2 Drafting

The employee's holiday entitlement should be specified in the service agreement to comply with the requirements for a statutory statement of employment terms to be given.

The service agreement should also make provision where holidays are with pay, as to how that holiday period accrues so that the employee can calculate the accrued holiday pay entitlement on termination. The employer should retain control as to when the employee takes the holiday entitlement. It may be advisable to provide that the holidays accruing to the employee will accrue in a specified holiday year, and that holiday entitlement cannot be carried forward into the next holiday year without the express consent of the company.

9.2.3 Precedents

Paid holiday

The Executive shall be entitled during every calendar year to the following holidays during which his remuneration [(including commission)] shall continue:

All bank and other public holidays and in addition:

Three weeks' holiday during the period from the First day of May until the Thirtieth day of September and one week's holiday during the remainder of the year to be taken at such times as the Company may agree *or*

Three weeks' holiday during the annual closure of the Company's factory *or*

Twenty-two working days' holiday of which not more than fifteen working days may be taken consecutively and the remainder may be taken either in one or more consecutive periods or in separate half and whole days the dates of absence to be agreed in advance by the Company.

Accrued holiday pay

If on leaving the Company's employment the Executive has an outstanding holiday entitlement he will, in addition to any other sums to which he may be entitled, be paid a sum representing salary for the number of days entitlement accrued. For these purposes holiday will be taken as accruing at the rate of [ ] days for each complete and continuous month during the calendar year

Unpaid holiday

IN addition to the paid holiday to which the Executive is entitled he may opt to take up to five working days additional holiday in any calendar year on dates agreed by the Company during which periods he shall not be entitled to be paid.

9.3 Expenses

9.3.1 Taxation

There are two alternative ways in which a service agreement may provide for the payment of an employee's expenses: either there can be an allowance of a fixed amount, or a reimbursement of the cost of particular items. Either way, the taxation consequences are the same. The money paid by the employer is liable to income tax in the employee's hands, unless he is allowed to deduct the cost of a particular item from his taxable income. For all company directors (except working directors without a material interest in the company) and all employees paid at least £8,500 a year, this even applies to sums paid by reason of their employment by someone other than their employer. Although strictly an employee receiving a general expense allowance should justify expenditure of at least the amount on allowable items to ensure that the allowance escapes a charge to tax, the inspector of taxes may well not insist upon that where the sum is reasonable in relation to the employee's job.

An employee who incurs expenses wholly, exclusively and necessarily in the performance of his duties is entitled to deduct that sum from his income before tax is calculated on it (Income and Corporation Taxes Act 1988, s 198). This applies whether or not the amount in reimbursed by the employer. Expenses incurred in business entertainment of anyone other than an overseas customer cannot be deducted unless the sum falls to be taxed in the hands of the employer (s 411). The result is that if a service agreement provides for the employer to pay more expenses than the employee is entitled to deduct, his taxable income is increased, just as if the agreement had treated the sum as additional emoluments.

The tax rule is interpreted strictly. This limits the expenses which are allowable. Examples of expenses which have been held not to be deductible are: a bank manager's subscription to a club, joined to obtain business (*Brown* v *Bullock* [1961] 1 WLR 1095);

the cost of a course attended by a teacher, which was relevant to the subject which he taught (*Humbles* v *Brooks* [1962] TR 297); the cost of an employed surveyor's clothes, which he claimed suffered wear and tear when visiting construction sites in the course of his work (*Ward* v *Dunn* [1979] STC 178). This means that even if the employer pays the amounts, the employee must pay tax and will be out of pocket to that extent. A service agreement term might be able to help the position, by making the activity for which the payment is made a compulsory part of the employee's duties. In practice there would be a few matters which could be foreseen to be dealt with in that way.

Travel to and from work is not a deductible expense (*Ricketts* v *Colquhoun* [1926] AC 1). Exceptionally, a hospital consultant was able to claim the cost of travel between his home and the hospital to deal with emergencies, because the facts established that his duties began before he left (*Pook* v *Owen* [1970] AC 244). In a case which might be treated similarly, a service agreement could be used to emphasise this time of commencement of the job, so that the travel is not to work, but in the course of it.

9.3.2 Employment abroad

There is special tax treatment of expenses in connection with employment abroad, in cases where the earnings are subject to United Kingdom tax. The cost of travel from the United Kingdom to take up the job, and the cost of the return trip when the job ends, are deductible expenses (Income and Corporation Taxes Act 1988, s 193). An employee with more than one job, at least one of which is outside the United Kingdom, can claim the cost of travel between jobs when the journey begins, ends or is wholly outside the United Kingdom. Neither of these concessions applies to journeys on leave. Deductible expenses for that purpose are closely defined. An employee who is absent from the United Kingdom for at least sixty days continuously can claim for the cost of a return journey to visit his spouse or a child, or for them to visit him. After a further qualifying period, a second return journey can be claimed in the same year of assessment, but no more. This only applies if the cost is borne or reimbursed by the employer, but not if the employee pays without the right to reimbursement (s 32(6), (7)).

An employee working abroad but subject to United Kingdom tax can also claim as a deductible expense the cost of his board and lodging. Nothing is allowed for the cost of board and lodging for his family. Again, this is an allowable expense only if the cost is paid or reimbursed by the employer (s 32(3), (4)).

In those cases in which expenses are only allowable as a deduction when paid or reimbursed by the employer, it is clearly to the employee's tax advantage that matters should be arranged in that way. The bargain between the employer and the employee should be, or be redrawn to be, such that the service agreement provides, if this is not to be an extra for which the employer pays, a fixed sum of expenses for the purpose with a balancing reduction in salary. There would be no increase in cost to the employer, but a tax saving for the employee.

9.3.3 Precedents

Expense allowance

THE Company shall pay to the Executive the monthly sum of £ . . . to reimburse him for the cost of entertaining the Company's customers and travelling on the Company's business [or such greater sum as the Executive shall show to the Company's satisfaction that he has spent for those purposes].

Reimbursement of expenses

The Executive shall be reimbursed the amount of all reasonable travelling and hotel entertainment and other expenses properly and necessarily incurred and defrayed by him in the discharge of his duties. The Executive shall produce to the Company at its request all supporting vouchers and documents in respect of such expenses.

Chapter 10

Fringe Benefits

10.1 Introduction

There will probably always be novel types of fringe benefits being offered to employees, either because they enable the employer to attract staff he needs but would otherwise not be able to recruit, or in the hope of some tax advantage. In particular, the employer may seek a way of remunerating employees without incurring a liability for National Insurance. With a contribution rate of 10.45 per cent and no upper limit on the total amount, National Insurance is a significant cost element for the employer to bear. Given the low rates of tax, and the gradual erosion of fringe benefit concessions, only some of the more common can be separately considered here.

10.2 Transport

10.2.1 Cars

A company director (other than a working director without a material interest in the company) or an employee paid at least £8,500 a year (Finance Act 1976, s 69; Finance Act 1978, s 23) is taxed on the benefit he receives when a car is available for his private use. This also applies if the car is provided for the use of a member of his family or household (Finance Act 1976, s 64). A cash equivalent is deemed to be added to the employee's income, and taxed as part of that income.

For the use of a car, the taxable cash equivalent from 6 April 1990 are as on page 108 (Income Tax (Cash Equivalents of Car Benefits) Order 1990).

The cash equivalent can be reduced in the following cases (Income and Corporation Taxes Act 1988, Sched 6, paras 2–5):

(i) A proportionate reduction of 1/365 per day is made to exclude any period before the car was made available to the employee, and for every day in a consecutive period of at least thirty days during which it is incapable of use.

(ii) The cash equivalent (after any reduction on the previous ground) is halved if the car is used for business travel of at least 18,000 miles during the year. That mileage is proportionately reduced to exclude any period for which a reduction is allowed on the first ground.

Table of Cash Equivalents of Car Benefits

Original market value	*Age of car at end of year of assessment* *Under 4 years old*	*4 years old and over*
Up to £19,250		
Up to 1,400 cc, or without cc rating less than £6,000	£1,700	£1,150
1,401–2,000 cc, or without cc rating £6,000 or more but less than £8,500	£2,200	£1,500
Over 2,000 cc, or without cc rating £8,500 or more but not more than £19,250	£3,550	£2,350
More than £19,250 but not more than £29,000	£4,600	£3,100
More than £29,000	£7,400	£4,900

These figures are adjusted periodically.

(iii) If the employee is required to make any payment for private use of the car, the cash equivalent, or any balance of it after previous reductions, is reduced by that amount. It can accordingly be eliminated.

On the other hand, if the car only has minimal business use—under 2,500 miles a year—and in the case of any second or subsequent company car, the cash equivalent is increased by half.

It will be cheaper for the employee to pay tax on the cash equivalent than to pay that sum to the employer to eliminate the cash equivalent. Not only is any payment to the employer of the full amount, rather than merely the tax on it, but it must be made from income which has already suffered tax.

10.2.2 Petrol

Car fuel—not just petrol—supplied by reason of his employment to an employee is treated as an additional emolument paid by his employer (Income and Corporation Taxes Act 1988, s 158). A cash equivalent is deemed to be added to the employee's income and taxed as part of that income. The taxable cash equivalents from 6 April 1990 are set out below.

The cash equivalents vary depending on the size of the car and are:

Cylinder capacity	*If none, original market value*	
Up to 1,400	Less than £6,000	£480
Over 1,400, up to 2,000	£6,000 and over, less than £8,500	£600
Over 2,000	£8,500 and over	£900

The cash equivalent can be reduced in the same way as in the case of cars, for non-availability of the car or for substantial business use. There is no tax on a cash equivalent of petrol benefit if fuel is made available only for business travel or if the employee has to pay for fuel used for business use.

10.2.3 Car parking

The payment or provision of parking facilities for an employee at or near the place of work is not regarded as part of the employee's income for the purposes of Schedule E (Income and Corporation Taxes Act 1988, s 197A).

10.2.4 Travel vouchers

Season tickets or any other documents or pass entitling the holder to passenger transport services is a taxable benefit if supplied to an employee by reason of his employment. The cost to the employer is treated as a taxable emolument (Income and Corporation Taxes Act 1988, s 158).

10.2.5 Car telephones

If a car phone is provided to an employee or director earning more than £8,500 a year, and it cannot be used separately from the car, it will not be regarded as a taxable emolument. However, if a telephone is provided for use in the employee's or director's own private car (or one belonging to a member of his family) then a taxable benefit will arise unless the full costs of private telephone calls are reimbursed (Inland Revenue Car Telephones Statement of Practice SP 5/88).

10.2.6 Directors

A director is not automatically entitled to his expenses in travelling to attend board meetings (*Young* v *The Naval Military and Civil Service Co-operative Society of South Africa Ltd* [1905] 1 KB 687). The company's articles of association may confer this right (as does art 83 in Table A to the Companies Act 1985).

10.3 Precedents

Car

The Company shall make available to the Executive, for his use in performing duties, and shall replace from time to time as necessary, a car of a type which it deems suitable. The Company shall maintain service tax and comprehensively insure the car as appropriate. The Company shall permit the Executive to use such car for private use [provided that the Executive shall pay the expenses directly attributable to such private use].

Petrol

The Company shall make arrangements for the supply to the Executive at the Company's expense of petrol for use in the car which it makes available for his use. [The Executive shall pay for all petrol attributable to his private use of the car].

Miscellaneous provisions

(i) The Executive shall ensure at all times, that when the car is driven on the road, it is in the state and condition required by law and that if so required a current test certificate is 'in force' in respect of it.

(ii) The Executive shall (so far as the law permits) at all times be the holder of a current driving licence entitling him to drive motor cars in the United Kingdom and shall produce it to the company on request.

(iii) Immediately upon the termination of the employment howsoever arising, the Executive shall return the car and its keys to the Company at its principal place of business (or any other place nominated by the Company for its return).

10.4 Financial

10.4.1 Loans

The Companies Act 1985 lays down very strict guidelines as to a Company's ability to make loans to its directors. Essentially the Act prohibits all loans but then allows certain limited exceptions. A loan made to a company director (other than a working director without a material interest in the company) or an employee earning at least £8,500 a year or to a relative of his, by reason of his employment, is a taxable benefit if it is interest free or at a beneficial interest rate (Income and Corporation Taxes Act 1988, s 160). Any part of a loan released or written off is also taxable (s 160(2)). An official interest rate is prescribed from time to time (currently 15.5 per cent: Income Tax (Official Rate of Interest on Beneficial Loans) Order 1982), and the extent to which the interest actually paid falls below this determines the amount of the taxable benefit. No tax is charged unless the benefit, or the sum of all benefits under this head, is over £200.

Where the employer's business involves lending and it charges interest on its loans at an amount less than the prescribed rate, an employee who takes a loan from the employer will still suffer tax as though he was in receipt of a beneficial loan, even though the provisions of the loan may not be a term of the employment.

10.4.2 Credit cards

An employee who is provided with a credit card by reason of his employment obtains a taxable benefit whenever he uses it. Its amount is equal to the cost charged to the person who provides the card, less any contribution the employee makes (Income and Corporation Taxes Act 1988, s 142). To the extent that the goods or services purchased constitute an allowable expense, the employee can set it off against his taxable income (ss 198 and 201). The Inland Revenue can give an employer a dispensation in respect of credit cards used by employees if the Inland Revenue is satisfied that their use would not give rise to a charge to tax. In such circumstances ss 141 and 142 do not apply and an employee can be given a credit card as a way to pay his expenses without either having to dip into his own money or having to obtain a cash advance from his employer, and it simplifies accounting.

10.4.3 Medical insurance

For company directors (other than working directors without a material interest in the company) and for employees earning at least £8,500 a year (Income and Corporation Taxes Act 1988, s 154), this will normally be a benefit charged under the general provision when supplied to him or members of his family or household. The amount charged is the cost of providing the cover. One exception to this is insurance for, or treatment, outside the United Kingdom where the need for treatment arises while the employee is outside the United Kingdom for the purpose of performing his duties (s 155(6)).

10.4.4 Pension

Detailed provision for payment of a pension is rarely appropriate in a service agreement. However, the service agreement clearly should ensure that the employee is given the right to participate in whatever pension scheme the employee is eligible to join by virtue of his employment. It would also be prudent to review the pension scheme provisions and consider and advise the employee of any consequences of him joining the new scheme. A pension arrangement without Inland Revenue approval will result in the employee being taxed immediately on the accruing benefit. This is to say, the cost of building up the pension rights is deemed to be included in the employee's current emoluments and is taxed accordingly. This applies whether the employer is actually contributing to a pension fund or insurance policy, in which case the sums paid are what is taxed, or the employer is not making specific provision, in which case the equivalent notional sum is taxed.

These difficulties are avoided where the pension is to be paid from a scheme approved by the Revenue under the provisions of chapter 1, part XIV of the Income and Corporation Taxes Act 1988, as amended by sched 7 to the Finance Act 1989 (retirement benefit schemes), or under the legislation contained in chapter IV, part XIV of that Act, as amended by sched 6 to the Finance Act 1989, (personal pension schemes).

The provision of a pension at the highest rate permitted by the Inland Revenue Rules can be a valuable and tax efficient method of rewarding employees.

10.5 Approved employee share schemes

10.5.1 Introduction

The ability of employees in general and the senior management in particular to purchase shares in the employing company in a tax efficient manner has become an important part of the total benefits package offered to many employees. It is a tax efficient way of providing benefits to the employee, if the scheme is approved by the Inland Revenue, as the employee can escape tax on the benefit as an emolument. It also gives the employee a vested interest in seeking the growth and financial success of the employing company. When drafting service agreements it will be necessary to make it clear that the employee will have the right to participate in whatever schemes the employing company operates. It is also necessary to review the terms of the scheme and in particular to ensure that they are approved Inland Revenue Schemes. It is beyond the scope of this book to deal in detail with such schemes, but the nature of each is set out below in brief terms.

10.5.2 Executive share options

An approved share option scheme is one which gives an employee the right to buy a certain number of shares at a fixed price at some time in the future. The price of the shares is fixed at the time the employee is given the option, and the price fixed at the time of granting them to the employee must not be less than the market value of the shares at that time. Income tax is not charged on the grant or exercise of the option provided that the exercise of the employee's right takes place within strict time limits. There are limits to the benefits given to employees under such schemes and an employee cannot hold options over shares where the aggregate value at the time the option is granted exceeds the greater of £100,000 or four times the employee's relevant emoluments for the current or preceding tax year. Judgment as to the size of the option granted to an employee is solely at the company's discretion. Employees do not have to exercise their rights but if the rights are exercised, and the shares sold at a profit there will be a capital gains tax liability at that time.

An approved profit sharing scheme requires the company to set up a trust fund to acquire shares in the company. Trustees receive payment from the scheme and apply the sums received to purchase scheme shares. These shares are then allocated by the trustees to eligible employees in accordance with the rules of the scheme. Employees cannot sell allocated shares during the first two years they are held by the trustees on their behalf. However, depending on the rules of the scheme, they normally can be sold at any time after this period, but there may be some income tax to pay otherwise the employee will not have to pay income tax on the value of the shares at the time either that they are set aside by the trustees on the employee's behalf or the value of the shares when they are sold; this requires the shares not to be sold for at least five years. Such schemes are not available to employees with less than five years full time employment.

10.5.3 Savings related share option scheme

This is a scheme which gives the employees the right to buy a certain number of shares at a fixed price. The shares under the share option scheme can only be bought from the proceeds of a Save as You Earn Contract (SAYE) either with the Department of National Savings or an equivalent contract administered by a Building Society. The price of the shares is fixed at the time the employees get their option. Share options can normally only be exercised in the period of six months following the maturity of the date of the savings contract, and generally cannot be exercised before that maturity date. Again, employees with less than five years service cannot take part in the scheme. The advantages to the employee are that they either receive the bonus and interest received under the SAYE contract tax free or do not have to pay income tax on the benefit they get from being given the option to buy the shares at a favourable price or any increase in the value of the shares between the date the option was given and the date which they use it. Naturally capital gains tax will be payable. A share option can normally only be exercised six months following maturity date of the savings contract. The options can normally only be used whilst the employees remain in the the employment of the employer, but if they have lost their jobs because of injury, disability or redundancy, or they retire on reaching pensionable age, or they have had to retire at any other age under the terms of their employment they have six months in which they may use their options to buy as many shares as the proceeds of their SAYE contract, including any interest, would allow. They cannot use any other money to buy shares through the option scheme.

Some schemes may allow employees to use their options within six months after they leave their employment for any other reason, but in this case they must normally have had the options for more than three years.

10.6 Accommodation

10.6.1 Tenure

An employer who provides an employee with accommodation faces the problem that any tenancy may constitute a regulated tenancy (Rent Act 1977, s 1), giving the employee security of tenure. Ways in which this can be avoided are:

(i) *Free accommodation*. Residential accommodation let without a rent falls outside the Rent Act (s 5). One way in which this is sometimes achieved is to charge nothing for the accommodation, but to make a compensating reduction in the employee's pay. This does not work if one level of salary is agreed, and is then reduced to take account of the accommodation: that immediately quantifies the rent (*Montagu* v *Browning* [1954] 1 WLR 1039). If this is avoided, by merely agreeing the duties and the cash wage and the accommodation to be given in exchange, it seems that the employee will not have protection (*Barnes* v *Barratt* [1970] 2 QB 657). It must be said that there are judicial dicta to the effect that the court can estimate the value of the services rendered in exchange for accommodation, thereby arriving at a rent, but they do not appear to have been acted upon.

(ii) *Licence*. An employer who grants a service occupancy, as distinct from a service tenancy, avoids creating a protected tenancy, which must be a tenancy in the technical sense and not a licence. It should normally both be a fact, and be said, that the employee occupies the premises for the better performance of his duties. The service agreement should reinforce that by imposing a positive obligation on the employee to live there. The employee's residence there should be of material assistance to the employer. That does not mean that occupation of that particular property must be essential, it is acceptable that other properties would be equally convenient (*Glasgow Corporation* v *Johnstone* [1965] AC 609). In drafting a licence, care should be taken to avoid all the verbal indicia of a tenancy (eg references to 'rent', 'tenancy', 'subletting'). A licence of this type comes to an end when the employee's job ends, even if the dismissal is wrongful (*Ivory* v *Palmer* [1975] ICR 340). Similarly, it will end, or be terminable, if the employment is brought to an end by the employer company going into liquidation (eg *RA Sanson Investments Ltd* v *Sanson* (1982) 132 NLJ 490). The employee's position is therefore insecure under this arrangement, even if the licence is to last as long as the job.

If a protected tenancy is granted, there is a special discretionary ground for possession on which the employer can rely. He must establish (Rent Act 1977, s 98(1), Sched 15, Case 8):

(i) that it would be reasonable to make a possession order;
(ii) that the premises were originally let to the employee in consequence of his employment, whether by his present or a former landlord;
(iii) that the employment has ceased; and
(iv) that the premises are reasonably required by the landlord for occupation by a full time employee or by someone else whom he has engaged on a contract of employment conditional on housing being provided.

Any tenancy agreement or licence should deal not only with the reasons for the grant of accommodation and its duration, but also with terms relating to outgoings and the maintenance of the property. It is generally more convenient to have a separate agreement for this purpose, rather than to add provisions to the service agreement.

10.6.2 Taxation

Where living accommodation is provided to an employee by reason of his employment, its value is charged to tax as an additional emolument of the employee, unless it falls into one of three excepted cases (Income and Corporation Taxes Act 1988, ss 145 and 146). The value taxed is the annual value of the property, ie the market rent on the basis of the tenant paying rates and the landlord paying for repairs or, if greater, any rent paid by the person providing the accommodation (s 145 (2)). An additional charge is made where the cost of providing the accommodation exceeds £75,0000 (s 146). This additional charge is related to interest on a notional loan of the amount by which the cost of providing the accommodation exceeds £75,000. Living accommodation provided by an employer is assumed to be provided by reason of the employee's employment, unless the employer is an individual providing it as a result of family, domestic or personal relationships, or the employee is a local authority and the terms on which the employee occupied are similar to those on which non-employees have accommodation (s 145(7)).

The three cases in which tax is not charged are (s 145(4)):

(i) where occupying the accommodation is necessary for the performance of the employee's duties; this is something that an express term of the service agreement can reinforce;

(ii) where it is the practice to provide accommodation for a particular class of employees, and it is provided to enable the employee the better to perform his duties;

(iii) where the accommodation provides special security and there is a special threat to the employee's security.

The first two exceptions only apply, in the case of a director of the company providing the accommodation or of an associated company, if he has no material interest in the company and he is a full time working director, or the company is non-profit-making or established for charitable purposes only (s 145(5)).

10.6.3 Precedent

Service occupancy

The Executive shall be required for the better performance of his duties under this agreement to occupy the premises at (*specify premises*) ('the Premises'). The Executive's occupation of such premises will be as a licencee and subject to the following terms:

(i) The Executive shall:

(a) be permitted to reside at the Premises,

(b) shall not assign; sublet or part with possession of the Premises or any part thereof,

(c) shall not have anyone to live with him in the Premises except with the prior written consent of Company,

(d) shall keep the interior of the Premises in a good and clean condition and in a good state of decorative repair (fair wear and tear excepted) and shall live quietly in the Premises.

(ii) The Company shall:

(a) pay all outgoings in respect of the Premises (other than telephone charges)

(b) have the right to enter the Premises at any time,

(c) The Executive's right to occupy the Premises shall cease immediately upon termination of the Executive's employment under this agreement and the Executive will forthwith vacate the Premises on the happening of that event.

10.7 Other Benefits

There is a general charge on all benefits, not otherwise specifically dealt with, provided by reason of his employment to a director (other than a working director without a material interest in the company) or an employee earning at least £8,500 a year (Income and Corporation Taxes Act 1988 s 154) or to a member of his family or household. The cash equivalent of the benefit is treated as an emolument of his employment (s 156). Expressly excluded from this charge are financial benefits for the employee or his dependants on his death or retirement, meals provided by the employer in a canteen in which meals are provided for staff generally and, in certain circumstances, accommodation (s 155).

The cash equivalent of a benefit, which is the amount taxed, is the cost of the benefit, less anything contributed or repaid by the employee and anything properly deductible by him as an allowable expense. The principle is that the cash benefit is what the benefit costs the employer, rather than the amount by which it benefits the employee. When the benefit concerned is the transfer of an asset, the market value of it at the date of the transfer is the cash value if it has been used or has depreciated since it was acquired or produced (s 156(3)). In the case of a loan, the annual value of the asset is the cash value (s 156).

Part IV

Safeguards for Employer

Chapter 11

Competition during Employment

11.1 Restrictions on employee

11.1.1 Full time work

A contract term by which the employee agrees not to undertake any other work while he is employed is perfectly valid. It does not suffer from the defect which invalidates many covenants restricting competition after a job finishes, that it prevents the employee from earning his livelihood. Nevertheless, there is a snag. For many years it was considered that an agreement not to take on other employment could not be enforced by injunction, because that would effectively amount to an order to work for the employer, a type of order against which the courts had always set their faces (*William Robinson & Co Ltd* v *Heuer* [1898] 2 Ch 451) as the courts would not give a specific performance of a contract of personal service, even though the injunction usually sought was negative in effect, it was found to be of such nature that it compelled the employee to return to work for his employer. It was thought that in appropriate cases, the employer's remedy was to summarily discharge the employee, or to claim damages (*Rely-a-Bell Burglar and Fire Alarm Co Ltd* v *Eisler* [1926] Ch 609). However, in certain very particular circumstances, it is possible to obtain an injunction against an employee to prevent him taking up employment with a competitor in breach of his obligations owed to the employer (*Provident Financial Group plc* v *Hayward* [1988] IRLR 84) considered below at **11.2**.

The employer can require an agreement that the employee does not take any other job in the same trade, while he is employed by the employer. As this restriction is narrower than a total ban, it must be equally valid. In some cases it might allow the employee sufficient freedom to overcome the objection to enforcement by injunction, but that cannot be guaranteed.

The mere fact that an employee has a full time job does not of itself prevent his doing other work, whether on his own account or for another employer, during his spare time (eg *Beloff* v *Pressdram Ltd* [1973] 1 All ER 241). Furthermore, there is nothing inherently objectionable in that other employment being of the same nature (*Hivac Ltd* v *Park Royal Scientific Instruments Ltd* [1946] Ch 169). However if the agreement expressly provides that the employee will not carry out such work, the employer has good reason for terminating the agreement.

11.1.2 Competition

In the absence of any express contractual restriction, the general duty of fidelity which the employee owes to the employer places limits on his spare time activities. They may be summarised:

(i) He must not place himself in such a position that he is tempted not to act in his employer's best interests. He should not, eg, be competing with his employer for the same contracts, or designing products to compete with other products which he designed for the employer.

(ii) He must not divulge any of his employer's trade secrets, or put himself in a position where that must inevitably happen (*Hivac Ltd* v *Park Royal Scientific Instruments Ltd* [1946] Ch 169).

This means that, as a generalisation, a manager may not engage in the same business as a spare time activity. Other employees, who do not have the same degree of responsibility for the conduct and direction of their employer's business, are free to do the same work for competitors, even if employing special skills, so long as they do not divulge or make use of the employer's confidential information.

This restriction on competing with an employer applies particularly to company directors, who stand in a fiduciary relationship to their companies. The directors of a railway construction company, who had been responsible for negotiating a number of contracts which the company had successfully completed, were not entitled to negotiate a further contract on their own behalf. When they purported to do so, they held the benefit of the new contract on trust for the company, and they were not entitled to use their votes as shareholders to procure the transfer of it to themselves (*Cook* v *Deeks* [1916] 1 AC 554). Again, when the managing director of a company was offered a design contract which his company had been seeking, on condition that he severed his connection with the company, he had to account to the company for the profit he made, notwithstanding proof that the company would never itself have been awarded the contract (*Industrial Development Consultants Ltd* v *Cooley* [1972] 1 WLR 443).

11.1.3 Interest in competitor

An agreement by an employee that while he is employed, or for the period that the employment is intended to last, he will not be interested in a competing business, eg as a shareholder, is in a different category. The employer is seeking to ensure that the employee has no financial interest, other than in carrying out his job successfully. The agreement does not, however, pose any threat to the employee's chances of employment. If the employee leaves his job before the end of a fixed term employment throughout which the restriction is to last, it can be enforced without preventing him being employed elsewhere. It is accordingly fully enforceable by injunction (*Rely-a-Bell Burglar and Fire Alarm Co Ltd* v *Eisler* [1926] Ch 609). The Financial Services Act 1986 and the Companies Securities (Insider Dealing) Act 1985 may also impose limitations on the employee's freedom to buy and sell shares.

11.1.4 Anticipating end of employment

While an employee's job continues he is not entitled to make arrangements to compete with his employer, even if that competition is to be after the job ends and at that time he will not be forbidden to compete. However, forming an intention to compete and seeking employment with a competitor will not automatically lead to a breach of contract (*Laughton and Hawley* v *Bapp Industrial Supplies Ltd* [1986] IRLR 245). Nevertheless, any steps the employee takes must be in his or her spare time and must not constitute a breach of the employee's duty of fidelity. '[The employee is] under the ordinary implied obligation . . . namely, that during the continuance of his employment he will act in his employer's interests and not use the time for which he is paid by the employers for furthering his own interests' (*Wessex Dairies Ltd* v *Smith* [1935] 2 KB 80, 84 per Greer LJ).

Acts which this principle has been held to forbid include:

(i) copying the names and addresses of the employer's customers from his order book, for use in a similar business which the employee proposed to set up (*Robb* v *Green* [1895] 2 QB 315);

(ii) personally canvassing the employer's customers to patronise the employee's own business once his employment had ended (*Wessex Dairies Ltd* v *Smith* [1935] 2 KB 80);
(iii) agreeing to undertake work for the employer's major client, in response to an unsolicited approach by that client, and offering to employ one of the employer's other employees even though she had expressed herself to be dissatisfied (*Sanders* v *Parry* [1967] 1 WLR 753).
(iv) taking from the employer a card index containing the names of customers (*Roger Bullivant Ltd* v *Ellis* [1987] 1 CR 464).

11.2 'Garden leave'–enforcement

The employee will continue to owe the employer his normal duties whilst he works out the period of notice. Where an employee is intending to leave to join a competitor, the employer may not wish the employee to continue to work for him during the notice period owing to fears that continued access to confidential information in relation to the employer's business may be valuable to the competitor when he joins that employer at the end of the notice period. Accordingly the employee was often instructed not to work during the period of notice but the employer agreed to continue to provide the employee with his contractual benefits during the notice period. Employees often object to being refused the opportunity to continue to work or being held to the contractual notice period and seek to leave before it expires. In such cases the employer did not appear to have an effective way of preventing the employee acting in breach of the service agreement. The decision in the case of *The Evening Standard* v *Henderson* [1987] 1CR 588, gave employers the right, in certain circumstances, to seek an injunction to restrain an employee from competition in such cases. In *The Evening Standard* case the employee was the production manager of a newspaper and was required under the terms of his contract of employment to give one year's notice to leave his employment. The employee received an offer of fresh employment with a competing newspaper and sought to give shorter notice than he was required under his contract. The employer refused to accept this notice and gave certain undertakings to the employee. The employer confirmed that he would receive all his contractual benefits during the notice period, he would be allowed to continue working if he chose to do so, and the employer also confirmed that they would not seek damages against him if he chose not to work out his notice. An injunction was granted to prevent him taking up the alternative employment.

It was said that it was essentially wrong that an employee can 'snap his fingers' at his employer and ignore the notice provision and obligations in the service agreement during the period of notice.

Having established an important principle, employers sought to make use of the provision to support other forms of non-competition provision, such as putting a long period of notice in the contract and expressly stating that the employer need not provide the employee with work but that the employee would be given contractual benefits during the period, provided the employee did not work for a rival employer in breach of contract. This gave the employer a buffer during which it was hoped that;

(1) the employee's knowledge of confidential information would become redundant and
(2) might of itself blunt the attractiveness of employees to others given the delay in their ability to recruit them to start work.

The use of the principle was recognised in the case of *Provident Mutual Financial Group Plc* v *Hayward* [1988] IRLR 84 as 'obviously capable of abuse'. In this case the Court emphasised that the enforcement of a clause in a contract preventing an employee from working with another during employment was a matter to be decided at the Court's discretion. The important question being what detriment is the employer going to suffer by virtue of the breach if no injunctive relief is granted. It was decided that the confidential information the employee had had access to would have been no use to the new employer. Simply helping the other business to run more effectively was not sufficient to be given the assistance of an injunction. However 'the risk of his going to a rival and fostering the rival business before the expiration of his notice is one against which the employers are entitled to be protected because of the damage that it would do to them' per Dillon LJ (*Provident Mutual Financial Group Plc* v *Hayward*). In such a case either an express covenant to prevent such activity would be enforced or if no such covenant existed there would be a breach of the implied duty of fidelity.

In fact in both cases there was an express term that the employee was not to compete with the employer during the course of the employment. The normal provisions of a service agreement concerning exclusive service may be sufficient to give a base for such claim. However, if the clauses are drafted more specifically, great caution must be taken as it is likely that the restraint of trade doctrine will apply to such provisions and accordingly, if the clause is deemed unreasonable, it may fail. The principle laid down by *The Evening Standard* case as modified by the decision of Provident Mutual Financial Group Plc will undoubtedly continue to develop and the progress of what has been referred to as the Evening Standard doctrine will have to be taken into account in drafting service agreements in future.

11.3 Drafting

The following points should be considered when drafting a service agreement:

(i) Insert a provision to the effect that the employee is expressly prohibited from working for anyone else.
(ii) Consider limiting the prohibition solely to competitors.
(iii) Consider carefully the period of notice the employer and employee are required to give under the terms of the agreement.
(iv) Insert a provision to the effect that the employer is not obliged to provide the employee with work during the period of notice whether given by employer or employee.
(v) State that express provisions are without prejudice to the restrictions placed on employees by their duty of fidelity which are automatically implied.
(vi) Where the employee's pay is dependent on being given work specify a formula to be adopted which the employee accepted provides a reasonable estimate of the amount he might otherwise have received.
(vii) Consider a requirement for the employee to disclose his family's interests

11.4 Precedents

No competing interests

The Executive shall not at any time during his employment be engaged or concerned either on his own behalf whether alone or in partnership or as an employee of any other person, firm or corporation or as director of a Company in any business other than that of the Company in the business of [*specify business*] (but the Executive may nevertheless become a minority holder of any securities in any company which is quoted on any recognised stock exchange provided that the Executive does not hold either directly or indirectly more than [*specify percentage*] per cent of the securities of the Company).

Devotion to duty

The Executive should devote the whole of his time, attention and abilities during normal business hours and at such other times as the Company or his duties may reasonably require to the business of the Company unless prevented by ill health from so doing.

No right to work

The Company shall be under no obligation to provide any work for the Executive during any period of notice either given by the Company or the Executive to terminate the Executive's employment under this agreement. The Company may at any time during the said period suspend the Executive from his employment or exclude him from any premises of the Company.

Note: Service Agreements should also incorporate provisions to protect confidential information (*see Chapter 12*) and the protection of staff (*see Chapter 14*).

Chapter 12

Protecting Trade Secrets

12.1 Introduction

The protection of confidential information and trade secrets confided to an employee is one of the major reasons why employers seek formal service agreements. Employers require protection both during the period of employment and after it ends. There are duties imposed on employees by the general law and the duty of confidentiality forms part of the more general implied duty of good faith and fidelity which the employee owes to the employer. Although the implied duty continues to bind the employee after the termination of employment, the implied term does not protect the employer against the disclosure of certain classes of information. Accordingly, it is advisable that the service agreement is prepared to supplement the implied duties owed by the employee. Some employees may also be required to be bound by the Official Secrets Act on taking up certain types of employment. Other employees may be subject to the provisions of the Financial Services Act 1986 and the Companies Securities (Insider Dealing) Act 1985. In both such cases employees may be subject to criminal prosecution should they use or disclose information covered by those Acts.

12.2 General duty

12.2.1 The equitable principle of confidence

Equity will protect the secrets of a person who imparts confidential information to someone else. This is a general principle, not confined to employer/employee relationships. 'The law on this subject. . . depends on the broad principle of equity that he who has received information in confidence shall not take unfair advantage of it' (*Seager* v *Copydex Ltd* [1967] 1 WLR 923, 931 per Lord

Denning MR). However in the Court of Appeals decision in the case of *Faccenda Chicken Ltd* v *Fowler* [1984] IRLR 69, suggests that the equitable duty of confidentiality will not be fully enforced in an employment situation.

12.2.2 Employment

Generally, an employee has a duty to respect his employers confidential and trade secrets. If he uses or discloses such information then both he and the receiver of that information may be liable in damages. This is an aspect of the duty of fidelity.

The employee's private circumstances may even disqualify him from giving a sufficient guarantee of performing his duty, although he has not in fact divulged information. A travel agent's booking clerk was dismissed shortly before her marriage to an employee of a rival agency. That dismissal was held to be fair. '. . . the basis of the employer's decision . . . was that the close association between husband and wife was such that there was a risk that confidential and damaging information would be exchanged between the two, even if inadvertently. A similar position could arise if, eg, two brothers or two sisters were living at home with their parents. There might be a risk of information being passed from one to the other which an employer would be justified in considering unacceptable' (*Skyrail Oceanic Ltd* v *Coleman* [1980] ICR 596, 600 per Slynn J).

There is no necessity for the employee's obligation to keep his employer's secrets to be expressly stated in his service agreement. '[This agreement] contains no express obligation not to divulge confidential information, but this makes no difference, for, if it were necessary, I would not hesitate to imply into the contract of employment . . . the relevant obligation' (*Cranleigh Precision Engineering Ltd* v *Bryant* [1965] 1 WLR 1293, 1320 per Roskill J).

'However, the implied term which imposes an obligation on the employee as to his conduct after the determination of his employment is more restricted in its scope than that which imposes a general duty of good faith' (*Faccenda Chicken Ltd* v *Fowler* [1986] IRLR 69). The Court of Appeals decision in Faccenda is now regarded as the leading authority on the law of confidentiality and employment cases. In that case Neil L J summarises the principles as follows:

(1) 'Where the parties are, or have been, linked by a contract of employment, the obligations of the employee are to be

determined by the contract between him and his employer. . . .

(2) In the absence of any express term, the obligations of the employee in respect of the use and disclosure of information are the subject of implied terms.

(3) While the employee remains in the employment of the employer, the obligations are included in the implied term which imposes a duty of good faith or fidelity on the employee.

(4) The implied term which imposes an obligation on the employee as to his conduct after the determination of the employment is more restricted in its scope than that which imposes a general duty of good faith. . . .

(5) In order to determine whether any particular item of information falls within the implied terms so as to prevent its use or disclosure by an employee after his employment has ceased, it is necessary to consider all the circumstances of the case.'

12.2.3 Information protected

The Faccenda case laid down certain principles to help determine what information would be covered by the duty of confidentiality. The application of those principles to cases is not always easy to do in practice, and as a starting point it is useful to consider the principles stated by McGarry VC in *Thomas Marshall (Exports) Ltd* v *Guinle* [1978] IRLR 174. He suggested that there were four elements which would help in identifying confidential information or trade secrets.

> First the information must be information the release of which the owner believes would be injurious to him or an advantage to his rivals or others. Secondly . . . the owner must believe that the information is confidential, or secret, ie that it is not already in the public domain. Third, the owners believe that the two previous heads must be reasonable . . . Fourth the information must be judged in the light of the usage and practices of the particular industry or trade concerned.

It should be noted that in this case the Court was considering an express confidentiality provision contained in the employee's contract of employment.

In the Faccenda case the Court of Appeal sought to clarify the position and suggested that in considering whether the information fell within the scope of the ex employee's duty of confidence, it was first necessary to consider the nature of the employment and whether the employee 'habitually handled' material, as the Court imposes a higher obligation of confidentiality than if he does not normally do so. Second the nature of the employment itself may suggest that any information is only protected if it can properly be classed as a trade secret or as material which is of a highly confidential nature. Third the employer must impress on the employee the confidentiality of the information. Finally, whether or not the relevant information can be easily isolated from other information which the employee is free to use or disclose must be taken into account.

At first instance Goulding J in the Faccenda case had distinguished three classes of information which an employee would become possessed of during the course of employment:

(1) Category 1—information which is of a trivial character or is easily accessible from a public source of information.
(2) Category 2—information which an employee was to treat as confidential because he or she was expressly told to do so or because it was obviously confidential, but which once learned necessarily remained in his head and became part of his own skill and knowledge.
(3) Category 3—information which was clearly a trade secret.

It was suggested that the information in category 1 could not be regarded by reasonable people as confidential and therefore did not require protection. He suggested that information in category 2 could not be used without a breach of contract during the employment, but the employee could use the information after he left employment unless the employer secured an express restrictive covenant preventing the employee using that information. Finally, information in category 3 was always confidential and capable of protection. The Court of Appeal made it clear that it did not consider that it was appropriate for information in the second category to necessarily be protected by a restrictive covenant unless there were trade secrets to protect.

The following are examples of matters which information was held capable of protection as trade secrets:

(1) Difficulties encountered with the design of aircraft instruments, and the consequent discussions with customers. (*Reid & Sigrist Ltd* v *Moss and Mechanism Ltd* (1932) 49 RPC 461);
(2) Manufacturing processes where the proportions, densities of the mixture and critical moments for mixing work are

important to the process. (*Amber Size & Chemical Co* v *Menzel* [1913] 2 Ch 239);

(3) The formula used in the manufacture of gold ink. (*Johnson & Bloy Holdings Ltd* v *Wolstenholm Rink Plc and Fallon* [1987] IRLR 499).

12.2.4 Conclusions

Given the difficulties that may be encountered in establishing whether information is or is not confidential when relying on the implied duty of confidentiality, it is advisable to draft a clause which expressly deals with the question of confidentiality. In the Faccenda case the Court of Appeal gave support to the idea that incorporating an express provision would be of assistance in supplying evidence of the nature of the information. 'First, although an employer cannot prevent the use or disclosure merely by telling the employee that certain information is confidential, the attitude of the employer towards the information provides evidence which may assist in determining whether or not the information can properly be regarded as a trade secret.' This was given support by the case of *Norbrook Laboratories Ltd* v *Smyth*.

Apart from any legal significance incorporating a clause, the clause is likely to have a psychological effect on the employee who may respect the obligation imposed on him.

12.3 Exclusions

There are exceptions to the general equitable duty and the general duty of fidelity which permits disclosure in certain instances. Such a disclosure may be limited merely to information about crimes and civil wrongs, or may go further. Lord Denning MR favoured a broad class of exceptions, when refusing to prevent a former public relations officer publicising in the press unfavourable information about his ex employer. 'It is a question of balancing the public interest in maintaining the confidence against the public interest in knowing the truth' (*Woodward* v *Hutchins* [1977] WLR 760, 764). There is also the question that such disclosures are permissible only if they are reported to the proper authorities or whether they may be made for instance to journalists (see *Initial Services Ltd* v *Putterill* [1968] IQB 396).

In the case of *In re a Company's Application* [1989] 1 All ER 248, it was accepted that an employee's duty of confidence did not extend to bar disclosure to FIMBRA and the Inland Revenue concerning matters that it is in the province of those authorities to investigate. The principle was also held capable of covering disclosure to a national newspaper and conducts of an appeal against an ex parte application (*Lion Laboratories* v *Evans* [1984] 2 All ER 417). But, as was said by Griffiths LJ; 'there is a world of difference between what is in the public interest and what is of interest to the public' (*British Steel Corporation* v *Granada Television Ltd* [1981] 1 All ER 417).

There was a thorough review of the law on confidentiality and public disclosure in the case of *Attorney General* v *The Observer Ltd and Others* (1988) 2 WLR 805. In refusing injunctions against newspapers the Court concluded that the worldwide disclosure of the information in question had destroyed the confidentiality of the information and so the confidence enjoyed by the Crown no longer bound third parties. Sir John Donaldson MR re-emphasised the point made by Griffiths LJ when he said 'The media should ponder the needs of the nation for a security service which was secret and the consequences of breaches of that essential secrecy. They should never forget how easy it was to confuse "self" with "public" when attached to "interest".'

12.4 Employee's expertise

The principle is well established that an employer has no right to protect himself against a former employee using his own expertise. This remains the case even though, almost inevitably, the employee's experience while in the job has added to his expertise. 'A servant cannot help acquiring a great deal of knowledge of his master's methods of business, and of the science which his master practises. The servant when he leaves cannot be restrained from using the knowledge so acquired, so long as he does not take any trade secrets or solicit customers' (*Stephenson Jordan and Harrison Ltd* v *McDonald and Evans* (1952) 69 RPC 10, 23 Denning LJ). '[The master] cannot prevent the outgoing servant from using the skill and expertise he has acquired over the years perhaps in his master's business. Those are the servant's own properties' (*Greer* v *Sketchley Ltd* [1979] IRLR 445, 446–7 per Lord Denning MR). This does not mean that an ex employee may freely use any information which he himself contributed to his former employer's business. For example, an engineering draughtsman who is employed to use 'such skill and inventive faculty as he may possess' (*Adamson* v *Kenworthy* [1931] 49 RPC 57 68 per Farwell J) may well design what becomes a pivotal part of the process of the business. A difficult distinction then has to be drawn between the secret devised by the draughtsman, which is the employer's secret, and the techniques which the draughtsman applies to solve the problem presented to him, which are his own expertise.

The principle has been more recently highlighted by the case of *Johnson and Bloy (Holdings) Ltd* v *Wolstenholme Plc and Fallon* [1987] IRLR 499. In that case the employee, who was also a director of the employing company, left his employment and joined one of the employer's suppliers. When he left, the employee took with him a number of documents containing information about the formulation of their product. The employer sought an injunction to restrain the employee and his new employers from making use of that information. The Court held, applying the guidelines in the Faccenda case, that it could not be accepted that it would be wrong to restrain the former employee from using the trade secret even though it could prevent him from using his general knowledge. Parker LJ commented that simply because an employee would be able to carry away such information in his head, could not mean that it became part of the ordinary skill and experience of the employee rather than a trade secret. He did not think that the decision of Scot J in *Balston Ltd* v *Headline Filters Ltd* (1987) FSR 330, laid down the general proposition of law that anything which is inevitably in somebody's head when they leave employment is something which they are free to use.

12.5 Confidentiality

Trade secrets are only protected if and so long as they are truly confidential. That involves both their being imparted to the employee in confidence and the information actually being secret.

The employer cannot stop a former employee from using or divulging information not given in confidence, even if it is of the nature which would otherwise be protected. 'However secret and confidential the information, there can be no binding obligation of confidence if that information is blurted out in public or is communicated in other circumstances which negative any duty of holding it confidential' (*Coco* v *A N Clarke (Engineers) Ltd* [1969] RPC 41, 47–8 per McGarry J). An employee who honestly and openly obtains information in the course of this employment, and is not warned that it is confidential, has no obligation to keep it secret (*E Worseley and Company Ltd* v *Cooper* [1939] 1 All ER 290). There could be circumstances in which the fact that the information is confidential should be obvious to the employee, so it would be wrong to assume that an express warning is necessarily essential to impose an obligation of secrecy. An employee who acquires such information surreptitiously or dishonestly is probably in breach of his duty of fidelity. He could not be allowed to take advantage of his wrongdoing by pleading the absence of a warning that the information was secret, when that was the result of his concealing from his employer the fact that he had the knowledge.

Difficult questions arise when information which the employer regards as secret is imparted to the employee confidentially, but is in fact not secret or at least available from other sources. In general, the employer is not entitled to any protection for facts publicly available, at least if the employee is using information derived from elsewhere. However if the employee is seeking to compete against his former employer using confidential information which he has obtained unlawfully in the course of his employment, eg by stealing or copying documents, and gains an unfair competitive advantage over the employer, the employee can be prevented by Court action from making use of the information. This is known as the 'springboard principle'. 'A person who has obtained information in confidence is not allowed to use it as a springboard for activities detrimental to the person who made the confidential communication, and springboard it remains even when all the features have been published or can be ascertained by actual inspection by any member of the public' (*Terrapin Ltd* v *Builders Supply Company (Hayes)* [1960] RPC 128, 130 per Roxburgh J). The rigidity of that rule must be modified if the employer releases the employee from his obligations of secrecy, or can be taken to have done so.

This was considered more recently in the case of *Roger Bullivant Ltd and Others* v *Ellis and Others* [1987] IRLR 491. In this case the employee took a card index listing the employer's trade contacts with him on leaving. It was accepted that the contents of the card index was not a trade secret, but was confidential information within category 2 of the Faccenda case which would have permitted the employee to use that information freely, but only in so far as he could carry away the information in his head. The fact that the employee had wrongfully taken the card index was sufficient for the Court to grant an injunction to prevent the use of that information as it had been gained in breach of his duty to his former employer. The injunction was limited to one year, as the springboard the employer gained by using the information was thought should be limited to the period the unfair advantage was likely to continue.

12.6 Documents

A former employee who takes documents concerning trade secrets from his employer will be ordered to surrender the documents as well as to respect the confidentiality of the secrets. The ownership of the documents themselves entitles the employer to have them back whatever they contain. There is no need therefore to establish that the information is a trade secret, entitled to protection from disclosure, in order to obtain physical re-delivery of the documents (*Roger Bullivant Ltd and Others* v *Ellis and Others* [1987] IRLR 491). Those considerations do apply to any order relating to the use of the information gained from them.

In these days when it is so easy to copy even the most complicated or lengthy document, or to transfer a great deal of information on to computer diskette, what the employee has in his possession may not be the employer's property, even though the copy has been made in breach of copyright and may contain trade secrets. Given proof of those facts, an injunction will be granted to restrain the misuse of the document or diskette, even if it is a copy made by the employee (*Printers and Finishers Ltd* v *Holloway* [1965] IRLR I). The copy which the employee makes need not be an exact or full one. Even if he merely copies out salient information such as names and addresses of customers from his employer's order book, he can be restrained from using it (*Robb* v *Green* [1895] 2 GB 315).

Any injunction to protect an employer from an employee taking unfair advantage of the springboard that they gain from the misuse of such information will not normally extend beyond the period for which the unfair advantage may reasonably be expected to continue. However such orders will be made even if they prevent the employee from using his acquired skill and knowledge, as in the case of *Johnson and Bloy (Holdings) Ltd and Johnson Bloy Ltd* v *Wolstenholme Plc and Fallon* [1987] IRLR 499 CA. In this case Fox LJ said

'I appreciate that the Court in granting injunctions in these cases has to be careful not unjustly to fetter the ability of an ex employee to compete;

but it seems to me that the difficulties in which Mr Fallon now finds himself were essentially of his making, through his conduct in improperly removing the plaintiff's documents. We have to consider not merely the position of Mr Fallon, but what is necessary for the proper protection of the Plaintiffs in relation to what are—it can reasonably be argued—their trade secrets, and if they are found to be trade secrets at trial, they constitute information which is vital to the effective continuation of the Plaintiff's business.

Employers now have a very effective remedy to protect their rights in addition to securing an injunction against employees. In certain limited and defined situations the employer can seek an order from the court permitting the employer to inspect the employee's home or business premises to search and recover documents belonging to the employer, this is known as the 'Anton Piller Order'. In both the Roger Bullivant and Johnson Bloy case, the Anton Piller Order was used to great effect to secure evidence of the employee's wrongdoing. However there has been some concern expressed that such orders are given too freely, and the Courts may not grant them as freely as they have been given in the past (*Lock International plc* v *Beswick* [1989] IRLR 481).

It is important to incorporate a provision into the service agreement placing on the employee an express obligation to return all documents or copies of documents, belonging to the employer and which he has obtained by virtue of the employment. This will assist the employer in any subsequent action taken against the employee. Particularly in the event that it is discovered that the employee does retain documents and it will then prove difficult for the employee to suggest that he was unaware of the need to return those documents and that he is entirely innocent of any wrongdoing.

If the employee improperly takes his employer's documents the criminal sanctions appropriate to theft may also be available.

12.7 Restrictive covenants to protect confidential information

The Courts have frequently expressed the view that a satisfactory and proper way to enforce an employee's duty of confidentiality, in respect of trade secrets or information which is of a highly confidential nature requiring the same protection as a trade secret, is by means of a covenant against competition.

'If [the managing director] is right in thinking that there are features in his process which can fairly be regarded as trade secrets and which his employees will inevitably carry away with them in their heads, then the proper way for the [employers] to protect themselves would be by exacting covenants from their employees restricting the field of activity after they have left their employment, not by asking the Court to extend the general equitable doctrine to prevent breaking confidence beyond all reasonable bounds' (*Printers and Finishers Ltd* v *Holloway* [1965] 1 WLR 1, 6 per Cross J).

The judgment in the Faccenda case suggests that it will only be proper to uphold a restrictive covenant on the basis that the status of the information which it is desired to protect is a trade secret or the equivalent of a trade secret. The Court declined to specify what would constitute a trade secret stating

> it is clearly impossible to provide a list of matters which will qualify as trade secrets or their equivalent. Secret processes of manufacture provide obvious examples, but innumerable other pieces of information are capable of being trade secrets, though the secrecy of some information may only be short-lived. In addition, the fact that circulation of certain information is restricted to a limited number of individuals may throw light on the status of the information and its degree of confidentiality.

In the case of *Balston Ltd* v *Headline Filters Ltd* [1987] FSR 330, it was observed that the Court of Appeal in the Faccenda Chicken case could not have intended to hold the confidential information that could not be protected by an implied term of that contract of employment and *ipso facto* could not be protected by a suitably limited express covenant. Accordingly, the fact that an employer has trade secrets to protect is a legitimate reason for the employer to seek a restrictive covenant. In this respect it is not necessary to show that each piece of information covered by the restriction is confidential—all the employer need show is that restriction is reasonably necessary to protect a trade secret or its equivalent. The fact that other information is thereby protected is irrelevant.

However, having established that there is a legitimate interest to be protected, this does not automatically validate such a covenant. The covenant the employer seeks to impose on the employee must be no wider than is strictly necessary to protect his interests in the circumstances and be reasonable when the public interest is taken into account. The test of reasonableness is considered in more detail in Chapter 15. A restriction which expressly recited that it was for the protection of trade secrets and secret processes, and prohibited the employee from engaging in any similar business involving such trade secrets and secret processes anywhere in the

United Kingdom during the 12 months following the end of his employment, was held to be void because the employer's business did not extend throughout the country (*Greer* v *Sketchley Ltd* [1979] IRLR 445).

An alternative form of covenant, which is sometimes appropriate, is one to prohibit an employee from working for a named rival during a limited period following the end of the current employment. Where it is possible to identify one competitor, or a small number of them as the only source of danger from the trade secrets if divulged, this type of restriction can be ideal because of its precision. Care is still needed, however, to ensure that the scope is no wider than necessary. In one case, a covenant of this nature was upheld, but only after implying a limitation restricting its application to that part of the competitor's business which truly overlapped with that in which the employee had worked. Indeed in the case of *Littlewoods Organisation Ltd* v *Harris* [1977] 1 WLR 1472, 1479, Lord Denning MR recommended this form of covenant as a way of overcoming the need to distinguish between confidential and non-confidential information. 'The difficulties [of distinguishing] are such that the only practicable solution is to take a covenant from the servant by which he is not to go to work for a rival in the trade'. This case concerned sensitive commercial information and was not disapproved of by the Court of Appeal in the Faccenda Chicken case.

Where an employee has access to trade secrets, it is clearly appropriate to seek a restrictive covenant and to obtain a specific commitment to the preservation of confidential information. Both can be effective simultaneously. It is possible that an express covenant will have the effect of limiting the extent of the general duty owed by the employee. Lord Denning MR opined that a service agreement imposing a year's restriction on former employees limited their general duty to keep trade secrets for the same period (*Potters-Ballotoni Ltd* v *Preston Bakers* [1977] RPC 202, 205).

A restrictive covenant preventing competition is only appropriate to protect the employer against the former employee divulging secrets. If express protection is required while the employee is still in employment, it will require the separate provision to be obtained. But even with such a clause, this can be attacked if it operates in an oppressive manner (*Schroeder Music Publishing Co* v *Macauley* [1974] 3 All ER 616).

12.8 Enforcement

The normal method of enforcing a duty to keep a confidence, whether express or implied, is by injunction. That obviously maintains the status quo which the employer requires. An interim injunction will also sometimes be granted. The court would also have the power to order the employee to deliver up the confidential information and, in certain cases, order the destruction of products produced illegally as a result of the use of the confidential information.

When seeking an injunction against the disclosure of trade secrets, as distinct from an injunction to enforce a restrictive covenant, it is normally necessary to specify precisely what the secrets are so that it is possible to determine whether they are indeed matters to which the duty of confidence extends (*John Zink Co Ltd* v *Lloyds Bank Ltd* [1975] RPC 385). This could also be required where the basis of validity of a non-competition covenant is the protection of confidential information. 'But if the plaintiffs, in seeking to protect their "know how", are anxious to enforce any injunction which may be granted to them by seeking the help of the court to punish a breach of it, it seems to me essential that they should make it absolutely clear what it is they are seeking to protect' (*P A Thomas & Co* v *Mould* [1968] 2 QB 913, 922 per O'Connor J). To refer simply to 'confidential material' is not enough.

Not only must the secrets be specified, but there must also be evidence that they are being improperly used or disclosed. '. . . unless the plaintiff can show that he has some basis for a reasonable belief in his assertion that the defendants are making use of his confidential information, then the action . . . ought not . . . to be allowed to proceed' (*Reinforced Plastics Applications (Swansea) Ltd* v *Swansea Plastics & Engineering Co Ltd* [1979] FSR 182 per Whitford J). The employer can apply to have the case heard in camera, so that his secrets are not revealed when evidence is given.

If the secret is out, and the harm done, the employer can sue for damages. It may only rarely be possible to calculate the direct financial loss incurred by reason of the information being divulged, although if it is, that would be the appropriate measure of damage.

Where the secret is in the nature of an invention, damages can be assessed in a manner similar to those for contravening a patent. The court cannot order the payment of a royalty, but the lump sum can be the equivalent to a capitalisation of an appropriate royalty. 'The value of the confidential information depends on the nature of it. If there was nothing very special about it, that is, if it involves no particular inventive step but was the sort of information which could be obtained by employing any competent consultant, then the value of it was the fee which a consultant would charge for it . . . But, on the other hand, if the information was something special, as, for instance, if it involved an inventive step or something so unusual that it could not be obtained by just going to a consultant, then the value of it is much higher' (*Seager* v *Copydex Ltd (No 2)* [1969] 1 WLR 809, 813 per Lord Denning MR).

The employer may also have the remedy of the Anton Piller order which is a very powerful weapon to search and seize evidence. However, in the case of *Lock International Plc* v *Beswick* [1989] 3 All ER 373, to search and seize evidence, it was made clear that the Court would only make such orders sparingly. In that case the order was discharged as there was no evidence to support the employer's allegation of misuse of confidential information and trade secret. It was suggested that in many cases it would be sufficient for the Court to make an order requiring the employee to deliver the employer's documents to his solicitor or, where the documents belong to the employee, and order that they be preserved pending further order or an order permitting the employer's solicitors to make copies.

If the parties simply wish to clarify the position and to test the enforceability of the provisions in question, the employee could seek a declaration from the court. The employer also retains the right to claim damages in respect of any breach of the contract. Alternatively the employer could claim an account. This entitles the injured party to the actual profits earnt as a direct consequence of the breach.

12.9 Drafting

The cases on the protection of trade secrets suggest, both in the decisions of the courts and by their facts, a number of guidelines to be followed when drafting service agreement clauses to protect the employer. They may be summarised:

(i) The general equitable duty to protect confidences can prove useful to protect trade secrets, and can be enforced in parallel with any contractual obligation. However, there is the danger that an agreement if badly drafted may reduce the scope of the general duty, or even supersede it, so any contractual duty should be expressed to be without prejudice to the employee's other duties.

(ii) The agreement should make it clear to the employee that information gained in the course of his employment is confidential. Merely to say that information is a trade secret does not automatically qualify it for protection, it must be treated by the employer as confidential and the employee must be told that it is confidential otherwise he will generally have no duty to keep it secret.

(iii) There is a distinction between not divulging confidential information and not using it. An agreement not to disclose information does not prevent the employee from making use of it for his own purposes (*Thomas Marshall (Exports) Ltd* v *Guinle* [1979] Ch 227). A comprehensive restriction should therefore prohibit both disclosure and use of the information.

(iv) A covenant restricting an employee from competing once his employment comes to an end may be an appropriate way to protect trade secrets. This may be in a general form, or it may restrict the former employee from working for one or more named competitors for a period. In either case, it is important that the scope of the covenant is not unreasonably wide and particular attention must be paid to the nature of the employee's work ie is he likely to have access to secrets? If it is, it will sometimes be enforced in a restricted form, but there is the danger of its being held invalid.

(v) In addition to a term governing the position once the employment comes to an end, it is useful to impose an express obligation to respect confidences while the job continues.

(vi) Documents supplied by the employer remain his property, as do documents created by the employee in the course of his duties. It can be useful to record the position, and to state expressly that they must be handed back when the employment comes to an end. To make sure that there is no misunderstanding, and to minimise the chance of dissemination of trade secrets, a term forbidding the copying of the employer's documents can be useful.

Given the wide use of computers by employers, employees can have access to, and can easily copy large quantities of information on to diskettes. The clause must therefore deal with such situations.

12.10 Precedents

Confidentiality recital

Given the nature of the work undertaken by the Company and the involvement the Executive will be given in all aspects of the Company's business, the Executive will have direct access to information all of which is confidential; the disclosure of which could be extremely damaging to the business of the Company. 'Confidential Information' means information relating to the business, products and affairs of the Company for the time being confidential to the Company or treated by the Company as such and trade secrets (including without limitation formulae, processes, methods, inventions, technical data and know how) relating to the business of the Company. To protect the confidentiality of that information without prejudice to every other duty which the Executive has, to keep secret all information given to him or gained in confidence, the Executive agrees as follows:–

Confidentiality

The Executive shall not, either during his employment under this agreement, otherwise than in the proper course of his duties, or thereafter, without the consent in writing of the Company being first obtained, divulge to any person firm or company and shall during the continuance of this agreement use his best endeavours to prevent the publication or disclosure of any Confidential Information of the Company or any of its secrets, dealings or transactions whatsoever which may have come or may come to his knowledge during his employment or previously or otherwise.

Delivery of documents

Upon the termination of the Executive's employment the Executive shall immediately deliver up to the Company or its authorised representative all plans, statistics, documents, records, papers, magnetic disks, tapes or other software storage media and all property of whatsoever nature which may be in his possession or control and relate in any way to the business affairs of the Company and the Executive shall not, without the written consent of the Company, retain any copies thereof.

Non-compete with specific competitor

The Executive shall not for a period of [*specify period*] [months/years] after termination of his employment (howsoever occasioned) [without the previous consent in writing of the Company be engaged or be interested (whether as principal, servant, agent, consultant or otherwise) in or give advice to [plc] or any company which is a subsidiary or associated company of [plc] which carries on business similar to that of the Company.

Non-compete

The Executive shall not for a period of [*specify period*] [months/years] after termination of his employment (howsoever occasioned) without the previous consent in writing of the Company be engaged or interested (whether as principal, servant, agent, consultant or otherwise) in any trade or business similar to or competing with any trade or business being carried on at the end of the employment by the Company with which the Executive shall have been directly connected during the preceding [*specify period*] [months/years] prior to the termination of the employment.

Chapter 13

Intellectual Property

13.1 Patents

13.1.1 Ownership

The Patents Act 1977 determines, as between employer and employee, which of them owns any invention which the employee makes. Inventions made in the course of the employee's duties belong to the employer in the following cases (s 39):

(i) in the course of normal duties, in circumstances when an invention might reasonably be expected to result;

(ii) in the course of duties specifically assigned to him, where the circumstances make an invention reasonably to be expected;

(iii) when the nature of the employee's duties and the particular responsibilities arising from them mean that he had a special obligation to further the interests of his employer's business. It is not clear whether a 'special' obligation means an unusual one, or one specially and expressly undertaken.

Any other invention belongs to the employee. He can assign it to his employer. The effect of an assignment is to make the employer the person to whom a patent may be granted, as he is in the case of inventions which originally belong to him (s 7(2)(*b*).

13.1.2 Compensation

An employee has a statutory right to compensation from his employer in respect to some inventions made by him which either originally belonged to the employer or were assigned to him (Patents Act 1977, s 40). This applies in two cases. First, there is compensation for any patented invention belonging to the employer which is of outstanding benefit to the employer, having regard inter alia to the size and nature of the employer's undertaking and it is just that compensation should be awarded. Secondly, an employer must pay compensation for a patented invention belonging to the employee, which was assigned or exclusively licensed to the employer by an agreement which does not adequately benefit the employee, having regard to the benefit the employer derives from the patent and it is just that compensation should be awarded. Benefit, here, means money or money's worth (s 43(7)).

The application for compensation to secure a fair share of any benefits or expected benefits for the employee may be made to the Comptroller-General of Patents, Designs and Trade Marks or to the court. An application to the Comptroller is made on Patent Form 26/77 (Patent Rules 1978, r60). Alternatively, the employee applies by originating summons to the patents court (RSC, O 104, r13). The time for an application is between the date of the grant of the patent and one year after it ceases to have effect. Little guidance can be given as to how these provisions will operate as there are no authorities to refer to.

13.1.3 Contracting out

There is a restriction on depriving the employee of his statutory rights. No contract can diminish an employee's rights in any invention, or his rights under a patent for it. To the extent that a contract would have that effect, it is unenforceable (Patents Act 1977, s 42(2)). Similarly, a contract under which an employee assigns a patent to his employer or grants him an exclusive licence of it, cannot prejudice his right to compensation (s 40(4)).

There is an important limit on these statutory rules, both as to the ownership of inventions and as to compensation. They do not apply unless the employee is mainly employed in the United Kingdom. For someone not mainly employed in any particular place, or where that place cannot be determined, the provisions apply only if he is attached to a place of business which his employer has in the United Kingdom, whether or not he is also attached elsewhere (s 43(2)). The employee may also face the practical difficulty of establishing that the invention has been of 'outstanding benefit' to his employer, particularly if the employer chooses not to exploit it, or exploit it without applying for a patent.

A collective agreement (as defined by the Trade Union and Labour Relations Act 1974) can contain provisions for compensation for employees' inventions superseding the statutory rules (Patents Act 1977, s 40(3)).

13.1.4 Drafting

An employer who employs people to carry out research into new products and processes, or any employer who employs people who are likely to invent something in the course of their employment will normally wish to ensure that he secures the benefit of all relevant inventions that such employee's make. Further, he may want to limit the payment of compensation to the extent that he is able, but despite the statutory limitations, there are a number of ways in which he may further those aims in drafting a service agreement:

(i) The definition of the employee's normal duties should be wide enough to ensure that most if not all inventions belong to the employer (*Reiss Engineering Co Ltd* v *Harris* [1985] IRLR 232 Ch Div) but the description must reflect the true employment situation as if the clause is drafted too widely then it may be argued that it is seeking to deprive the employee of his rights (s 42). Such a clause may also create additional problems, eg when it is necessary to decide whether an employee is redundant.

(ii) All relevant inventions which belong to the employee should be assigned to the employer. There can be disputes as to the time at which an invention was made, and whether or not the employee was then on duty. Assigning all inventions to the employer effectively equates those which the Act declares to be the employee's with those which are the employer's.

(iii) The agreement could also provide the employer with the option of purchasing the employee's invention and to be compensated, the compensation to be calculated in accordance with an alternative compensation system similar to the statutory scheme. Clearly, it would be necessary for such a compensation scheme to provide the employee with similar rights to the statutory scheme otherwise it would be void under s 42. A simple reward scheme may be sufficient in itself to provide employees with sufficient compensation to dissuade them from exercising their full statutory rights.

(iv) Ensure that the agreement contains a comprehensive confidentially provision as s 42(3) provides that nothing derogates from the employee's obligation owed to the employer by virtue of any rule of law or otherwise. If the invention belongs to the employee, he may be unable to apply for a patent or exploit the invention if it relies on the disclosure or use of the employer's confidential information.

13.1.5 Precedent

Intellectual property

(i) The Executive's duties include the review of the Company's manufacturing processes with a view to improving them by new and original inventions and implementing improvements by means of such inventions and of applying established techniques, designs, processes and manufacturing methods not previously used, or in that particular application, by the Company.

(ii) In this Clause the expression 'Intellectual Property' shall mean (a) every invention, discovery, design or improvement, (b) every work in which copyright may subsist and (c) moral rights as defined by s 77 and s 80 of the Copyright Design and Patents Act 1988.

(iii) The Executive shall forthwith communicate to the Company in confidence all Intellectual Property which the Executive may make or originate either solely or jointly with another or others during his employment.

(iv) In the case of such Intellectual Property as is made or originated hereunder wholly or substantially in the course of his normal duties or in the course of duties specifically assigned to him and which relate to the affairs of the Company the following sub-clauses of this Clause shall apply.

(v) Such Intellectual Property (or in the case of Intellectual Property made or originated by the Executive jointly with another or others to the full extent of the Executive's interest therein so far as the law allows) shall be and become the exclusive property of the Company and shall not be disclosed to any other person, firm or company without the consent of the Company being previously obtained which if given may be subject to conditions. The provisions of this sub-clause shall not entitle the Executive to any compensation beyond the salary hereinafter mentioned except that in the case of any invention on which a British Patent has been granted or assigned to the Company and the Company has derived outstanding benefit from such patent, the Executive may be entitled by virtue of s 40 of the Patents Act 1977 to claim additional compensation.

(vi) The Executive shall if and when required by the Company and at the expense of the Company do and/or combine with others in doing all acts and sign and execute all applications and other documents (including Powers of Attorney in favour of nominees of the Company) necessary or incidental to obtaining maintaining or extending patent or other forms of protection for such Intellectual Property in the UK or elsewhere or for transferring to or vesting in the Company or its nominees the Executive's entire right title and interest to and in such Intellectual Property or to and in any application, patent or other form of protection or copyright as the case may be including the right to file applications in the name of the Company or its nominees for patent or other forms of protection or for registration of copyright in any country claiming priority from the date of filing of any application or other date from which priority may run in any other country.

13.2 Copyright

13.2.1 Ownership

The ownership of the copyright in works created by employees, prior to 1 August 1989, is governed by section 4 of the Copyright Act 1956. The statutory rule can be varied or excluded by agreement (s 4(5)).

The statutory position can be summarised in this way. Apart from two special cases, the employer has the copyright in everything his employee creates in the course of his employment. The first exception is that employed journalists, including photographers and illustrators, keep the copyright in their work so far as it relates to reproduction in other forms. The second exception is that the copyright in a commissioned photograph, or a commissioned portrait by an employee, vests in the person giving the commission rather than in the employer.

The ownership of the copyright in works created by employees after 1 August 1989, is governed by the Copyright Design and Patents Act 1988.

The general rule is that when a literary, dramatic, musical or artistic work is made by an employee in the course of his employment, his employer is the owner of the copyright on that work, subject to any agreement to the contrary (s 11.2). This only applies to these specified works and the owner of the copyright on a sound recording, broadcast or film in broad terms is the person by whom the arrangements necessary for making the recording, transmission or film are undertaken.

'Literary work' so widely defined as 'any work . . . which is written, spoken, or sung' and includes a table or compilation and a computer program, (s 3(1)). 'Artistic work' is defined as meaning 'a graphic work; photograph . . . work of architecture . . . or a work of artistic craftsmanship.' (s 4(1)).

The Act also vests in the employer any design rights created by the employee in the course of his employment. The Act abolished the copyright protection for industrial designs and created new rights (s 213).

The Act also created new rights called 'moral rights' essentially these rights entitled a copyright author to be identified, for his work not to be subject to derogatory treatment, for a work not to be falsely attributed to him and finally the right of privacy in certain photographs and films. These rights do not apply where copyright vests in the employer, however (s 79(3) and s 82(1)).

13.2.2 Express assignment

Subject to the two exceptional cases, there is no need for an employer to take special action in relation to the copyright in work done by the employee in the course of his employment. That does, however, raise the question of the scope of the employee's employment. Where the production of material which is subject to copyright or design rights is the essence and purpose of the employment, it will be vital to the employer to ensure that the interpretation of that phrase causes no difficulty. Examples would be: fashion designers, advertising copywriters, musical arrangers, computer programmers.

Material the employee produces may be outside the scope of his employment, even though it is on the subject matter of the employee's employment and its composition was known to or encouraged by the employer. In one case, lectures written and delivered by an employee employed as a 'management engineer' about his job, which his employer welcomed for their publicity value and for which he gave the employee clerical facilities, were held to be outside the scope of the employee's employment so that the copyright remained his (*Stephenson Jordan & Harrison Ltd* v *Macdonald & Evans* [1952] 1 TLR 101). Similarly, a newspaper employee translated a letter for use in an advertisement to be published in the newspaper. He did so at his employer's request, but was paid extra and made the translation in his own time. The copyright in the translation remained the employee's (*Byrne* v *Statist Co* [1914] 1 KB 622).

While an obvious solution to any dispute about the scope of the employment is to incorporate into a service agreement a blanket assignment of all rights, or those of all relevant material, whether or not the work was made in the course of employment, there can be difficulties. Blanket assignments in situations other than employment have been held invalid as in restraint of trade (*Instone* v *A Shroeder Music Publishing Co Ltd* [1974] 1 WLR 1308). The possibility of undue influence being exerted can also arise, and if established, invalidates the agreement (*Clifford Davis Management Ltd* v *WEA Records Ltd* [1975] 1 WLR 61).

13.2.3 Held in trust

In some cases, although the employee remains owner of the copyright, he holds it in trust for his employer and is obliged to assign it to him on demand. An example of this was the managing director of a company who made furniture design drawings. His duty of fidelity to the company entitled the company to the benefit of the designs (*Antocks Lairn Ltd* v *I Bloohn Ltd* [1972] RPC 219). The company does not have a right to take action for breach of copyright in such a case unless there has been an actual assignment to the company.

13.2.4 Drafting

The employer's object will be to ensure that he both has the benefit of, and can sue to protect, all matter subject to copyright and design that his employee produces. To achieve this, the following should be considered in drafting a service agreement:

(i) The definition of the employee's job should be as broad and as specific as possible, to enable the maximum amount of material to be claimed as produced in the course of employment. Where an individual is expected to contribute items subject to copyright outside the main job on which he is engaged, they should be expressly mentioned.

(ii) There should be an express assignment to the employer of the copyright in any relevant material which would otherwise be vested in the employee.

13.2.5 Precedent

Copyright

The Executive shall promptly disclose to the Company all works in which copyright or design rights may exist which the Executive may make or originate either solely or jointly with others during the Executive's employment. Any such copyright works or designs created by him in the normal course of his employment or in the course of carrying out duties specifically assigned to him which relate to the affairs of the Company shall be the property of the Company whether or not the work was made by direction of the Company or was intended for the Company and the copyright in it and the rights in any design shall belong to the Company and to the extent that such copyright or design rights are not otherwise vested in the Company the Executive hereby assigns the same to the Company.

Chapter 14

Poaching Employees

14.1 General restrictions

One way in which employers increasingly fear competition from former employees is that they will leave with, or entice away, other employees to work with them or for them. The loss of an entire team or group of employees working on a specific project, or for a particular client, can have a severe impact on the employer's business. In such cases the employer not only loses the investment he has made in recruiting and training the employees, but it may have a considerable effect on the employer's ability to maintain the stability of his business.

There is little authority on the effectiveness of clauses drafted specifically to deal with such situations. It has been held that '. . . an employer has no legitimate interest in preventing an employee, after leaving his service, from entering the service of a competitor merely on the ground that the new employer is a competitor' (*Kores Manufacturing Company Ltd* v *Kolock Manufacturing Ltd* [1959] Ch 108, 125 per Jenkins LJ) but a reasonable restraint should have some effect. The clause will have to be reasonable as, although there is no decided authority on the point, it would appear that the restraint of trade doctrine will apply. If it was simply a matter of contract then there would be little difficulty in drafting and enforcing such provisions. However, if it is correct that the restraint of trade doctrine applies to such clauses then great care must be taken in drafting the provision.

14.2 Restrictions during employment

While a person is employed it will generally be a breach of his duty of fidelity to his employer to seek to recruit fellow employees to work for him once he has left that employment. This is not because of any interference with an existing employment contract. It applies even if the suggestion is that the recruited employee should work out his full notice. It is simply not proper for an employee to undermine his employer's business by taking other employees away.

In one case, an assistant solicitor offered his secretary a job once she had left his employment. She had been discontented with her current employment, but that was no justification for the solicitor's action. The proper course was for the solicitor to have reported the position to his employer, yet only nominal damages of £2 were awarded (*Sanders and Parry* [1967] 1 WLR 753). In view of the radical changes in the job market since that time, it may be easier for employers to show more substantial damage being caused by the wrongful action of its employees.

14.3 Post-termination obligations

An express provision contained in the service agreement to restrain an employee's activity after his employment has ended will probably have to be justified within the restraint of trade doctrine. The basic principle is that a contract of restraint of trade is *prima facie* void, but may be held valid if it is proved that the clause is reasonably necessary to protect a recognised legitimate interest of the employer and they are reasonable with reference to the interests of the parties and are not contrary to public policy. The two interests which are normally regarded as requiring protection are the employer's trade secrets or his trade connection (*Herbert Morrison Ltd* v *Saxelby* (1916) AC 688).

14.3.1 Trade secrets

In the case of *G D Searle and Co Ltd* v *Celltech Ltd* (1982) FSR 92 CA, it was held that 'information concerning the aptitudes of characters and fields of specialisation of staff does not normally amount to confidential information which is covered by the implied common law duty of confidentiality.' Accordingly, an employee's knowledge of the abilities of his fellow employees may be regarded as part of his own general knowledge gained in the course of his employment, which the employer cannot ordinarily prevent him exploiting. However, it may well be possible for an employer to show that to allow a former employee from employing others whom he formerly employed, could result in them divulging trade secrets. To take action successfully against the ex-employee, the employer must show that he realised the information which the other employees would disclose constituted the employer's trade secrets. Just to show that the other employees knew is not enough (*British Industrial Plastics Ltd* v *Fergusson* (1940) 1 All ER 479). It is not uncommon for employers, when dealing with secret processes, to restrict the information employees have of the process so that even those working on the same project are not aware of all aspects of the development work. In such cases it may well be possible to show a legitimate interest and that securing the employment of others within the team enables an ex-employee to exploit his employer's trade secrets in an unacceptable way.

There is an advantage in being able to restrain a former employee who was not himself privy to those secrets, but proposes to organise a new, competing business which will take advantage of them. If the restriction is imposed, and can be seen as likely to be fully enforceable, it acts as a deterrent. The employer may in that way avoid the disruption to the business caused by the departure of the employees, which is better than merely restraining their competitive activities later (*G D Searle & Co Ltd* v *Celltech Ltd* (1982) FSR 92 CA).

14.3.2 Trade connections and goodwill

The second ground on which the employer may be able to rely to justify the restraint is the protection of his trade connection. The protection of this interest may be argued as protecting the stability of the employer's workforce, which is essential for the employer to be able to retain and service customers. Such a legitimate interest may well exist where an employer forms a specific sales team to direct its marketing effort towards a particular group of customers. At present there is no authority suggesting that the Courts will recognise the stability of a workforce as a legitimate interest that an employer is entitled to protect. However, given the investment made by employers in training and developing the skills of its employees, we may see this interest develop as a legitimate interest which the employer is entitled to protect, particularly given the obvious attempts that are sometimes taken by competing employers to recruit staff with the intention of securing a presence in a new market.

14.4 Reasonableness

Once the employer has established a legitimate interest that requires protection, it is of course then necessary to demonstrate that the provision is reasonable ie that it goes no further than is necessary to protect that interest and that it does not offend against the public interest. Factors that will be considered are likely to be similar to those when dealing with non-soliciting or non-competition provisions. It is therefore unlikely that a blanket restraint preventing an ex-employee from soliciting any of the employer's employees will be enforceable. It will be necessary for the employer to demonstrate that the ex-employee has some influence over the employee being approached. There must be a time limit for the operation of the clause. Further it may be more difficult to demonstrate that the covenant should cover employees who are unskilled as this may again reflect on the appropriateness of the legitimate trading interest the employer is seeking to protect.

14.5 Interference with contract

In the absence of an express provision limiting an employee from poaching staff there is no implied obligation on an employee not to try to persuade his former colleagues to leave their employment after he himself has left (*Horcal Ltd* v *Datland* (1983) IRLR 459, QBD). However, to procure a person to break a contract of employment with a third party is an actionable tort (*Lumley and Guy* (1853) 2 E and B 216). This may provide a sanction to be used against a former employee poaching his former colleagues from his ex-employer. There are exceptions to the tort in connection with trade disputes, which are not relevant here (*Quinn* v *Leathem* [1901] AC 495, 510 per Lord Macnaghten).

The limits on this principle must be noted. First, simply to recruit another persons employee is not wrong, as long as the employee will not be in breach of contract. There must be no question of the employee leaving in the middle of a fixed term contract, or without giving proper notice. There is a limited exception to this when the person doing the recruiting is still employed by the same employer.

Secondly, it is essential if the person doing the recruiting is to be held liable, that he knows the facts that will mean that the employee breaks his contract. It is no defence to claim he was acting in good faith (*Pratt* v *British Medical Association* [1919] 1 KB 244, 265–6).

Thirdly, the recruiter's action must be the cause of damage to the former employer. An action failed when an employee voluntarily left his job without giving notice, and the facts showed that he had no intention of returning. As soon as the new employer was alerted to the fact that he was still under contract to the old employer, the new employer could have been guilty of tort, but because, even if the new employer relinquished the employee, he would not have gone back to his old job, the new employer's acts did not themselves cause any damage (*Jones Brothers (Hunstanton) Ltd* v *Stephens* [1955] 1 QB 275).

The amount of damages to which an employer is entitled as a result of employees being enticed away is measured by the harm which he suffers. So, where a number of key workers are taken at the same time and the employer's whole business is undermined, he may be able to recover his consequent loss of profit (*Gunter* v *Astor* (1819) 4 Moore 12).

14.6 Drafting

14.6.1 Principles

(i) While the employment continues, a total ban on recruiting fellow employees should be effective.

(ii) It would be helpful for employees in a prime position to recruit fellow employees ie senior managers, team leaders etc to ensure that it is made evident in their agreements that they are aware of the terms upon which the employees in their group are employed. Examples might be where all employees engaged in a certain category are employed on terms requiring that they give three months notice, or employees are required not to work in a competing business. Once could also expressly provide that employees should not discuss the terms of their own contracts with other employees so treating individual terms of contract as confidential information of the employer.

(iii) Incorporate in all agreements of the employees the employer wishes to protect notice periods, which may inhibit recruitment, or provide longer term contracts. Consider incorporating into such contracts the right to terminate summarily and pay money in lieu of notice and to put in place during the notice period non-competition provisions for the period of notice.

(iv) As the clause is likely to be governed by the restraint of trade doctrine so it must:
  (a) seek to protect the legitimate interests of the employer, and
  (b) must be reasonable in the interests of an employee and public policy.

(v) Given the difficulties of evidence of solicitation, the clause may need to cover both non-solicitation and non-employment.

(vi) To emphasise the legitimate interest point the clause must either show that the target employees have had access to trade secrets, enjoy a particular trade connection or control elements of their employers goodwill with customers.

(vii) The preservation of the stability of the workforce may be an insufficient reason justifying such a clause.

(viii) To ensure it is reasonable it must strictly limit the target group of employees, to those with whom the former employee had a personal connection or those over whom he could exercise some personal influence.

(ix) The protections sought must be limited in time and cannot be open-ended.

(x) A clause which seeks to prevent recruitment of all employees employed by the employer including skilled and unskilled employees is unlikely to be up-held.

(xi) If the employer has made a specific and recognisable investment in training, a clause dealing with the recovery of training expenses may further inhibit the poaching of staff. The amount to be recovered must be a genuine pre-estimate the employer will suffer.

(xii) Consider the implications and use of 'garden leave' with non-poaching where an employer reserves the right for the employee not to work during the notice period to prevent the departing team organising a programmed staggered departure.

(xiii) Ensure the clause can be severed from other clauses in the employment agreement.

14.7 Precedent

14.7.1 Non solicitation of Staff

(i) The Executive acknowledges that he understands and accepts that it is the employment policy of the company:

(a) to develop and adopt employment practices which seek to provide a stable and quality workforce; and

(b) to promote personal and individual contract negotiations with its employees.

(ii) Accordingly the terms and conditions of employment of staff employed by the Company are regarded by the Company as confidential information and the Executive accepts he will treat all such information as confidential and shall not at any time disclose to any person, firm or company such confidential information.

(iii) The Executive shall not during the course of his employment with the Company (whether on his own account or for any other person, firm or Company) solicit or endeavour to entice away from or discourage from being employed by the Company any other employee of the Company, nor will the Executive employ any other employee.

(iv) The Executive shall not for a period of [*specify period*] after the termination of his employment (howsoever occasioned) whether on his own account or for any other person, firm or Company, solicit or endeavour to entice away from or discourage from being employed by the Company any of its employees (specify group by salary range or job description) who are employed by the Company at the date of the termination of the Executive's employment and with whom the Executive had contact during his employment with the Company.

Chapter 15

Competition After Employment

15.1 Introduction

It is now common practice for employers to seek to limit an employee's ability to compete against his employer on leaving employment. This is particularly true where service agreements are drafted when a business has been sold and an essential feature of the sale of the business is the need to secure the senior management team to ensure the continuity of the business and to safeguard it from unfair competition. In such cases protection will be often sought by incorporating provisions in both the sale and acquisition agreement and the service agreements of the employees deemed important by the purchasers. However, such provisions are equally relevant when employees develop a strong trade connection with customers which the employer wish to protect when the employee leaves his employment.

There are a number of different types of provision used to gain protection. These are similar to the clauses already considered with regard to the protection of trade secrets and confidential information (Chapter 13) and are also often used in conjunction with a clause seeking to prevent the non-poaching of staff (Chapter 14). They include provisions to prevent the employee soliciting or dealing with customers and to prevent the employee being employed or setting up his own business in competition with his employer. All such provisions will be subject to the restraint of trade doctrine and accordingly great care must be taken in the preparation of such clauses as they must be tailored to cope with the particular factual circumstances of each employment situation.

15.2 The restraint of trade doctrine

An employer has no right to extract from an employee an agreement which is simply designed to protect the employer from the effect of the employee competing with him after the employee has left his employ. An agreement of that type is in restraint of trade and void. It is not the restriction on competition that makes the covenant bad; but the lack of legitimate justification, '. . . the fact that a legitimate covenant may also operate to prevent competition does not mean that the covenant is a bad one' (*Routh* v *Jones* [1947] 1 All ER 758, 761 per Lord Green).

The leading authority on the scope of the restraint of trade doctrine is *Esso Petroleum Co Ltd* v *Harpers Garage (Stourport) Ltd* [1968] AC 269. In that case Lord Wilberforce made the following statement:

> There will always be certain general categories of contracts as to which it can be said, with some degree of certainty; that the doctrine does or does not apply to them. Positively, there are likely to be certain sensitive areas as to which the law will require in every case the test of reasonableness to be passed. Such an area has long been and still is that of contract between employer and employee as regards the period after the employment has ceased.

What the employer can validly do is to obtain an agreement restricting the employee in a way which is both reasonable and protects the legitimate interests of the employer. '. . . Restraints of trade . . . may be justified by the special circumstances of a particular case. It is a sufficient justification, and indeed it is the only justification, if the restriction is reasonable—reasonable, that is, in reference to the interests of the parties concerned and reasonable in reference to the interests of the public' (*Nordenfelt* v *Maxim Nordenfelt Guns and Ammunition Co Ltd* [1984] AC 535, 565 per Lord Macnaghten). Whether or not a restriction is reasonable is a question of law. This has a practical effect on the preparation of cases. 'Evidence cannot be given on the question of validity or reasonableness, although evidence can be given as to the nature of the business and the employment and, I think, also as to any practice which is usual among businessmen as regards the terms of employment' (*Mason* v *Provident Clothing and Supply Co Ltd* [1913] AC 724, 732 per Viscount Haldane).

Deciding whether or not a particular restriction is enforceable is an uncertain matter and has provoked considerable litigation. The decisions of the Courts are not all consistent. A contract term must be judged according to its effect rather than its form (*Stenhouse Australia Ltd* v *Phillips* [1974] AC 391) where a term requiring a former employee to pay to the former employer half the commission he earned from the latter's clients for five years was viewed as a competition restriction, rather than a mere obligation to pay money. See also *Sadler* v *Imperial Life Assurance Co of Canada Ltd* [1988] IRLR 389 where it was said 'that a financial incentive to limit a former employee's activities amounts to a restraint of trade' (per Mr P J Crawford QC).

The way in which a restriction should be approached by the Court has been summarised in this way.

> . . . First, that it is for the covenantee to show that the restriction sought to be imposed upon the covenantor goes no further than is reasonable for the protection of his business; secondly, that the restraint must be reasonable not only in the interests of the covenantee but in the interests of both the contracting parties; and thirdly, that an employer is not entitled by a covenant taken from his employee to protect himself after the employment has ceased against his former servants competition, although a purchaser of goodwill is entitled to protect himself against such competition on the part of the vendor (*Gledhow Autoparts Ltd* v *Delaney* [1956] 1 WLR 1366, 1372 per Sellers LJ).

There is one type of case in which the greater freedom to impose restrictions enjoyed by the purchaser of goodwill applies between employer and employee. If the vendor of a business is employed by the purchaser—as is not infrequently the case on the takeover of a small concern—then any restriction in the service agreement made between the purchaser and the vendor as employer and employee can limit competition by the vendor/employee once the employment ends (*Systems Reliability Holdings plc* v *Smith* [1990] IRLR 377 Chd). The purchaser will also ensure that there are restrictions in the sale and acquisition agreement bind the vendor for a period of time immediately after the completion of the acquisition.

In the *Esso Petroleum* case (see above) Lord Morris of Borth y Gest said:

> If someone has sold the goodwill of his business, some restraint to enable the purchaser to have that which he has bought may be recognised as reasonable. Some restraints to ensure the protection of confidential information may be similarly regarded. The law recognises that if business contracts are fairly made by parties who are on equal terms such parties should know that business best . . . yet the law, in some circumstances, reserves the right to say that a contract is in restraint of trade and that to be enforceable it must pass a test of reasonableness. In the competition

between varying possible principles applicable, that which makes certain covenants in restraint of trade unenforceable will in some circumstances be strong enough to prevail. Public policy will give it priority.

The validity of any particular restriction depends on the circumstances of the case. Subject to that overall qualification, there are a number of aspects of it which can be examined to assess the likelihood of its enforceability. However, it must be stressed that to draft provisions which are likely to be enforced it is essential for the draftsman to understand that the employee's business is, how it is conducted, and what the employee's role is. This work needs to be completed before the clause is drafted and a list of relevant questions appear in Appendix F. But as Stevenson LJ said in the case of *Spafax Ltd* v *Harrison* [1980] IRLR 442 'the law in this area is easier to state than to apply'.

15.3 The employer's legitimate interest

Whatever an employer's motive in imposing a restriction it is common and advisable to aim at a particular target, because a clause merely aimed at preventing an employee from competing will not generally be enforceable. The first stage in drafting the clause must therefore be to identify the interest the employer is seeking to protect and establish whether it is a legitimate interest recognised by the Courts as one the employer is entitled to seek to protect. The protection of trade secrets is an acceptable interest for the employer to protect, and this is dealt with separately (Chapter 12). The protection of trade connections is also a legitimate interest (*S W Strange Ltd* v *Mann* [1965] 1 WLR 629).

In the case of *Stenhouse Australia Ltd* v *Phillips* (see above) Lord Wilberforce said:

> The employer's claim for protection must be based on the identification of some advantage or asset interest in the business which can properly be regarded as, in a general sense, his property, and which it would be unjust to allow the employee to appropriate for his own purposes, though he (the employee) may have contributed to its creation.

15.4 The test of reasonableness

15.4.1 Employees freedom

No restriction can be so wide as totally to prevent the employee from obtaining employment elsewhere. Enforcing such a restriction would be tantamount to requiring specific performance of the contract, which a Court will not do in the case of a service agreement (*Whitwood Chemical Co* v *Hardman* [1891] 2 Ch 416). On the other hand, a restriction not to work for anyone else in a particular capacity is not void, if there are other ways in which the employee can earn his living (*Warner Bros Pictures Inc* v *Nelson* [1937] 1 KB 209).

15.4.2 Period of restraint

A restriction can be valid even though there is no time limit on it (*Fitch* v *Dewes* [1921] 2 AC 158, a restriction on a solicitor's managing clerk against practicing within a defined area). This may now be regarded as an exceptional case and normally, however, a time limit is necessary. It should be related to the interest being protected. Where the employer's clientele is in regular contact with the business, so that it should within a short time be able to secure its loyalty as part of its goodwill rather than that of a departed employee, a short period is appropriate. The seniority of the employee and the degree of influence the employee has over the clientele are also relevant factors in judging the reasonableness of the period chosen. A one year restriction was valid in the case of a ladies hairdressing assistant (*Marion White Ltd* v *Francis* [1972] 1 WLR 143), and a milk roundsman (*Home Counties Dairies Ltd* v *Skilton* [1970] 1 WLR 526). For an estate agents manager, in a practice to which many clients returned, three years was a reasonable period (*Culvert Hunt and Barden* v *Elton* (1974) 233 EG 391). A five year restriction on the managing director of an insurance broking company against canvassing the company's clients was upheld (*Stenhouse Australia Ltd* v *Phillips* [1974] AC 391).

15.4.3 Area of restraint

The area in which the restriction on a former employee's activities is to operate must be strictly related to the extent of the business to which the employer can legitimately protect, or the area in which the employee himself has worked. In the case of *Greer* v *Sketchley Ltd* [1979] IRLR 445 the employer sought to enforce a 12 month non-competition provision covering all of the UK in the case of a company director with knowledge of trade secrets. However, as the employer traded in the South of England, (exclusively Devon and Cornwall), the Cardiff and Midlands areas the restraint was held to be unreasonable. Generally a restriction without a geographical limit is invalid (*Dowden and Pook Ltd* v *Pook* [1904] 1 KB 45, a departmental manager for a medium sized West Country cider business; *Commercial Plastics Ltd* v *Vincent* [1965] 1 QB 623, a specialist in PVC calendering), but in the exceptional case where a business is worldwide, and the employees concerned in it on that scale, no limit is needed (*Nordenfelt* v *Maxim Nordenfelt Guns and Ammunition Co Ltd* [1894] AC 535). In *Norbrook Laboratories Ltd* v *Smyth*, Kelly J gave guidance as to when a wordwide restraint would be enforced where evidence was given to the effect that the employer's products were sold in 46 countries and the areas and countries was sufficient to show a substantial worldwide market. Where the objective is to secure the goodwill of customers with whom the employee dealt, it should be considered whether in fact they came from a defined area. Where a bookmaker did his business largely by telephone, a restriction on his manager affecting a 12 mile radius was held to be unenforceable (*S W Strange Ltd* v *Mann* [1965] 1 WLR 629), it also failed because the manager was unlikely to acquire personal goodwill when dealing with customers by telephone).

15.4.4 Employers customers

An employee who has personal contact with the employer's customers may well build up a personal following among what is the employer's trade connection. A restriction against the employee in a case like that dealing with or soliciting those customers for a reasonable time after the employment ends is generally enforceable. This does not apply if the nature of the employee's job, even if he speaks to the customers, makes it unlikely that he will have attracted their loyalty (*S W Strange Ltd* v *Mann* [1965] 1 WLR 629, where all the dealing were on the telephone). The normal form for this restriction is not to deal with, serve, solicit, or seek custom from any person who was a customer of the employer while the employee was employed by him. Appropriate time and area limitations are added. Both non-dealing and a non-solicitation clause can be justifiable provided there is a legitimate interest which requires protection (*London and Solent Ltd* v *Brooks* CA 27 October 1988). The clause is likely to be unenforceable if it covers a wider range of goods and services than those in which the employee dealt (*Marley Tile Co Ltd* v *Johnson* [1982] IRL 75). Accordingly, the dealings restricted should only be those related to the business the employee did for the employer. A non-dealing provision is wider in its effect than a non-solicitation clause as it will apply even if the first contact is made at the initiation of the customer and not the employee (*John Michael Design Plc* v *Cook and Foley* [1987] ICR 445 CA). Clearly, this ban will often cover people who were potential customers of the employer or people who were the employer's customers, even though the employee did not know it. This is not a ground for rejecting the restriction as unreasonable (*T W Plowman and Son Ltd* v *Ash* [1964] 1 WLR 568). The Court exercises the discretion in enforcing this type of restriction, to ensure that an innocent former employee is not punished. 'The covenantor might inadvertently solicit one of that class of customers, but in such case the Court would not grant an injunction against him or commit him for contempt of any injunction already granted' (*Guildford Motor Co Ltd* v *Horn* [1933] Ch 935, 964 per Lawrence LJ).

Generally the clause should cover customers with whom the employee had direct contact in the course of the employment (*Home Counties Dairies Ltd* v *Skilton* [1970] 1 All ER 1227). The claim can be limited to client contact within a specified period during and before the termination of the employment which will be of assistance in showing the reasonableness of the provision. If it is desired to cover any customer of the employer during the employee's period of employment it may be prudent to limit the period during which no client contact can be made.

15.4.5 Direct competition

Although, without further provisions, a former employee cannot be stopped from competing with his ex-employer, some restrictions are intended to do that. A foreman toolmaker's agreement forbade him to take employment within two years with any competitor of the employer. This was invalid because 'competitor' was so wide that it would not be limited to cases which protected the employer's legitimate interests (*Vandervell Products Ltd* v *McLeod* [1957] RPC 185). Even the restriction which was more specific, not to work for any competitor of the employer in the field of PVC calendering, failed because the employer's speciality and the employee's work had been in PVC calendaring specifically for adhesive tape (*Commercial Plastics Ltd* v *Vincent* [1956] 1 QB 623). In this type of case, 'competitor' is construed to mean someone in that category at the date the employment ends.

A successful restriction on competition was imposed on a clerk to a commission merchant who imported goods. He was forbidden for five years to deal, in the UK, in any goods of continental manufacture dealt in by the employer before the employment ended. That was construed to mean while the employee had been employed, and the effect of the agreement was limited to dealings as commission agent (*Moenich* v *Fenestre* [1892] 627 LT 602). Presumably, in practice, dealing in the same range of goods would have meant dealing with the same suppliers, and perhaps also the same customers, as the employee had done on the employer's behalf. If such clauses are considered necessary it is essential they should be limited in time and area. In judging the appropriate limitation some knowledge of the employer's business is necessary. In the case of *Spencer* v *Marshington* [1988] IRLR 392 it was held that a provision which restricted competition within an area in 25 miles of the Defendant's office was too wide to be enforced. It was said that the object of the rule of public policy against too wide a restriction on a former employee's future activities is not primarily to protect the employee but to protect the market open to prospective customers and to promote competition. A restriction is too wide to be enforced if its area was more than was adequate to protect the employer's legitimate interest. In that case, the 25 mile restriction was more than enough to protect the employer's legitimate interest. It was not necessary to extend the area beyond 20 miles at the most. All but one of the employer's existing customers worked within that narrower area and there was nothing to justify extending the area of restriction beyond where possible future customers might have been won or to places from where they could have been reached. It was also suggested that the goodwill of the business could have been protected by taking a non-solicitation restriction from the employer.

15.5 Construction

15.5.1 Introduction

Whether or not a covenant restricting a former employee's future activities is enforceable depends not only on the circumstances of the case, but also on how the covenant is construed in context. The Courts have from time to time adopted various methods, which have allowed them to enforce provisions which might otherwise have been void. The enthusiasm which the Courts show for a flexible approach, seeking a construction more likely to uphold a restriction than to reject it, waxes and wanes. In recent years the tendency has been to uphold covenants whenever it is reasonable to do so. This does not involve any formal alteration in the rules which the Courts apply. It is rather the way in which they are likely to exercise their discretion, judged from the tenor of the decision.

15.5.2 Context of the agreement

Conditions which might, on a literal interpretation out of context, be held to be too sweeping, can be interpreted in a narrower, acceptable sense by reference to the context in which they appear. A milk roundsman's agreement restricted him from serving or selling milk or dairy produce to certain former customers of his employer. That could, taken literally, have caught a number of unrelated employments, eg selling cheese in a grocery, or serving in a milk bar. However, it was held to be limited to actions as a milk roundsman, because that was the context in which the agreement was made (*Home Counties Dairies Ltd* v *Skilton* [1970] 1 WLR 526).

Again, the restriction placed on a commercial traveller required him not to call on or solicit anyone who had been a customer of his former employer to transact business, without limiting the type of business which he might be seeking to do with them. The breadth of that term is reduced by considering its intended purpose. 'The object of the [employer's] was to prevent the [employee] from being allowed to do anything which would be detrimental to their business; and I think that "transact business" ought to be construed as confined to business similar to that of [employer's]' (*Mills and Dunham* [1891] 1 Ch 576, 587 per Lindlay LJ). A similar type of restriction, against canvassing an employer's customers, was limited by interpretation to doing so in connection with the type of goods which the employee had handled for the employer (*G W Plowman and Son Ltd* v *Ash* [1964] 1 WLR 568).

A different type of clause is one forbidding the employee to accept employment from another, named, company. That company traded both as a rival to the employer and in other fields. The restriction was construed as applying only to the part of the other company's business as was in competition with the employer (*Littlewoods Organisation Ltd* v *Harris* [1977] 1 WLR 1472).

It is difficult to forecast when this principle will apply. One employer sought to safeguard his trade secrets by forbidding an employee from engaging 'in any part of the UK in any business which is similar to any business involving such trade secrets and/or secret processes carried on by the company . . .'. The area of the restriction was too wide, because they did not have branches throughout the UK. However notwithstanding the obvious intention of the clause, the Court would not limit its effect by implying the word 'competing' to qualify the business which the employee was forbidden to join (*Greer* v *Sketchley Ltd* [1979] IRLR 445).

15.5.3 Main effect

If the main effect of a restriction is reasonable and otherwise enforceable, it is not held void merely because it is possible to imagine outlandish and unlikely circumstances which could theoretically be caught and would make the clause wider than should be enforced. '. . . a covenant in restraint of trade is not to be rendered invalid simply by putting forward unlikely or improbable contingencies in which it might operate unreasonably . . . if such an unlikely or improbable end should happen, the Court would not enforce it so as to create injustice' (*Office Overload Ltd* v *Gunn* [1976] 120 SJ 147, per Lord Denning MR, quoted in *Littlewoods Organisation Ltd* v *Harris* [1977] 1 WLR 1472, 1479).

This principle has also been expressed with considerable sympathy for the draftsman of service agreements who, when concerned with this type of clause, can justifiably feel beleaguered.

> It is in practice extremely difficult to frame restrictions which will adequately protect a trade connection and may at the same time cover some cases where a breach will not injure the trade connection. If the Court can see that the restriction has been carefully framed for a legitimate purpose, I do not think it should be held void as contrary to public policy in favour of an ex-employee who is in flagrant breach of it on such narrow grounds . . . (*Home Counties Dairies Ltd* v *Skilton* [1970] 1 WLR 526, 538 per Cross LJ).

In judging whether a clause is reasonable it must be judged in the circumstances applying at the date of the contract, and one must 'not examine it ex-post facto in the light of the circumstances applying at the date of trial' (*NIS Fertilisers* v *Trevor Neville* per Carswell J).

15.5.4 Severance

Where a single clause contains both a legitimate restriction and an extension which is too wide to be enforceable it may be possible to sever the two, enforcing the one and jettisoning the other. Although there have been cases in which the Courts have severed such clauses and others in which they have declined to do so, no simple test to determine when the terms of an agreement can be severed has emerged.

In the case of *NIS Fertilizers* v *Trevor Neville* the part of the clause which defined the area read as follows: 'in an area which covers the territory within which you represented the Company and any area outside this territory which stands at a distance of less than 20 miles from the boundary of . . .'. The Court was asked to strike out the 20 mile extension it—refused to do so, stating—'although it could grammatically be done without any difficulty. In my judgement the promise is a single and indivisible one, extending over a specified area, and one cannot split this area up and regard it as being one promise in respect of the territory and another in respect of the 20 mile extension'. In the case of *Business Seating (Renovations) Ltd* v *Broad* [1989] ICR 729 the Court upheld a non-solicitation provision clause which referred to customers of 'the Company or any associated company' by severing the reference to 'any associated company'.

One suggestion has been that the part severed must be distinct and that without it the underlying meaning of the clause must remain intact. '. . . if one severs the two restrictions . . . that would give the severed part a meaning and object different in kind as well as an extent from that which it possesses in its collocation with the other restrictions, and if this is so, . . . the different parts cannot be said to be distinct' (*T Lucas and Co Ltd* v *Mitchell* [1972] 1 WLR 938, 1043 per Pennycuick V-C). Nevertheless, that often does seem to be the effect of severence, but maybe this is because the distinction between differences of kind and those of extent can only be a matter of opinion.

Alternatively there is what has been called the 'blue pencil' approach, which removes the offending words in a clause without having to substitute something else and which leaves the remaining words capable of a sensible and reasonable interpretation.

It is important to be able to use the approach to be able to demonstrate that the covenant can be deleted without re-writing the covenant (*Mason* v *Provident Clothing and Supply Co Ltd* [1913] AC 724) and that the covenant is divisible into two or more covenants (*NIS Fertilisers Ltd* v *Neville* [1987] 342 IDS). The Courts have a reluctance to use the approach except in very clear cases, it should therefore not be relied on in drafting such clauses. In the case of *Attwood* v *Lamont* [1920] 3 KB 571 a restraint clause provided that the employee was 'not to engage in the trades of tailor, dressmaker, general draper, milliner, hatter, haberdasher, gentleman's lady's or children's outfitter'. The clause was held to be too wide, and the Court refused to cut it down using the 'blue pencil' approach as it was considered to be one indivisible covenant and could not be cut down. However in the case of *Rex Stuart Jefferies Parker Ginsberg Ltd* v *Parker* the Court was prepared to delete words from an otherwise unreasonable clause so that the clause became valid and enforceable. In this case the clause was a non-solicitation provision which was to apply 'to any person who is or has been a customer during the employment'. It was argued that the words 'or is' could refer to future customers. The Court allowed the deletion of the words.

It is not possible to guarantee that a Court would sever any particular restriction. The draftsman's main object must naturally be only to impose restrictions which are wholly valid. To cope with the possibility of invalidity, the style of an agreement should be such that restrictions are imposed separately and individually, both to help their being construed as independent, and to make severance easy. However care must be taken to ensure that in following this approach the clauses are not rendered too uncertain or vague for them to be enforced. Often clauses are now drafted where a series of restraints linked to different areas and times are stated in a progressively restricted format. Whether the approach will receive the Courts' approval and necessarily its assistance is yet to be decided.

15.6 An express acceptance of the reasonableness of the provision

It is common to add a clause to the provisions relating to the employee's post-termination obligations to the effect that the parties accept the clauses as being reasonable and if any of the provisions are held to be unreasonable the clause with the unacceptable parts deleted shall continue to apply if they are capable of being enforced. The effectiveness of such a provision was questionable as it was thought to be too vague to be given effect to but in the case of *Hinton and Higgs (UK) Ltd* v *Murphy* [1989] IRLR 519, it was accepted by the Judge that the statement made by the parties reinforced the justification for using the 'blue pencil' test. However the Court also held that the mere statement that the clause was reasonable had no effect and the Court would do no more than delete words and would not re-write the provisions.

15.7 The consequences of the employer's breach of contract

A restriction on an employee after his employment ends is not enforceable if he is wrongfully dismissed. The employer has then repudiated the contract, and cannot take the benefit of part of it (*General Billposting Co Ltd* v *Atkinson* [1909] AC 118, and *Unigate Dairies (Western) Ltd* 21 July 1982 Lexis). Various steps are now taken to draft clauses to avoid the consequences of this decision so that certain matters are defined as being matters that will by agreement not constitute a repudiation of a contract. However, as such clauses are likely to be interpreted against the employer, great care must be taken in drafting them to limit the scope for judicial interpretation. The use of phrases such as 'howsoever occasioned' or 'for whatever reason' are likely to be interpreted as being limited to an 'occasion' or 'cause' which is lawful within the terms of the service agreement (*Lawrence David* v *Ashton* [1989] IRLR 22). In the case of *Briggs and Oats* (unreported) Scott J, commenting on a clause containing a phrase 'for whatever reason', said 'the breach of contract..was adopted by the Defendant as putting an end to the contract. In such a case outstanding contractual obligations of the injured party are in law discharged together with the contract. The result does not depend on the construction of the contract.' He also considered 'grossly unreasonable' a contract under which an employee could be wrongfully dismissed but would nevertheless still remain bound by the restraint of trade provisions.

However, there has been approval given by the Courts to one type of clause designed to avoid the consequences of the *General Billposting* decision. In the case of *Rex Stuart Jefferies Parker Ginsberg Ltd* v *Parker* the employee's contract contained a provision that he was entitled to receive six months notice or receive salary in lieu of notice. The Court held that as the contract contained two alternative contractual means of lawfully terminating the service agreement the restrictive covenants could be enforced in the circumstances where the employee was paid money in lieu of notice. Payments made under such a provision will be taxable as an emolument under Schedule E.

15.8 Enforcement

Although an action for damages can be maintained by an employer against a former employee who contravens a restriction on his future activities, it seldom is. That necessitates proving actual loss, which can be difficult, and it does not give the employer the remedy he really wants, which is compliance with the terms of the covenant. For this reason, an injunction is the remedy normally sought, and it will generally be granted if the covenant is valid. An interim injunction can usually be obtained. The limitation on the jurisdiction to grant interim injunctions, stemming from *American Cyanamid Company* v *Ethicon Ltd* [1975] AC 396, does apply (*Lawrence David* v *Ashton* [1989] IRLR 22), provided the plaintiff employer seeks a speedy trial and it is likely that the hearing of the trial will occur before the expiry of the restriction. So the employer must show there is a serious issue to be tried and that on balance the circumstances favour granting the injunction. Generally the employer will be able to show that on this test the injunction should be granted.

In one case, the employer obtained a declaratory judgment condemning the employee's action even though the period of restriction had by then expired. This was justified because the employer had imposed the same restriction on other employees in similar positions, so it was in the nature of a test case (*Marion White Ltd* v *Francis* [1972] 1 WLR 1423). Equally it is possible for an employee to seek a declaration as to the validity of a restriction before acting in breach of its terms (*Greer* v *Sketchley Ltd* [1979] FSR 197).

15.9 Taxation

Income tax is charged on any payment by an employer to an employee as consideration for entering into a covenant restricting him from competing (Taxes Act 1988 s 313). An employer who makes such a payment cannot deduct it from his profit as a business expense because the payment is of a capital nature (*Associated Portland Cement Manufacturers Ltd* v *Kerr* [1946] 1 All ER 68).

15.10 Special situations

15.10.1 Temporary workers

An employment agency which supplies its employees as temporary workers for its clients is forbidden to impose any prohibition or restriction on an employee which is calculated to deter the employee from terminating his contract with the agency and starting to work for the agency's client direct (Conduct of Employment Agencies and Employment Business Regulations 1976, 9(9)).

15.10.2 Restrictive trade practices Acts

The relevant Acts are the Restrictive Trade Practices Act, the Restrictive Trade Practices (Sale and Purchase and Share Subscription Agreements) (Goods) Order 1989, the Restrictive Trade Practices (Services) (Amendment) Order 1989.

These Acts apply to agreements for goods or services between two or more persons carrying on business within the UK and where restrictions are accepted by two or more parties. In situations where there is a sale of a business, and as a condition of the sale of the business, the employee is required to enter into service agreements which contain restrictions as to their future activities, and restrictions are also accepted by the purchaser such restrictions may fall within the scope of the Act. Accordingly it is considered advisable to furnish the Director General of Fair Trading for entry on the register of restrictive trading agreements, such service agreements. If this step is not taken within the time prescribed by the Act, then the agreements are void and unenforceable.

15.11 Drafting

The ideal is undoubtedly that every restriction should be separately drafted, expressly to cover the relations between one employer and one employee, and having regard to the facts of their particular situation. That will often not be possible, but it has to be recognised that a common form, standard restriction will be viewed with suspicion by the Courts, and will be even less readily enforced than one which is tailor made (*Instone* v *A Schroder Music Publishing Co Ltd* [1974] 1 WLR 1308).

Bearing in mind that general point, the following guidelines should be taken into consideration:

(i) The clauses must be validly incorporated into the service agreement (See Chapter 3).

(ii) The protection given to the employer should be limited to the protection of his legitimate interest. It may be an advantage to recite the circumstances justifying the restriction.

(iii) Both time and area limits on the restriction should be carefully considered, and conservative ones should be inserted in both cases where appropriate.

(iv) Where the employer's undertaking extends more widely than the business in which the employee worked, the restriction on the employee should relate only to that business.

(v) If more than one form of restriction is to be placed on the employee, each should be physically separated and a clause drafted so that they can easily be severed if necessary.

(vi) Clauses seeking to protect trading connections should focus on the employee's personal influence over the trade connection.

(vii) Steps should be taken to incorporate provisions, which seek to avoid the consequences of the *General Billposting* decision.

(viii) It may be advisable to incorporate a provision in which the employer and employee acknowledge the need for the restrictions and that those sought are reasonable.

(ix) It is worthwhile incoporating a provision to permit the re-structuring of the restraint provisions if found to be unreasonable for some reason, despite the present uncertainty about the effectiveness of such provision.

(x) The burden of proof of reasonableness is on the party seeking to enforce it.

(xi) The reasonableness of the provision will be judged at the date of the service agreement.

15.12 Precedents

Non solicitation of customers

The Executive shall not for a period of (*specify period*) [months/years] after termination of his employment (without the previous consent in writing of the Company and whether on his own account or for any other person, firm or company) solicit or endeavour to entice away from the Company any person, firm or company (a) who or which in the preceding (*specify period*) [months/years] shall have been a customer of or in the habit of dealing with the Company and (b) with whom or which the Executive had contact during [the period of (*specify period*) months prior to the end of] his employment.

Non dealing

The Executive shall not for a period of (*specify period*) [months/years] after termination of his employment (howsoever occasioned) [without the previous consent in writing of the Company] and within (*specify area*) directly or indirectly do any business with or have any dealings with any person, firm or company who was a client customer supplier [agent or distributor] of the Company during the period of his employment provided that nothing contained in this sub-clause shall prohibit the Executive's activities which are not in direct or indirect competition with any business carried on by the Company at the date of the termination of this agreement.

Non compete

The Executive shall not for a period of (*specify period*) [months/years] after termination of his employment (howsoever occasioned) [without the previous consent in writing of the Company] be engaged or interested (whether as principal, servant, agent, consultant or otherwise) in any trade or business which is situated within (*specify area*) and which is similar to or competing with any trade or business being carried on at the end of his employment by the Company or any other Group Company with which he shall have been directly connected during the preceding (*specify period*) [months/years].

Severance provision

The Executive acknowledges:

(i) that each of the foregoing sub-clauses of this clause constitutes an entirely separate and independent restriction on him; and

(ii) whilst at the date of the agreement the duration, extent and application of each of the restrictions are considered by the parties no greater than is necessary for the protection of the Company's interests and reasonable in all the circumstances it is acknowledged that restrictions of such a nature may be valid because of changing circumstances and accordingly if any of the restrictions shall be adjudged to be void or ineffective for whatever reason but would be adjudged to be valid and effective if part of the wording thereof were deleted or the periods thereof reduced or the area thereof reduced in scope they shall apply with such modifications as may be necessary to make them valid and effective.

Part V

Termination

Chapter 16

Ending Employment

16.1 Terminating the employment contract

There are five ways in which a service agreement can come to an end:

(i) *Expiry*. A service agreement made for a fixed period automatically ends when that time expires. No action is required either on the part of the employer or of the employee. An agreement which is terminable on notice, but lays down a retirement date or age for the employee, effectively runs for a fixed period until that date unless notice is given earlier. A contract engaging the employee to work on a particular project expires when the work comes to an end.

(ii) *Notice*. A service agreement which does not state that it is to last for a definite period can be brought to an end by either party giving notice to the other. The period of notice may be prescribed by the contract, be governed by an implied term or be subject to a statutory minimum period.

(iii) *Agreement*. The parties may come to a later agreement which supersedes the earlier one.

(iv) *Rule of law*. Some supervening circumstances have the effect of bringing a service agreement to an end independently of any actions of the parties. If there is frustration by some outside event, no action of the parties is required. 'The contract is terminated automatically by the event giving rise to frustration' (*Egg Stores (Stamford Hill) Ltd* v *Leibovici* [1977] ICR 260, 264 per Phillips J).

(v) *Breach*. A breach of the terms of a service agreement can bring it to an end, or may be such as to justify the innocent party in ending it.

A sharp distinction must be drawn between the termination of employment which puts an end to the contract and the suspension of the employee. Suspension is often useful as an interim measure in the course of disciplinary proceedings, or while allegations are investigated. The vital difference is that the contract remains in full force, except only in so far as it relates to the performance of the employee's duties. 'When a man is suspended from the office he holds it is merely a direction, that so long as he holds the office and until he is legally dismissed he must not do anything in the discharge of the duties of the office' (*Boston Deep Sea Fishing and Ice Co Ltd* v *Ansell* (1888) 39 Ch D 339, 357 per Cotton LJ). The employee whilst under suspension must receive full pay unless there is a specific contractual term providing that suspension can be without pay.

16.2 Expiry

Although the expiry of a fixed term service agreement does not constitute a breach of contract at common law—indeed it is, on the contrary, the fulfilment of its purpose—it is deemed to be dismissal for certain statutory purposes. For compensation for unfair dismissal, 'an employee shall be treated as dismissed by his employer if . . . (*b*) where under that contract he is employed for a fixed term, that term expires without being renewed under the same contract' (Employment Protection (Consolidation) Act 1978, s 55(2)). The same provision applies in the case of redundancy (s 83(2)). That does not mean that the non-renewal of a fixed term agreement automatically entitles the employee to compensation or a redundancy payment, but merely that one of the qualifying conditions for making a claim, that the employee was dismissed, has been satisfied. Therefore, it may be possible for the company to justify the dismissal on one of the grounds prescribed by the Employment Protection (Consolidation) Act 1978 eg some other substantial reason (*North Yorkshire County Council* v *Fay* [1985] IRLR 247, [1986] ICR 133).

It seems that non renewal of a service agreement intended to last the duration of a particular task will not be deemed to be a dismissal for the statutory purposes (*Wiltshire County Council* v *NAFTE and Guy* (1980) IRLR 198). Further a contract terminable on the happening or non-happening of a future event has been held to terminate automatically and did not constitute a dismissal (*Brown* v *Knowsley BC* (1986) IRLR 102).

A service agreement for a fixed term of one year or more can contain a provision validly excluding rights to compensation for unfair dismissal and/or redundancy payments, but only where the dismissal is due to the expiry of that term without its being renewed (Employment Protection (Consolidation) Act 1978, s 142). A term to that effect cannot be used in a contract for the duration of a project. Employment on a job to job basis is not a fixed term contract for this purpose (*Ryan* v *Shipboard Maintenance Ltd* [1980] ICR 88). It is suggested that a way to overcome the difficulty is to express the contract to be for one year or until the work is finished, whichever is the later. The efficacy of that cannot be guaranteed.

16.3 Notice

16.3.1 Form

It is normal for a service agreement to specify that notice to end it must be given in writing. In the absence of a term of that sort, any unequivocal notice, whether written or oral, suffices.

With certain exceptions, an employee who is given notice has a statutory right to a written statement giving particulars of the reasons for his dismissal. The employer must give such a statement within fourteen days of being requested to do so (Employment Protection (Consolidation) Act 1978, s 53). That statement is not part of the notice, although no doubt it could be incorporated into the notice in anticipation of a request. The fact that the statement must be in writing does not mean that the notice must also be.

16.3.2 Effect

For a notice to end employment, it must clearly state the date on which the contract comes to an end. To give general advance notice that dismissal is coming, and to suggest that the employee seek employment elsewhere, is not good enough. A warning of that nature does not constitute dismissal either for the purpose of claiming compensation for unfair dismissal (*Haseltine Lake & Co* v *Dowler* [1981] ICR 222) or for claiming a statutory redundancy payment (*International Computers Ltd* v *Kennedy* [1981] IRLR 28).

A notice takes effect when it is received by the intended recipient *Brown* v *Southall and Knight* [1980] IRLR 130. Generally service agreements contain express provisions, which may lay down presumptions about the receipt of notices served in a prescribed manner (in the manner of the Law of Property Act 1925, s 196, or the Interpretation Act 1978, s 7). Any such terms will bind the parties. They are obviously useful for an employer who loses touch with an employee who quits without giving notice. It may also be important to establish the precise date for the dismissal when an employee has at sometimes in the future the right to exercise share options.

A notice to end an employment contract probably does not have to end on a day on which wages or salary is payable (*Ryan* v *Jenkinson* (1855) 25 LJQB 11). That is not totally free from doubt, so an agreement should make it clear when notice may take effect. It will often be easiest to permit a notice to end the employment at any time. Sometimes specific dates or times of year are more convenient than others, eg school teachers' agreements ending at the end of a term.

Once notice has been served, whether by the employer or the employee, it cannot be withdrawn unilaterally by the party who served it. 'It will of course always be open to the other party to agree to his withdrawing the notice, but in the absence of agreement the notice must stand and the contract will be terminated on the effluxion of the period of notice' (*Harris & Russell Ltd* v *Slingsby* [1973] ICR 454, 455 per Sir Hugh Griffiths). The effect of a notice may nevertheless be suspended. This was the effect of an employee availing himself of the employer's internal appeal procedure against a dismissal on medical grounds. On the failure of the appeal, the date the employment ended was the original date of dismissal (*Crown Agents for Oversea Governments and Administrations* v *Lawal* [1979] ICR 103).

16.3.3 Minimum length

Statute prescribes minimum periods of notice for terminating employment contracts, after a qualifying period of one month's continuous employment, which is employment under an agreement for at least sixteen hours' work a week disregarding any week during which the employee is on strike (Employment Act 1978, s 49 (1)). To prevent evasion, any contract for a term certain of one month or less is, for the purposes of ascertaining whether the minimum notice provisions apply, treated as if it were granted for an indefinite period once the employee has been continuously employed for twelve weeks (s 49(4)). This applies where a series of short agreements are entered into.

The minimum period of notice which the employer has to give the employee increases with the length of the employee's continuous employment. The periods of notice are (s 49(1)):

Continuous employment	*Minimum notice*
At one month and less than two years	One week
At least two years and less than twelve years	One week for each year of continuous employment
At least twelve years	Twelve weeks

The minimum notice which the employee must give the employer is one week (s 49(2)).

A service agreement which provides for less notice than the statutory minimum is effectively varied, so that the minimum applies. Either party is at liberty to waive his right to notice, to accept a payment in lieu and to treat the agreement as terminable summarily if the other party's conduct justifies it (s 49(3), (5)). Further, the service agreement can expressly provide for the employment to be determined by giving notice or the payment of salary in lieu of notice (*Rex Stewart Jefferies Parker Ginsberg Ltd* v *Parker* [1988] IRLR 483). In that case it was held that such a clause offered two alternative methods of lawful termination.

16.3.4 Length by contract

An express term of a service agreement may prescribe the length of notice required to end it. A different period may be prescribed for the employer and the employee. An express contract term overrides any provision which would otherwise be implied into the agreement. A contractual term is subject to the statutory minimum, but only as and when it applies.

For example, say an agreement requires either party to give to the other one month's notice to bring it to an end. Until the employee has worked for four weeks, there is no statutory minimum but the contract term applies. At the end of the first four weeks' continuous employment, the employee is bound by the Act to give at least one week's notice, a minimum which does not increase. The statutory minimum which the employer must give the employee does not exceed the month that the contract requires until the employee has been continuously employed for five years.

Only then will the Act take effect to vary the contract, and only in respect of notices which the employer gives.

In the absence of any express provision in the agreement, or a custom of the trade, the common law implies a term that reasonable notice will be given. The former general custom which assumed a yearly hiring no longer applies (*Richardson* v *Koefod* [1969] 1 WLR 1812). In certain very limited circumstances the courts have accepted that the parties intended the employment to be for life. *Eric McClelland* v *Northern Ireland General Hospital Services Board* [1957] 2 All ER 129.). Factors in fixing what notice is reasonable include: the seniority and responsibility of an employee's position; the difficulty he would encounter in finding another suitable post (*SW Strange Ltd* v *Mann* [1965] 1 WLR 629, 642); his length of service; the difficulty the employer will face in replacing him; his importance in the employer's business.

Examples of periods which have been held to be required for reasonable notice are:

(i) *one year* for the chief officer of a ship (*Savage* v *British India Steam Navigation Co Ltd* (1930) 46 TLR 294), a newspaper editor (*Grundy* v *Sun Printing and Publishing Association* (1916) 33 TLR 77);

(ii) *six months* for a photographer and journalist (*Bauman* v *Hulton Press Ltd* [1952] 2 All ER 1121);

(iii) *three months* for a bookmaker's credit manager (*SW Strange Ltd* v *Mann* [1965] 1 WLR 629), a salesman (*Fisher* v *WB Dick & Co Ltd* [1938] 4 All ER 467), a director of a small garage company (*James* v *Thomas Kent & Co Ltd* [1951] 1 KB 551), a port engineer (*Cowey* v *Liberian Operations Ltd* [1966] 2 Lloyd's Rep 45 (*Mayor's and City of London ct*), a superior clerk (*Mulholland* v *Bexwell Estates Co Ltd* (1950) 66 TLR (pt 2) 764), and a private tutor (*Wilson* v *Ucelli* (1929) 45 TLR 395).

16.3.5 Drafting

The length of notice which either party must give to bring a service agreement to an end is one of the matters which must be expressly stated if the agreement is to take the place of the statutory statement of particulars of terms of employment (Employment Protection (Consolidation) Act 1978, ss 1(3)(*e*), 5), or to avoid the court implying a period of notice. Apparently, the requirement would be satisfied, in a case where the parties had not expressly agreed upon a precise notice period, by a statement that 'reasonable notice' was required to end the employment (*Cuthbertson* v *AML Distributors* [1975] IRLR 228 (*IT*)). A statement in that form would certainly be less informative than the legislation intends.

Since the introduction of the statutory minimum periods of notice, there has been a tendency to treat them as a norm to be adopted. But, as will have been seen, to do so will often reduce the period of notice to which a senior employee would otherwise be entitled at common law. That reduction in the employee's benefits is often unintended.

Should the intention be to give no more than the statutory entitlement, it must be borne in mind that the qualification periods are laid down as periods of 'continuous employment'. Such a period can be extended if a week during which the employee is on strike has to be disregarded (Sched 13, para 15). Accordingly, if the agreement lays down the dates on which the period of notice required is to increase, or states qualification periods in years without referring to the Act, the result may be to give the employee more than his statutory entitlement. When relying on the statutory minimum periods of notice, provision should be made for the period before they apply. It may also be appropriate where the employee is engaged on probation that different periods of notice will apply during and after the initial probationary period.

16.3.6 Precedents

Minimum notice

This agreement may be brought to an end at any time by notice as follows:

(i) If served by the Executive on the Company, by one week's notice

(ii) If served by the Company on the Executive, by notice of the appropriate period according to the length of his period of continuous employment (as defined by the Employment Act 1982) as follows:

Length of continuous employment	*Period of notice*
Less than two years	One week
At least two years but less than twelve years	One week for every completed year of continuous employment

At least twelve years	Twelve weeks

Mutual rights to formal notice

Either party shall be entitled to end this agreement by giving at least two months' written notice to the other to take effect at any time PROVIDED THAT:

(*a*) The first three months employment shall be a probationary period and during the first three months after the commencement of the Executive's employment by the Company the period of notice shall be one month and

(*b*) After the Executive shall have been continuously employed (as defined by the Employment Protection (Consolidation) Act 1978) by the Company for at least nine years the period of notice to be given by the Company to the Executive shall be at least one week for every completed year of his continuous employment taking no more than twelve years into account for this purpose.

Service

ANY notice given under the provisions of this agreement shall be duly served on the Executive if handed to him personally or left at or sent by ordinary letter post to his last known address in England/Wales or on the Company if handed personally to [the personnel manager] or left at or sent by ordinary letter post to the Company's registered office. And it shall be assumed that any notice sent by post shall be delivered on the day on which the letter would have been delivered in the ordinary course of post.

16.4 Agreement

The parties to a service agreement can reach a later agreement to cancel it. The later agreement may be a new service agreement superseding the earlier arrangements (*R* v *Inhabitants of Bottesford* (1825) 4 B & C 84). A later agreement which is not inconsistent with the earlier one does not cancel it (*R* v *Inhabitants of Buckingham* (1834) 5 B & Ad 953).

Termination by consent contrasts with termination by the employer. It generally deprives the employee of any statutory rights. 'If the parties agree consensually . . . to rescind it and substitute a new contract of employment, the plain fact is that the contract is not terminated by the employers, but by consent' (*Marriott* v *Oxford and District Co-operative Society Ltd (No 2)* [1970] 1 QB 186, 191–2 per Lord Denning MR). However, it is extremely difficult to draft a clause to provide that the employment will terminate on the occurrence of a particular event, because of the value of the statutory rights, the courts are now reluctant to construe circumstances as terminating employment by agreement (*Igbo* v *Johnson Matthey Chemicals Ltd* [1986] IRLR 215). To ensure that such a provision is effective it is necessary to be able to prove that the employee understood the nature of the term, and that the clause is not rendered void under s 140(1)(a) of the Employment Protection (Consolidation) Act 1978.

This is particularly true where the employee is under notice and leaves before it expires (*Lees* v *Arthur Greaves (Lees) Ltd* [1974] ICR 501). '. . . it would be a very rare case, indeed, in which it could properly be found that the employer and the employee had got together, notwithstanding that there was a current notice of termination of employment, agreed mutually to terminate the contract, particularly when one realises the financial consequences to the employee involved in such an agreement' (*McAlwane* v *Boughton Estates Ltd* [1973] ICR 470, 473 per Sir John Donaldson P). A person with authority to dismiss an employee on behalf of the employer also has authority to abridge a notice already given to the employee. The early departure of the employee will normally still be the result of the original dismissal (*Glacier Metal Co Ltd* v *Dyer* [1974] 3 All ER 21).

16.5 Rule of law

16.5.1 Frustration

The doctrine of frustration will apply to a contract of employment. As a contract of employment imposes an obligation of personal service on the employee, a contract may be terminated by frustration if outside events prevents the employee from performing his obligations. The main statement of principle by the Courts in applying the doctrine to contracts of employment is that in the case of *Pall Wilson and Co* v *Partenreederei* (1983) AC 854. In that case it was stated that,

> . . . there are two essential factors which must be present in order to frustrate a contract. The first essential factor is that there must be some outside or extraneous change of situation, not foreseen or provided for by the parties at the time of contracting, which either makes it impossible for the contract to be performed at all, or at least renders its performance something radically different from what the parties contemplated when

they entered into it. The second essential factor is that the outside event or extraneous change of situation concerned, and the consequences of either in relation to the performance of the contract, must have occurred without either the fault or the default of either party to the contract.

The two most common situations in which the doctrine is applied, arise due to the employee's illness, or imprisonment.

(i) Illness. The commonest cause is illness as in the case of an opera singer unable to appear at the opening of a new opera (*Poussard* v *Spiers and Pond* (1876) 1 QBD 410). It is often difficult to judge precisely what moment in time the contract has been frustrated, but helpful guidance was given by Sir John Donaldson in the case of *Marshall* v *Harland and Wolff Ltd* [1972] IRLR 90 in which he said:

> In the context of incapacity due to sickness, the question of whether or not a relationship has come to an end by frustration sounds more difficult than it is. The Tribunal must ask itself: was the employee's incapacity, looked at before the purported dismissal, of such a nature, or did it appear likely to continue for such period that further performance of its obligations in the future would either be impossible or would be a thing radically different from that undertaken by him and agreed to be accepted by the employer under the agreed terms of his employment? In considering the answer to this question the Tribunal should take account of:
> (a) the terms of the contract, including the provisions as to sickness pay . . .
> (b) how long the employment was likely to last in the absence of sickness . . .
> (c) the nature of the employment . . .
> (d) the nature of the illness or injury and how long it has already continued and the prospects of recovery . . .
> (e) the period of past employment . . .
>
> These factors are inter-related and cumulative, but not necessarily exhaustive of those which have to be taken into account. The question is and remains: was the employees incapacity, looked at before the purported dismissal, of such a nature, or did it appear likely to continue for such a period, that further performance of his obligations in the future would either be impossible or would be a thing radically different from that undertaken by him and accepted by the employer under the agreed terms of his employment? Any other factors which bear on this issue must also be considered.

Further guidance was given by Phillips J in the case of *In Egg Stores (Stamford Hill Ltd)* v *Leibovici* [1976] IRLR 376.

(ii) Imprisonment. It was suggested that following the principles in *Pall Wilson and Co* v *Partenreederei* Hannah Blumenthal [1983] 1 AC 854, that imprisonment could not be a frustrating

event, as it was caused by the default of one of the parties but in the case of *F C Shephard and Co Ltd* v *Jerrom* [1986] IRLR 358, it was held that the party against who frustration is asserted cannot rely on his own misconduct by way of answer. It is suggested that to permit an employee to improve his position by asserting that an event which would otherwise bring about mutual discharge by frustration does not do so because it was caused by his own fault would be an affront to common sense and infringment of what Diplock L J in *Hong Kong Fur Shipping Company* v *Kishen Kaisha* (1962) 2 QB 26, described as 'the fundamental legal and moral rule that a man should not be allowed to take advantage of his own wrong.'

A service agreement may be frustrated by the threat of an interruption to the performance of the contract which does not actually come about, eg a sentence of imprisonment on the employee which is mitigated on appeal to a non-custodial sentence. The position has to be judged when the original potentially frustrating event occurs.

> . . . the question of frustration has to be decided by finding the answers to the following questions: (1) Looking at the matter from a practical commercial point of view, when was it necessary for the employers to decide as to the employee's future and as to whether a replacement driver would have been engaged? (2) At the time when the decision had to be taken, what would a reasonable employer have considered be the likely length of the employee's absence over the next few months? (3) If in the light of his likely absence it appeared necessary to engage a replacement, was it reasonable to engage a permanent replacement rather than a temporary one? (*Chakki* v *United Yeast Co Ltd* [1982] ICR 140, 145 per Neill J).

Similarly, a contract can be frustrated by the likelihood of the employee becoming unfit to continue to perform his duties, although he is fit to do so for the time being (*Condor* v *Barron Knights Ltd* [1966] 1 WLR 87).

(iii) Death. The death of the employee necessarily ends the contract of employment, and the death of the employer may have the same effect in the absence of contract terms to the contrary (*Farrow* v *Wilson* (1968) LR 4 CP 744) unless the Transfer of Undertakings (Protection of Employment) Regulations 1981 apply.

(iv) Legal Impossibility. An employment contract will be frustrated if it becomes illegal to continue to perform it, as one of the party becomes an enemy alien on the outbreak of war. The

question whether the suspension from registration for 12 months for part-time consultant psychiatrists frustrated the contract for his employment was left open (*Tarnesby* v *Kensington, Chelsea and Westminster Area Health Authority (Teaching)* [1980] ICR 475). Legal intervention may also render further performance impossible (eg *Reilly* v *R* [1934] AC 176: the abolition of the Federal Appeal Board frustrated the employment contract of a member of it).

(v) The right to pay. In most cases, the employee's pay will accrue for the period until frustration. However, if the contract provided only for payment on completion of the job, and the job was never finished, the employee should have a claim under the Law Reform (Frustrated Contracts) Act 1953, s 1(3). Having conferred a valuable benefit on the employer, he is entitled to such benefit as the Court considers just having regard to the value of the benefit. In cases of illness, the contract will normally provide for this to occur in the event of the illness of the employee.

16.5.2 Employer's insolvency

Bankruptcy of the employer does not ipso facto terminate employment contracts to which he is a party (*Thomas* v *Williams* (1834) 1 Ad & E 685). Apprenticeship contracts and articles of clerkship become terminable by notice to the trustee in bankruptcy (Bankruptcy Act 1914, s 34(1)).

In the case of a company employer, any of the following ends employment contracts to which it is a party:

(i) the court making a compulsory winding-up order (*Re Oriental Bank Corporation, MacDowall's Case* (1886) 32 Ch D 366);

(ii) the court appointing a receiver and manager of the company's property (*Reid* v *Explosives Co* (1887) 19 QBD 264);

(iii) the passing of a resolution to wind up voluntarily, but only if de facto it involves the ending of the activities in which the employee is engaged (*Midland Counties District Bank Ltd* v *Attwood* [1905] 1 Ch 357);

(iv) the appointment of a receiver and manager who acts on behalf of the debenture holder (*Hopley-Dodd* v *Highfield Motors (Derby) Ltd* [1969] ITR 289 (*IT*)).

The appointment of a receiver and manager out of court does not normally of itself terminate an employee's contract, if the appointee acts on the company's behalf (*Re Mack Trucks (Britain)*

Ltd [1967] 1 WLR 780). There are three exceptions. 'The first situation is where . . . the appointment is accompanied by a sale of the business; . . . The second situation is where it happens that, simultaneously or very soon after the appointment . . . a receiver and manager enters into a new agreement with a particular employee . . . The third situation . . . is where . . . the continuation of the employment of a particular employee is inconsistent with the role and functions of a receiver and manager' (*Griffiths* v *Secretary of State for Social Services* [1974] QB 468, 485–6 per Lawson J).

16.6 Breach

There is dispute as to the precise effect of a breach of contract. The proper view in principle appears to be that if one party breaks the terms of the agreement, and that breach is sufficiently fundamental, it entitles the innocent party to repudiate the contract (*London Transport Executive* v *Clarke* [1981] ICR 355). The innocent party has an option. He can decide to ignore the breach, in which case the contract continues in force. 'In accordance with the ordinary principles of contract law, the employee's options in that situation are, himself to treat the contract as at an end and crystallise his remedy then and there, or, to treat the contract as still subsisting and go on working under it' (*WPM Retail Ltd* v *Lang* [1978] ICR 787, 790 per Bristow J). Where the innocent party decides to accept the repudiation and to end the contract, it is treated as terminated by the party in breach. 'If the employer is guilty of conduct which is a significant breach gong to the root of the contract of employment, or which shows that the employer no longer intends to be bound by one or more of the essential terms of the contract, then the employee is entitled to treat himself as discharged from any further performance. If he does so, then he terminates the contract by reason of the employer's conduct' (*Western Excavating (ECC) Ltd* v *Sharp* [1978] QB 761, 769 per Lord Denning MR).

This theoretical position, that the wronged party has the choice of ending the contract or continuing it, is hard to reconcile with the circumstances of the majority of wrongful dismissals. The employee is discharged and has no practical choice of continuing in employment. Lord Denning MR advanced the view, in a dissenting judgment, that cases fall into two groups: those where a party's conduct is so grave as to operate to end the contract, and lesser misconduct which justifies the innocent party in ending it if he chooses (*London Transport Executive* v *Clarke*, supra, pp 363–4).

In one case, regarded at the time as exceptional, an employee obtained an injunction restraining the employer from treating the notice he had been given as having terminated the employment (*Hill* v *CA Parsons & Co Ltd* [1972] Ch 305). That ties in with the theory that a breach does not automatically end the contract. Certainly there is now authority for suggesting that an employee may have a choice between damages or a declaration that the contract subsists where the employer is in breach of the procedure to be followed on dismissal (*McClelland* v *NI General Health Services Board* [1957] 1 WLR 594). In the case of *Dietman* v *London Borough of Brent* [1987] IRLR 259, the court held that a wrongful dismissal does not unilaterally determine the contract of employment. The contract remains in force until the repudiatory breach is accepted by the employee. However, the court will readily find acceptance and if the employee wishes to challenge the employer's action, it will be necessary for the employee to both make his position clear and seek interlocutory relief immediately. Generally the employee must also show that there has been no breakdown in the trust and confidence between the employer and the employee to succeed. The court will not normally give a remedy which requires such an agreement to continue. Even the statutory remedy of reinstatement in the case of unfair dismissal is effectively only a power to recommend reinstatement (Employment Protection (Consolidation) Act 1978, ss 69, 71).

The most obvious breaches of service agreements which amount to a repudiation of the contract are a refusal by the employee to work, and the employer purporting to end the contract by less notice than he was obliged to give. In other cases it may be less obvious whether the law would regard the breach as sufficiently grave as to amount to a repudiation. Examples of such breaches are:

(i) a reduction in the employee's wages (*Marriott* v *Oxford & District Co-operative Society Ltd* [1970] 1 QB 186);

(ii) the employee borrowing money from the till, which although not dishonest was an act he knew would be against the employer's wishes (*Sinclair* v *Neighbour* [1967] 2 QB 279);

(iii) the employee's disobedience to a lawful and reasonable order (*Pepper* v *Webb* [1969] 1 WLR 514).

16.7 Directors

16.7.1 Effect of termination of employment

Employees who are also directors will not automatically cease to be so on termination of the employment. In such cases it is necessary to comply with either any procedures set out in the company's articles or in accordance with the provisions of s 303 of the Companies Act 1985. To avoid the requirements of these provisions it is common to include in the service agreement an express provision requiring the employee to resign any directorships he holds solely by virtue of his employment with the employer.

16.7.2 Precedent

Resignation as a director.

The Executive shall on the termination of the employment under this agreement at the request of the Company resign without claim for compensation from all offices held by him in the Company and any other offices held by him by virtue of his employment should he fail to resign when requested to do so the company is hereby irrevocably authorised to appoint some person in his name and on his behalf to sign and execute all documents or things necessary or requisite to give effect thereto.

Chapter 17

Financial Consequences

17.1 Introduction

As discussed in Chapter 6, the traditional approach to providing an employee with security on termination of employment, has been to prepare service agreements incorporating either a long period of notice, or to specify that the employment is for a fixed period. In the event that the employment is terminated by the employer, in breach of the terms of the service agreement then the employee may have a substantial financial claim against the employer. There may be compensation for unfair dismissal, whether or not the employer has abided by the contract terms. When the circumstances constitute redundancy within the statutory definition, the employee may also be able to claim a statutory redundancy payment.

This traditional approach to the granting of security to the employee, was adopted for a number of reasons, but the principal reason was that it provided the employee with the most tax advantageous way of receiving the compensation. Any express contractual arrangement for payments to be made to the employee in the event of termination, did not secure the tax benefits provided by s 148 and s 184 of the Income and Corporation Taxes Act 1988 as amended by the Finance Act 1988 s 74, discussed below and accordingly alternative ways of providing security were not pursued. However there are now a number of reasons why the traditional approach may not always be the appropriate method, and alternative methods of providing security to the employee can be advantageous.

Although there continue to be tax advantages in receiving compensation as a compensation payment under these provisions, as current tax rates are low the tax factor is less relevant, and an employee may be prepared to accept a tax penalty of £12,000 (ie 40 per cent tax on the tax free amount of £30,000 at current rates) in exchange for greater security that he will receive a fixed amount on termination.

Employees have also become increasingly aware that employers do not consider that providing an employee with a long period of notice or a fixed term contract gives the employee an absolute right to compensation in line with the terms of the service agreement. The employee is always under a duty to mitigate his loss on the service agreement being terminated, and generally employees are being put under increased pressure to actively mitigate their losses. This is particularly so in the case of directors of public companies, where payments of compensation are much more likely to be subject to scrutiny by the shareholders. In such cases the company must be able to show it has acted reasonably and has determined whether the employee has taken proper steps to minimise the damage that has been caused by any breach of the employment contract. As employees will often not join a company leaving secure current employment unless they are satisfied that they will secure adequate compensation for the loss of the new employment, different approaches are being adopted to ensure that they are given comfort.

Claims for compensation on termination of employment is a subject which is outside the scope of this book, but it is important to give some basic information as the nature of such claims do have an influence in the way in which service agreements are drafted. Certainly for the employee the financial security he believes the agreement affords him is the prime reason for seeking a formal service agreement.

17.2 Compensation on termination

17.2.1 Contract

In normal cases where an employee's service agreement is terminated without giving the employee the proper notice required by the agreement or by breach on the part of an employer amounting to a repudiation, or dismissal during a fixed term contract, then the employee can claim damages for the losses arising from the employer's breach. The damages will be assessed on the basis that the employee is to be compensated for the financial loss directly flowing from the breach, on the footing that the employer, if the contract had continued, would have fulfilled only his minimum obligations consistent with his own interest. Damages will not be enhanced by the manner of the employee's or by the consideration that the fact of dismissal makes it more difficult for the employee to obtain future employment (*Addis* v *Gramophone Co Ltd* [1909] AC 488, affirmed by *Bliss* v *N E Thames RHA* [1985] IRLR 308. In assessing damages the following factors will be taken into account:

(i) The gross loss of prospective earnings over the unexpired period (that is, the period from the date of dismissal or breach to the earliest date on which the contract could lawfully have been terminated by the employer) will be the principal loss suffered by the employee. So prospective increments or bonuses expressly provided for in the contract (eg a cost of living increment) will be taken into account. On the other hand, deductions should be made for expenses to be incurred by the employee for the purpose of earning his remuneration. Where future remuneration depends on variable factors (eg commission by reference to profits), a projection will be made as to probable earnings.

(ii) The loss of fringe benefits may be significant. The employee may enjoy a number of benefits in kind eg the use of a car private medical care, which may be of considerable value to him (even though by concession or otherwise they may not be taxed as emoluments or are only taxed at a fraction of the true value for the employee). These are only taken into account if there is a contractual entitlement but not otherwise.

(iii) The loss of prospective retirement benefits and life assurance benefits is assessed on the basis of the cost of purchasing an annuity to make up the rights already accrued (and available) to the employee to the level of those which would have accrued at the end of the unexpired term taking into account the effects of any contractually stipulated increase (or decrease) in pensionable emoluments and deducting the present value of the employee's contributions (if any) which would have been payable during the unexpired term.

Having calculated a figure for the losses the employee has to suffer by virtue of the wrongful termination, the amount is then reduced to take account of tax and that the employee will receive the money earlier than he would have otherwise been entitled to receive it. The ruling in *British Transport Commission* v *Gouerley* [1956] 2WLR 41, required that the amount of tax which the employee would not incur as a result of loss of earnings and other tax benefits, should be deducted from the amount of the loss arrived at. This is based on the premise that a damages award is compensatory and not punitive so that the award is reduced by the employee's estimated tax liability on the assumption that the award is in fact income under schedule E.

The damages are ultimately taxable in the hands of the employee—see Clause 17.4. below so all sums over £30,000 would be grossed up to provide a figure to be then paid to the employee which will result in the employee retaining the calculated figure after tax. (*Shove* v *Downs Surgical* [1984] 1AER 7).

Where a dismissed employee is a participant in a share option or share incentive scheme of any kind, his dismissal may occasion the loss of the potential benefit under the scheme in respect of his existing participation, and loss of expected opportunities of future participation. Loss of benefits from existing participation should normally be a subject of compensation unless this is precluded by the terms of the scheme; opportunities for future participation are in the most case dependant on the exercise of a discretion, and their loss is unlikely to give rise to a claim.

Having calculated the gross loss in respect of earnings and loss of retirement benefits etc, the court will then consider when and how far such losses have been or could have been reasonably mitigated by the employee obtaining alternative employment, and the time taken to obtain them. Although a dismissed employee cannot be expected to accept alternative employment which is not reasonably comparable in status with that from which he has been dismissed or, in the case of a specialist employee, which does not enable him to make use of his specialised knowledge. However, it will be necessary for the employee to show that positive steps have been taken by him to find alternative employment. The circumstances and manner of the dismissal may play an important part in how easy it has been for the employee to find that alternative employment.

17.2.2 Statute

In the event that the employee establishes that his dismissal is unfair, a tribunal can award compensation under a number of heads. First, a basic award, which is calculated with reference to the employee's age and length of service at the effective date of termination. The maximum award is £5,520.00. Second, the tribunal has power to award a special award where dismissals are regarded as unfair by reason of s 58 or 9(a) of the Employment Protection (Consolidation) Act 1978. Third, the tribunal can award a compensatory award which the tribunal considers just and equitable to compensate the employee for all losses arising from the termination. The maximum compensatory award is £8,925.

Given the limited compensation available even if a statutory claim is successful, the contractual claim, ie wrongful dismissal, may often be of greater importance. However such claims have a number of features which make them important, and they provide a quick and effective remedy, there are few costs penalties imposed against the employee if he does not succeed in his claim, (apart from having to bear his own legal costs) and they have significant nuisance value.

What is also important in considering such claims, is whether any *ex gratia* payment made by an employer on termination will be taken into account in reducing the potential compensation that an employee could hope to receive from the tribunal. Section 75(3) of the Employment Protection (Consolidation) Act 1978 provides that 'a limit imposed by this section applies to the amount which the Industrial Tribunal would, apart from this section, otherwise award in respect of subject matter of the complaint after taking into account any payment by the Respondent to the complainant in respect of the matter and any reduction in the amount of the award required by any enactment or order of law'. However this is not always the case, as the tribunal should first assess the total loss suffered by the employee, then deduct the *ex gratia* payment from the maximum loss figure, and then apply the statutory maximum. Accordingly, although the *ex gratia* payment is taken into account in working out the overall loss, it may not have an impact on the final award, if the loss is in excess of the statutory maximum.

17.3 Liquidated Damages

17.3.1 Introduction

For the reasons set out in the Introduction to this section (17.1) the parties may be attracted by the idea of providing in a service agreement for the financial consequences which would follow any premature termination, commonly known as a 'golden parachute'.

The attraction of this, as in the case of any other contract providing for liquidated damages, is that it gives certainty and avoids much of the need for time consuming negotiations. It seems unlikely that a term that the employee should pay the employer if he left the job without giving proper notice would be very practical. Consideration will therefore be confined to a requirement under which the employer compensates the employee for premature termination of the agreement. The feasibility and desirability of this must be examined.

17.4 Validity

17.4.1 Contract

The law generally is that a contractual provision for liquidated damages is valid and enforceable if it is a genuine pre-estimate of the loss likely to be suffered by the wronged party. The alternative is that the amount would be a penalty, which is unenforceable. 'If the intention is to secure performance of the contract by the imposition of a fine or penalty, then the sum specified is a penalty; but if, on the other hand, the intention is to assess the damages for breach of the contract, it is liquidated damages' (*Law* v *Redditch Local Board* [1892] 1 QB 127, 132 per Lopes J). An enforceable contract term for liquidated damages can declare that the employee is not entitled to any other damages as a result of the early end to the agreement (*Dunlop Pneumatic Tyre Co Ltd* v *New Garage and Motor Co Ltd* [1915] AC 79).

If this type of clause is included in a service agreement of any length, and the agreement provides for the employee's salary to increase or it is expected that increases will be agreed, a fixed sum payable on breach of contract might not be regarded as a realistic pre-estimate of damage. The figure could, as an alternative, easily be made a multiple of the current annual salary.

17.4.2 Company law

Such a clause was considered by the Privy Council in the case of *Taupo Totara Timber Co* v *Rowe* [1977] 3 All ER 123. where the court took the view that the provision was quite proper.

17.4.3 Statutory rights

A contract provision of this type cannot exclude the statutory right to compensation for unfair dismissal. In a fixed term contract of one year or more, the employee's right can be excluded in the case of dismissal which merely consists of non-renewal of the term (Employment Protection (Consolidation) Act 1978, s 142(1)). However, we are here concerned with premature termination. In that case, the service agreement cannot exclude the right to compensation (s 140(1)).

Notwithstanding that the employee's right to compensation cannot be excluded, a term in a service agreement laying down what the employer must pay to end it may render the statutory right largely otiose. The compensatory award of compensation is intended to make good any loss which the employee suffers. In calculating that sum, the employee must bring into account anything he has received by reason of the termination of his employment, whether as wages or salary in lieu of notice, or as an ex gratia payment, or both (*UBAF Bank Ltd* v *Davis* [1978] IRLR 442). There seems no reason why this rule should not apply to payments received by the employee as of right under the contract, in the same way as it does to ex gratia payments.

If the employer pays the employee as much or more than the compensation to which he would otherwise be entitled, he has no claim to a compensatory award (*Wellman Alloys Ltd* v *Russell* [1973] ICR 616). Therefore, leaving aside the basic award, which will be small, the practical effect of a reasonably generous contractual right to liquidated damages can be to avoid a claim to compensation for unfair dismissal. However, this will not always be the case where the compensation awarded is greater than the permitted maximum award. Ex gratia payments are deducted from the total gross award, for example if the compensation award was found to be £20,000 and an ex gratia payment of £15,000 had been made, the Tribunal would still award a sum of £5,000. Further, if the employee insists on his right to reinstatement, the Tribunal would still be bound to hear the claim even though there may be no possible compensation award due to the ex gratia payment.

A contractual payment to be made in the event of an employee being made redundant does not reduce any statutory redundancy payment to which the employee is entitled, except where there is a collective agreement as to redundancy payments which the Secretary of State has approved by order. In that case, there is no right to a statutory payment (Employment Protection (Consolidation) Act 1978, s 96), and the agreement is valid (s 140(2)(*f*)). However, although the employer cannot contract out of the statutory obligation, he can presumably, so to speak, contract into it.

That is to say, no service agreement can say that in consideration of a certain payment the employee surrenders his statutory rights; but what it can do is to impose an obligation to pay a sum on account of the statutory payment. If the statutory entitlement is greater than the contractual one, the difference must still be paid. Otherwise, the statutory duty has been satisfied.

A payment made under a service agreement because the employee has been made redundant is also relevant if the employee makes a claim for compensation for unfair dismissal. An employer who pays an employee on the ground that he was dismissed by reason of redundancy can, where the sum paid exceeds the amount of any statutory redundancy payment, set any excess off against the compensatory award (s 74(7)). In this type of case, the agreement should make clear that the payment is due as a result of redundancy.

17.5 Taxation

17.5.1 General charge

A distinction must be made for tax purposes between emoluments payable to an employee by reason of his employment, and payments as a result of the termination of his employment. Both sums are liable to income tax under Sched E, but the latter are subject to valuable reliefs. When only the former was liable to tax, a payment which the employer contracted to make when a service agreement came to an end was held to be taxable as a perquisite of his office (*Dale* v *De Soissons* [1950] 2 All ER 460). This followed a decision where tax was charged on a payment due to a director on resignation, under the company's articles of association (*Dewhurst* v *Hunter* (1932) 146 LT 510).

It may be that these decisions were influenced by the fact that a payment for loss of office, not contracted for, then wholly escaped tax (as in *Henley* v *Murray* [1950] 1 All ER 908). Also, in *Dewhurst* v *Hunter*, the article made a payment due to all directors who had served for five years, unless the reason for their going was one of a small number, eg bankruptcy or incompetence. However, it is important to ensure that payments are not taxed as emoluments. It is therefore suggested that including an obligation to pay compensation in a service agreement is not necessarily a safe course of action to follow. Protection for the employee should be secured by careful drafting of the notice provision in the contract, so giving the employee the possibility of the tax advantages of the Income and Corporation Taxes Act 1988 s 148 and s 188.

17.5.2 Reliefs

Schedule E income tax extends to 'any payment . . . which is made, whether in pursuance of a legal obligation or not, either directly or indirectly in consideration or in consequence of, or otherwise in connection with, the termination of . . . employment' (Income and Corporation Taxes Act 1988, s 148(2)). The rules governing such exceptions only apply where the sums paid are not otherwise chargeable to tax under Schedule E, and charge to tax only payments exceeding £30,000 which is made directly or indirectly in connection with the termination of an office or employment or payments on death, injury or disability, certain pension fund benefits and some payments for those employed abroad. Payments in excess of £30,000 are chargeable to tax at the employees normal rate of income tax.

17.5.3 Foreign employment

There is an exception from tax on terminal payments for loss of employment to those employed abroad, provided they can bring themselves within certain conditions, these are dealt with in more detail in Chapter 18.

17.6 Precedent

Liquidated damages

In the event that the Company terminates the Executive's employment before the expiry of the [four] years for which he has been engaged, otherwise than in circumstances in which the Executive's conduct justifies his summary dismissal, the Company shall compensate the Executive by paying to him as liquidated damages in full settlement of any claims which he has against the Company by reason of the termination of this agreement a sum equal to eighteen months' salary at the rate to which the Executive shall have been entitled immediately prior to that termination.

PART VI

Overseas Employment

Chapter 18

Special Considerations

18.1 Statutory rights

The statutory employment protection rights conferred on employees are generally not available to those who work outside Great Britain, although the form of the restriction varies.

(1) *Written particulars of terms of employment and minimum periods of notice.* These rules do not apply while the employee is engaged in work wholly or mainly outside Great Britain, unless the employee ordinarily works in Great Britain and the work outside it is for the same employer (Employment Protection (Consolidation) Act 1978, s 141(1)).

(2) *Compensation for unfair dismissal, written statements of reasons for dismissal, itemised pay statements, guarantee payments, payments during suspension on medical grounds, time off, maternity rights, rights on employer's insolvency.* An employee who ordinarily works outside Great Britain under his contract does not enjoy these rights (s 141(2)). For this purpose, a person employed to work on board a ship registered at a port in Great Britain has a contract under which he works in Great Britain, unless either the employment is wholly outside Great Britain or he is not ordinarily resident in Great Britain (s 141(5)).

(3) *Redundancy payment.* An employee whose contract provides for him ordinarily to work in Great Britain is entitled to a redundancy payment even if he is outside Great Britain when the contract ends. Otherwise, an employee outside Great Britain on that date is not entitled to a payment. An employee who, under his contract, normally works outside Great Britain does not generally qualify for a redundancy payment. He is entitled to one if on the date the contract ends he is in Great Britain on the employer's instructions (s 144(3), (4)).

To determine whether an employee 'ordinarily works' outside Great Britain, the test to apply is where the employee is based. That is normally the country in which he ordinarily works for this purpose (*Wilson* v *Maynard Shipbuilding Consultants AB* [1978] QB 665). In deciding this, the following have been suggested as possible factors: where the employee's headquarters are; where his travels in his employment begin and end; where he makes his home; where and in what currency he is paid; whether he has to pay national insurance contributions in Great Britain.

A declaration in a service agreement as to the place in which the employee ordinarily works is unlikely to be conclusive. If the aim is to demonstrate that the employee will be working abroad, the following terms should help: financial assistance with fares to the overseas posting and on repatriation referring to travel before the appointment begins and after it ends; provision of accommodation on the spot referring to the establishment of the employee's home there; obligations for the employee to take instructions from and to report to locally based management.

The employer may well want to exclude the employee's statutory rights, and the employee may accept that as a result of overseas employment he should do so. It should be remembered, however, that to the extent that the intention is that any similar rights should apply as a matter of contract, they must be expressly stated in the service agreement.

Further, regardless of what law governs the contract of employment, the employee may gain statutory employment rights in the country in which he works.

18.2 Taxation

18.2.1 Salary

A major attraction of overseas employment for many employees is the escape from United Kingdom income tax. Complete exemption from Sched E tax is allowed to an employee whose duties are wholly or partly performed outside the United Kingdom, where the duties are performed during a 'qualifying period' of at least 365 days falling at least partly into the year of assessment (Taxes Act 1988 Sched 12, para 3). The key rests in ensuring that there is a long enough qualifying period.

A qualifying period is a continuous period consisting of days of absence from the United Kingdom, with or without days in the

United Kingdom sandwiched between two periods of absence, as long as there was a previous qualifying period. To qualify, the days in the United Kingdom must neither exceed 62, nor one sixth of the total number of days in the whole qualifying period. This means that the timing of any periods in the United Kingdom is as important as the length of them.

Examples

Out of UK	200 days	Qualifying period of 330 days, of whch 30 in the UK (first three lines)
In UK	30 days	
Out of UK	100 days	
In UK	30 days	
Out of UK	10 days	
	370 days	Qualifying period of 370 days. Both 30 day periods can count, because the first was in a qualifying period and the second preceded by one.

Out of UK	60 days	*Not* a qualifying period. 130 days of which 30 (of over 23 per cent) in UK. (first three lines)
In UK	30 days	
Out of UK	40 days	
In UK	30 days	
Out of UK	210 days	
	370 days	Qualifying period of 280 days. The absence of 40 days is a qualifying period, but the earlier 90 days cannot be added. The qualifying period is therefore less than the 365 days needed for tax exemption.

18.2.2 Termination

There is an exception from tax on terminal payment for loss of employment to those employed abroad, provided they can bring themselves within the conditions set out in s 188(3) of the Income and Corporation Taxes Act 1988. The conditions that have to be fulfilled are that at least three quarters of the whole period of service was spent by the employee in foreign service. If this condition is not fulfilled then, in a period exceeding 10 years, the whole of the last 10 years must have been spent in foreign service or, in a period exceeding 20 years, at least half of it, including any 10 of the last 20 years must have been spent in that way.

The other case in which relief was given is being phased out, the relief being withdrawn for payments where the relevant date falls after 13 March 1984, except where the payment was made before 1 August 1984 pursuant to an obligation incurred before 14 March 1984.

18.3 Employer

18.3.1 Overseas subsidiary

Although employees may often not appreciate the significance of the distinction, an employer may seek to have his overseas staff employed by an overseas subsidiary. This may be for reasons of organisation, taxation or to satisfy the government of the country in which the work is to be done. An employee who freely negotiates for employment with a subsidiary company accepts any inherent risks. But one who accepts an offer of an overseas posting from his current employer cannot be taken without more to have consented to a transfer of employer. 'No contract of service can be transferred from one employer to another without the servant's consent: and this consent is not to be raised by operation of law' (*Denham* v *Midland Employers Mutual Assurance Ltd* [1955] 2 QB 437, 443 per Denning LJ).

Among the disadvantages from the employee's point of view of what would otherwise be simply a secondment are: the possibility of the disposal, nationalisation or even disbanding of the subsidiary; and the lack of continuity of pension fund membership. The major practical difficulty is the lack of recourse the employee has against the subsidiary. If the employment comes to an end for any reason, it is likely that the employee will return to the United Kingdom. He may hope to be reengaged by the parent company, but that company may not make him such an offer or have no employment that the employee deems equivalent. The latter is more likely to be the case, as often employees with foreign subsidiaries are given more responsibility and secure better benefits than they would have done if they had continued their United Kingdom employment. The employee will not usually have the resources for making a claim against a company which is overseas, nor for conducting litigation there. For that reason, it is suggested that where the employer insists on an overseas company being the formal employer, the employee should require assurances that the parent company accepts an obligation to find suitable alternative employment or agrees to pay compensation to the employee if it is unable to preserve the employee's employment. Where the employment is not a continuation of current employment, but is fresh employment it may still be advisable for the employee to require the United Kingdom parent company to act as guarantor indemnifying him against loss as a result of any breach of contract, on the basis that he has a direct claim against the parent.

18.3.2 Drafting

If the parent company agrees to give a guarantee, it will have to join in the service agreement as a party. The agreement should be under seal, to avoid any possible argument that the parent company's guarantee is not supported by consideration.

18.3.3 Precedent

Guarantee

The Parent Company covenants with the Executive that the Company will at all times observe perform and comply with its obligations as employer under and by virtue of this agreement and agrees to indemnify the Executive against all loss damage costs and expenses suffered or arising as a result of any failure by the Company so to observe perform or comply with its obligations. To the intent that this covenant shall be performed and may be enforced in England.

18.4 Premature termination

The premature termination of an overseas employment contract needs consideration, both because there are extra reasons why it might happen and also because it poses special problems.

18.4.1 Repatriation

A prudent employee will wish to ensure that he will be repatriated, whatever the circumstances in which the agreement comes to an end. Although it may seem illogical that, if he so neglects his duties that he is dismissed, he can still claim expensive fares from an innocent employer, an employee who cannot guarantee to get home will feel vulnerable and may not give of his best. However, it may be appropriate in certain circumstances to reserve the right to recover part of the cost of repatriation from the employee to deter the employee from making rash decisions to return, particularly at the commencement of a contract period. Possibly the most efficient way of solving the problem is to provide for a terminal bonus which is only secured on completion of the full term of the overseas contract, so giving the employee an incentive to remain.

There is a technical difficulty in guaranteeing repatriation. Many events that may make it a necessity at short notice—revolution, nationalisation, serious illness—will normally act to frustrate the contract. Frustration not only operates independently of the will of the parties, but it has the effect of completely and immediately bringing the contract to an end. In other words, it is not possible to exclude from the frustration a single term of the contract, the one guaranteeing repatriation. While it may be unlikely that any responsible employer would not honour the arrangement, yet the reason for having an agreement is to ensure that the parties can enforce the rights it appears to give them.

Two possible ways to overcome this difficulty may be considered. First, it is possible to prevent frustration if events are foreseen and the agreement deals with their consequences. It could provide that notwithstanding events which would normally frustrate it, the obligation to pay the salary continues until the employer repatriates the employee. This is somewhat uncertain, because there may be unforeseen events necessarily not covered, and there may be the risk of importing the employee's statutory rights because he appears to be based in Great Britain. The alternative, where the parent company acts as guarantor, is to incorporate an agreement by that company to repatriate the employee. Although in the same document, it should be possible to make this independent of the principal agreements so that the frustration does not operate to end it.

18.4.2 Precedents

Payment until repatriation

This agreement shall continue in full force and effect notwithstanding the happening of any event which prevents the employee from carrying out his duties whether by reason of his illness or incapacity or the action of any Government or competent authority war riot civil commotion act of God or force majeure or any other event which might in other circumstances frustrate this agreement but in such case the Company shall be at liberty (after ensuring that the Executive [and his family] and his/their possessions (if practicable) is/are repatriated to the United Kingdom free of expense to him or offering to do so) to give to the Executive not less than [one month's] notice to terminate this agreement

Repatriation by parent company

In consideration of the Executive initially agreeing to work for the Company the Parent Company agrees with the Executive as a separate contract promptly to repatriate the Executive to the United Kingdom with [his family and] his/their possessions (if practicable) in the event of the agreement between the Company and the Executive being frustrated.

Re-employment and liquidated damages clause

On the termination of the agreement, other than on grounds that justify the Company terminating the employment summarily, the Parent Company will offer alternative employment to the Executive of an equivalent status and level of responsibility and on terms which are reasonably equivalent save that no account will be taken of the benefits the Executive secured solely by virtue of the overseas nature of the appointment. In the event that the Parent Company is unable to make a suitable offer, save where the Executive has already indicated that he does not wish to be considered for such a position, then the Parent Company will pay to the Executive a sum equivalent to six months base salary at the rate paid to the Executive immediately prior to the termination of the overseas appointment.

18.4.3 Taxation

Premature repatriation to the United Kingdom can have disastrous tax consequences for the employee. It can result in his being liable to United Kingdom income tax in a year when he would otherwise have been free of tax. Given time, it may be possible for the employee to arrange to leave his country of employment for a different destination to maintain the continuity of his period outside the United Kingdom. In some emergencies, this will not be possible.

An attractive solution for the employee is for the employer to guarantee that he receives the same net sum that he would have received without United Kingdom tax, if he unexpectedly becomes subject to it. This could prove so expensive for the employer that it cannot be recommended. Not only would he become liable to pay to the employee the tax on the original income, but also tax on that sum, and so on.

Chapter 19

Contents of Agreement

19.1 General

Assuming that an employee working overseas enjoys none of the statutory rights, his service agreement must expressly spell out all the terms which might otherwise be implied, eg the notice needed to end it, maternity rights, etc. This section will not go through every clause which should be included, but will rather concentrate on those posing particular problems.

19.2 Proper law

19.2.1 Principle

Any agreement in an international context should specify what is to be the proper law of the contract, to avoid confusion. If it does so, by English law that is conclusive. Necessarily, the law of other jurisdictions may be different.

In the absence of a declaration as to the proper law, it is judged to be the law which the parties intended to apply. The connection of the contract and the parties with a particular country is indicative. But the facts that the employee is British, the contract written in English and the salary payable in sterling are not conclusive. In a case where the employer was a Dutch company using the same form of contract to employ Europeans of many nationalities for work wholly outside the United Kingdom, the proper law was held to be Dutch (*Sayers* v *International Drilling Co NV* [1971] 1 WLR 1176).

19.2.2 Precedent

Proper law

This agreement shall be interpreted and enforced in accordance with the laws of England.

19.3 Pay

19.3.1 Calculation and payment

Both the currency in which the salary is to be calculated and the currency and place of payment should be made clear. Exchange fluctuations can make the choice of currency for calculating the amount important. If the employee is working in a country with a notoriously weak currency, he will wish to choose a stronger one. An employer with a contract under which he is paid in local currency will obviously want the salaries which are part of his overheads to be expressed in the same currency.

An employee working abroad should consider the possible impact of local exchange control regulations which could prevent his taking out of the country any saving he has made from his salary when his job ends. Clearly, he will need part of his pay for current use locally, but an option to direct that part should be credited to him elsewhere could be useful.

19.3.2 Precedent

Salary

The Company shall pay the Executive a salary at the rate of [ ] pounds sterling a year to be paid by equal monthly payments on the last day of every month at the Company's local office in [ ] in local currency (the amount of each payment to be calculated at the rate of exchange ruling seven days before payment) Provided always that the Executive may from time to time opt by at least one month's notice to the Company and until further notice to have up to one half of his salary credited at his expense to any bank account in his name in any part of the world and in any currency (the exchange being effected by the Company's bank when remitting at the rate of exchange then ruling) so long as it is lawful for the Company to make such payments.

19.4 Time

19.4.1 Years

Expressions as to time in a service agreement of which the proper law is English will normally be interpreted according to the Gregorian calendar. It should not be overlooked that as well as other calendar systems celebrating new year on different dates, the years themselves vary in length. Jewish years vary between 353 and 385 days, and the Moslem hejira calendar has years of 354 or 355 days. Ambiguity is possible in the period for which the agreement is to last when it is expressed in years, and in salary entitlement when it is expressed as an annual sum. An express term should be included to avoid doubt.

19.5 Local customs and holidays

19.5.1 Principle

In many areas of the world it is of great importance to the employer that the employees obey and respect local laws, customs and religious practices. Misconduct by employees could lead to serious consequences both to employee and employer. It is therefore of importance to stress to employees the need to behave responsibly.

19.5.2 Precedent

Summary dismissal

The Company may dismiss the Executive summarily if he is guilty of conduct prejudicial to the Company's interests or gross incompetence or of any offence against the laws, customs or religious practices of the Government and people of the country in which he is employed.

19.5.3 Holidays

Feast days and public holidays vary from country to country. It is probably best for a service agreement to provide that local normal working hours and days shall apply, or where appropriate that the employee shall work when the local office is open or the site at which he is to be employed is working. A reference to locally observed holidays may not be clear. In North Africa, eg, Moslem shopkeepers observe Friday as the sabbath and close their shops. Jewish shopkeepers do the same on Saturdays, and

Christians on Sunday. There is therefore never a day when all are shut, and there are three days a week when not all are open.

PART VII

Precedents of Agreements and Checklists

A—Managing Director

This agreement for a managing director has been drawn generously from the employee's point of view. There are a lot of benefits: eg, a rolling contract term to give security, an index linked salary, a commission related to profit and sick pay which is not abated after a lengthy absence. There are express restrictions on the disclosure of confidential information and the non solicitation of employees and customers on termination. But there is no express restriction on competition when the employment ends. Minor regulations such as producing a driving licence for inspection, which might seem inappropriate for a managing director, have been omitted.

The type of agreement may well be adopted for a managing director who has already proved himself to be an able and efficient manager and whose loyalty it is considered vital to secure for the long-term good of the company. More reciprocity would be normal in an agreement negotiated completely at arm's length and where the employees value to the company had yet to be judged.

DATE:

PARTIES:

(1) [ ] [Limited] [plc](registered number) having its registered office at [ ] ('the Company').

(2) [ ] of [ ]('the Executive').

Operative Provisions

1 Definitions and interpretation

1.1 In this Agreement:

'The Board' means the Board of Directors of the Company and includes any committee of the Board duly convened by it.

'The Commencement Date' means the [ ] day of [ ] one thousand nine hundred and [ ].

'Group Company' means any company which for the time being is (*a*) a holding company (as defined in s 736 of the Companies Act 1985) of the Company, or (*b*) a subsidiary (as defined by s 736 of the Companies Act 1985) of the Company.

'Confidential Information' means information relating to the business, products and affairs of the Company (including without limitation marketing information) for the time being confidential to the Company or treated by the Company as such and trade secrets (including without limitation formula, processes, methods, inventions, technical data and know how) relating to the business of the Company.

'The Employment' means the Employment established by this Agreement.

'Termination Date' means the effective termination date of the Employment hereunder as defined by the Employment Protection (Consolidation) Act 1978.

1.2 The headings in this Agreement shall not affect its interpretation or construction.

1.3 Any reference in this Agreement to any statutory provision includes any statutory modification or re-enactment of it or the provision referred to.

2 Employment

The Company shall employ the Executive and the Executive agrees to act as Managing Director or in such other office or offices as the Company may from time to time reasonably direct.

3 Period

3.1 The Executive's employment under this agreement is for a fixed period of four years from the Commencement Date, subject to termination by the Executive during the fixed period by not less than six months prior written notice to the Company, such notice to expire on any anniversary of the Commencement Date provided that the period of the fixed term shall be extended automatically on each anniversary date of the Commencement Date for a further period of one year unless either party shall have given written notice to the other not less than six months before any anniversary date of its or his desire to terminate the further extension of the fixed term in which event the period of employment shall (subject to prior termination by the Executive as above mentioned) be the expiration of four years from the anniversary date immediately preceding the giving of such written notice.

3.2 The Executive's previous employment with (*specify employer*) counts as part of the Executive's period of continuous employment with the Company.

4 Duties

The Executive shall well and faithfully serve the Company and use his utmost endeavours to promote the interest thereof and shall perform such duties and exercise such powers in relation to the conduct and management of the affairs of the Company and its subsidiaries (if any) that may from time to time be assigned to or vested in him by or at the direction of the Board and shall give to the Board such information concerning the affairs of the Company and its subsidiaries (if any) as the Board shall require and at all times shall conform to the reasonable directions of the Board. Further the Executive shall at all times comply with all the rules and regulations of the Company for the time being in force.

5 Devotion to duties

The Executive shall devote the whole of his time attention and abilities during normal business hours and at such other times as the Company or his duties may reasonably require to the business and affairs of the Company and its subsidiaries (if any) unless prevented by ill health from so doing and shall not during the term of this Agreement either on his own account or as the employer of others or otherwise be engaged or concerned in any business or engagement other than that of the Company or any Group Company except with the prior consent in writing of the Company but the Executive may nevertheless be or become a minority holder of any securities which are quoted on a recognised investment exchange.

6 Place of work

6.1 The Executive will initially work at the offices of the Company at [*specify place*] but the Executive shall if required to do so work in such place or places as the Board may reasonably require for the proper performance of his duties hereunder and shall reside in such place in the United Kingdom as will enable him in the reasonable opinion of the Board to fulfil his duties efficiently.

6.2 The Executive shall not be required (except for travel on the business of the Company or any other Group Company) to go to reside in other parts of the world.

6.3 If the Executive is required to move his place of work in accordance with this clause and the Company requires the Executive to change his residence as a consequence the Company will reimburse the Executive such removal and other expenses incidental to such change of residence as the Company may consider fair and reasonable in the circumstances.

7 Hours of work

The Executive is required to work at such times and for such periods as the efficient and conscientious discharge of his duties hereunder requires. There are no fixed working hours for the Employment.

8 Remuneration

During the Employment the Executive shall receive as remuneration a salary at the rate of £[*specify amount*] per annum (or at such higher rate as the Company shall from time to time decide) to be paid by equal monthly instalments on the last day of each calendar month. The said salary shall unless otherwise agreed in writing by the Company be inclusive of all fees and other remuneration which the Executive may receive for his services from the Company or any Group Company.

9 Adjustment of salary

9.1 On every anniversary of the start of the Executive's employment his salary shall be reviewed and the annual amount of it payable immediately before that review date shall be increased as from that date by such percentage (if any) as the last figure of the Index of Retail Prices ('the Index') published by the Department of Employment prior to that date shall have increased over the figure of the Index current one year previously.

9.2 If during the year immediately prior to any review date the basis of computation of the Index shall have changed any official reconciliation between the two bases of computation published by the Department of Employment shall be binding on the Executive and the Company.

9.3 In the absence of such official reconciliation adjustments shall be applied to the latest Index figure to make it as nearly as practicable fairly comparable with the figure with which it is being compared.

9.4 If the Index is no longer published an alternative method of periodically adjusting the Executive's salary shall be adopted either by reference to other published statistics or otherwise.

9.5 If the parties are unable to agree on any question arising under clauses *9.3* or *9.4* the dispute shall be referred for a decision to an independent Fellow of the Institute of Chartered Accountants of England and Wales nominated and paid by the Company whose decision shall be final and binding on the parties.

9.6 In this clause any reference to the Department of Employment includes the body for the time being officially responsible for publication of the Index and any reference to the Index includes any Index expressly published to replace the Index of Retail Prices.

10 Bonus

10.1 In addition to his salary the Company shall pay to the Executive a bonus of [*specify percentage*] per cent of the Company's net profit throughout the Employment to be paid to him within one month of the adoption of the Company's accounts by its annual general meeting in each year.

10.2 For this purpose the Company's net profit means profit after paying or making adequate reserve in respect of:

(i) The Company's liability to corporation tax.

(ii) Depreciation of the Company's plant and equipment.

(iii) Directors' fees and salaries of working directors including the salary of the Executive.

(iv) The Company's future requirements of working capital or for such other purposes as the Board considers it desirable to create reserves and after deducting notional interest in accordance with clause 10(*c*) if applicable but before payment of the bonus payment under this clause or the payment of any bonus calculated as a percentage of the net profit of the Company now or at any time payable to any other director or employee of the Company.

10.3 If the Company has issued shares for cash or other valuable consideration after the date of this Agreement notional interest shall be charged in respect of the net proceeds of every such issue of shares at the rate of one and a half per cent above the base rate for the time being of [*specify Bank*] Bank plc (or if that rate shall no longer be published at such other rate as the Company's auditors shall determine).

10.4 The Company shall cause its auditors to certify on or before the date of each annual general meeting of the Company the amount of the net profit of the Company for the purpose of this clause for the period covered by the accounts presented to that meeting and such certificate shall be conclusive and binding on the parties.

10.5 For the purpose of calculating the Executive's bonus the net profit of the Company shall be deemed to accrue without fluctuation from day to day and shall be apportioned on a daily basis.

11 Car

11.1 The Company shall make available to the Executive for his use in performing his duties and shall replace from time to time as necessary a car of a type which it deems suitable and authorises the Executive to use it for his private purposes. The Company shall maintain service tax and comprehensively insure the car as appropriate and shall arrange for the supply of the Executive of petrol for his use in it. The Director shall ensure that he has at all times a current valid licence to drive private motor cars.

11.2 Immediately upon the termination of the Employment howsoever arising the Executive shall return the car and its keys to the Company at its principal place of business (or any other place nominated by the Company for its return).

12 Expenses

In addition to his salary hereunder the Executive shall be reimbursed the amount of all reasonable travelling, hotel, entertainment and other expenses properly and necessarily incurred and defrayed by him in the discharge of his duties hereunder. The Executive shall produce to the Company at its request all supporting vouchers and documents in respect of such expenses.

13 Pension and medical insurance expenses

During the Employment the Executive shall be entitled:

(*a*) to become and remain a member of the [*specify name of scheme*] Pension Scheme full details of which shall be provided to the Executive;

(*b*) at the Company's expense become a full member of the Company's health scheme (or such other plan or scheme as the Board may decide is preferable);

(*c*) participate in the Company's total disability/long term sickness benefit scheme subject always to the rules of the scheme.

14 Holidays

The Executive shall be entitled (in addition to public holidays) to [*specify number of days/weeks*] [weeks/months] holiday in each calendar year at such times as shall be convenient to the Company and such additional holidays as the Board shall approve.

15 Sickness or injury

15.1 The Executive is entitled to be paid during any period of absence from work due to sickness or injury, subject however to the provisions of clause 19 and also subject to the right of the Company to deduct from the remuneration of the Executive the amount of income benefit which he is entitled to claim in consequence of sickness or accident under any scheme for the time being in force of which by virtue of his employment by the Company he is a non-contributory member.

15.2 In the event that the Executive is incapable of performing his duties by reason of injury sustained wholly or partially as a result of actionable negligence nuisance or breach of any statutory duty on the part of any third party all payments made to the Executive by the Company by way of remuneration shall to the extent that compensation is recoverable from that third party constitute loans by the Company to the Executive (notwithstanding that as an interim measure income tax has been deducted from payments as if they were emoluments of employment) and shall be repaid when and to the extent that the Executive recovers compensation for loss of earnings from that third party by action or otherwise.

16 Confidentiality

The Executive shall not either during the Employment otherwise than in the proper course of his duties or thereafter without the consent in writing of the Board being first obtained divulge to any person firm or company and shall during the continuance of this Agreement use his best endeavours to prevent the publication or disclosure of any Confidential Information concerning the business accounts affairs or finances of the Company and its subsidiaries or any of their secrets dealings or transactions which have come or may come to his knowledge during the Employment or previously or otherwise.

17 Delivery of documents

Upon the termination of the Employment the Executive shall deliver up to the Company or its authorised representative all plans, statistics, documents, records, papers or property of whatsoever nature which may be in his possession or control and relate in any way to the business or affairs of the Company and its subsidiaries and no copies of documents shall be retained by him.

18 Summary termination

In any of the following cases the Company may terminate the Executive's Employment by written notice taking effect on the date of its service in which case the Executive shall not be entitled to any further payment from the Company accept such sums as shall then have accrued due:

(*a*) if the Executive shall be guilty of gross dereliction of duty or non-observance of any of the provisions of this Agreement;

(*b*) if the Executive shall be guilty of a criminal offence and sentenced (except in a case not involving dishonesty) to a term of imprisonment;

(*c*) if the Executive be adjudged bankrupt or prohibited by law from being a director.

19 Short notice

If the Executive shall at any time become or be unable properly to perform his duties hereunder by reason of ill health accident or otherwise for a period or periods aggregating at least 180 days in any period of 12 consecutive calendar months the Company may by not less than three months notice in writing determine this Agreement.

20 Resignation of offices

Upon the termination of the Employment howsoever arising the Executive shall at any time or from time to time thereafter upon the request of the Company resign without claim for compensation from all offices held by him in the Company and its subsidiaries and should he fail to do so the Company is hereby irrevocably authorised to appoint some person in his name and on his behalf to sign and execute all documents or things necessary or requisite to give effect thereto.

21 Prior rights

The termination of the Employment shall be without prejudice to any right that the Company may have in respect of any breach by the Executive of any of the provisions of this Agreement which may have occurred prior to such determination.

22 Notices

Any notice given under this Agreement shall be deemed to have been duly given if despatched by either party hereto by registered post addressed to the other party as in the case of the Company its registered office for the time being and in the case that the Executive his last known address and such notice shall be deemed to have been given on the day on which in the ordinary course of post it would be delivered.

23 Prior agreements

This Agreement is in substitution for all previous contracts of employment express or implied between the Company or any Group Company and the Executive which shall be deemed to have been terminated by mutual consent as from the date on which the Employment commenced.

24 Fixed term

Pursuant to s 142(1) and (2) of the Employment Protection (Consolidation) Act 1978 the Executive hereby agrees that no rights shall arise under ss 54 and 81 respectively of that Act in relation to this Agreement if the term of the Executive's Employment under it expires without being renewed.

25 Post termination obligations

25.1 The Executive shall not during the period of one year after termination of the Employment (howsoever occasioned) solicit or endeavour to entice away from, or discourage from being employed by, the Company any [*specify category of employee by job description or by salary range eg salesman—senior executive whose base salary exceeds £20,000*] who to his knowledge was an employee thereof at the date of such termination or whom to his knowledge has at that date agreed to be engaged as an employee of the Company.

25.2 The Executive shall not for a period of [*specify period*] [months/years] after termination of the Employment (howsoever occasioned) (without the previous consent in writing of the Board and whether on his own account or for any other person, firm or company) solicit or endeavour to entice away from the Company any person, firm or company (*a*) who or which in the preceding [*specify period*] [months/years] shall have been a customer of or in the habit of dealing with the Company and (*b*) with whom or which the Executive had contact during (the period of [*specify period*] months prior to the end of) the Employment.

25.3 The Executive acknowledges:

(i) that each of the foregoing sub-clauses of this clause constitutes an entirely separate and independent restriction on him; and

(ii) whilst at the date of this Agreement the duration, extent and application of each of the restrictions are considered by the parties no greater than is necessary for the protection of the Company's interests and reasonable in all the circumstances it is acknowledged that restrictions of such a nature may be invalid because of changing circumstances and accordingly if any of the restrictions shall be adjudged to be void or ineffective for whatever reason but would be adjudged to be valid and effective if part of the wording thereof were deleted or the periods thereof reduced they shall apply with such modifications as may be necessary to make them valid and effective.

26 Disciplinary and grievance procedure

There are no fixed rules for the resolution of grievance or disciplinary problems. In the event of the Executive being dissatisfied with any decision taken against him, or have any grievance relating to the Employment, he should apply in the first instance, to the Chairman who will either propose a solution or refer the matter to the Board of the Company for a final decision.

27 Reconstruction or amalgamation

If before the termination of this Agreement the Employment shall be determined by reason of the liquidation of the Company for the purpose of reconstruction or amalgamation and the Executive shall be offered employment with any concern or undertaking resulting from such reconstruction or amalgamation on terms and conditions no less favourable than the terms of this Agreement than the Executive shall have no claim against the Company in respect of the determination of the Employment.

B—Area Sales Manager

This is an agreement for an area sales manager, paid a basic salary plus a commission on sales.

In this agreement the area sales manager is paid commission on all sales generated by the sales force in the sales territory. The commission rate and the rate paid to the manager for personal rather than group sales will need to vary geared to the degree the manager retains an active sales role. The agreement also draws a distinction between types of customer. Often in large organisations purchasing decisions are taken centrally. Accordingly decisions taken concerning sales in the sales territory may be made by an employee of the customer without the direct involvement of the manager or his sales force. It is also important to retain the right to terminate or vary the terms of the commission arrangements.

The nature of this type of work makes a car essential. The agreement assumes that it is provided by the employer. The employee has an obligation to maintain a current driving licence.

An employer is particularly vulnerable to competition from a salesman who has left his employ. The appropriate restriction is on canvassing former customers. A separate ban on using or divulging trade secrets is needed in a case where the salesman has been made privy to those secrets in order to sell effectively.

DATE:

PARTIES:

(1) [ ] [Limited] [plc] a Company registered in England (under registered number) whose registered office is at [ ] ('the Company').

(2) [ ] of [ ] ('the Executive').

Operative provisions

1 Definition And interpretation

1.1 In this Agreement:

'the Commencement Date' means [*specify the date of the commencement of the employment*].

'Confidential Information' means information relating to the business products and affairs of the Company or any Group Company (including without limitation marketing information) for the time being confidential to the Company and any Group Company and trade secrets (including without limitation formula, processes, pricing policies, methods, inventions, technical data and know how) relating to the business of the Company and any Group Company.

'The Employment' means the employment established by this Agreement.

'Group Company' means any company which for the time being is:

(i) a holding company (as defined in s 736 of the Companies Act 1985) of the Company or

(ii) a subsidiary (as defined by s 736 of the Companies Act 1985) of the Company

'The Territory' means [*specify the sales territory the Executive will be responsible for*].

'The Termination Date' means the effective termination date of the employment hereunder as defined by the Employment Protection (Consolidation) Act 1978.

1.2 The headings in this Agreement shall not affect its interpretation or construction.

1.3 Any reference in this Agreement to any statutory provision includes any statutory modification or re-enactment of it or the provision referred to.

2 Employment

The Company shall employ the Executive and the Executive agrees to act as an Area Sales Manager.

3 Period

3.1 The Employment shall commence on the Commencement Date and shall (subject as hereinafter provided) continue until terminated by either party giving to the other not less than [*specify number*] [weeks/months] written notice.

3.2 The Executive's previous employment with [*specify employer*] counts as part of the Executive's period of continuous employment with the Company.

4 Duties

The Executive shall well and faithfully serve the Company and use his utmost endeavours to promote the interest thereof and shall be responsible for the initiation, organisation and implementation of the sales strategy of the Company and for the performance of other members of the sales staff responsible to him in the Territory. Further the Executive shall at all times comply with all the rules and regulations of the Company for the time being in force.

5 Devotion to duties

The Executive shall devote the whole of his time attention and abilities during normal business hours and at such other times as the Company or his duties may reasonably require to the business and affairs of the Company (if any) unless prevented by ill health from so doing and shall not during the term of this Agreement either on his own account or as the employer of others or otherwise be engaged or concerned in any business or engagement other than that of the Company or any Group Company except with the prior consent in writing of the Company but the Executive may nevertheless be or become a minority holder of any securities which are quoted on a recognised investment exchange.

6 Place of work

6.1 The Executive will work at the office of the Company at [*specify place*] but the Executive shall if required to do so work in such place or places as the Company may reasonably require for the proper and efficient performance of his duties hereunder.

6.2 The Executive will be required to travel on the business of the Company anywhere within the Territory or [*state area*].

7 Hours of work

The Executive is required to work at such times and for such periods as the efficient and conscientious discharge of his duties hereunder requires. There are no fixed working hours for the Employment.

8 Remuneration

During the Employment the Executive shall receive as remuneration a salary at the rate of £[*specify amount*] per annum (or at such higher rate as the Company shall from time to time decide) to be paid by equal monthly instalments on the last day of each calendar month.

9 Commission

9.1 In addition to his salary the Executive shall be entitled to receive a commission of [*specify percentage figure*] per cent of the retail price (excluding VAT) of all orders for goods obtained by him or by the sales force employed in the Territory provided that commission is only payable on goods actually sold and paid for by the customer.

9.2 Commission will not be payable as provided in sub-clause *9.1* above in respect of orders received for customers designated by the Company in its absolute discretion, national account customers. In respect of orders received and goods sold to national account customers the Executive shall receive a commission of [*specify percentage figure*] per cent of the price (excluding VAT) for orders placed by the national account customer in the Territory after deducting actual discounts given to the said customer.

9.3 On the termination of the Employment (howsoever occasioned) entitlement to commission shall cease other than with regard to orders received and completed prior to the date of the Termination.

9.4 The Company reserves the right in its absolute discretion to terminate or vary the commission arrangements set out in this clause on giving the Executive one month's written notice of its decision.

10 Car

10.1 The Company shall make available to the Executive for his use in performing his duties and to replace from time to time as necessary a car of a type which it deems suitable and authorises the Executive to use it for his private purposes. The Company shall maintain service tax and comprehensively insure the car as appropriate and shall arrange for the supply of the Executive's petrol for his use in it.

10.2 The Executive shall ensure that he has at all times a current valid licence to drive private motor cars and shall comply with any guidelines issued by the Company in respect of the use of Company cars.

10.3 The Executive shall immediately report to the Company any order of any court to endorse his driving licence or to disqualify him from holding a driving licence.

10.4 Immediately upon the termination of the Employment (howsoever arising) the Executive shall return the car and its keys to the Company at its principal place of business (or any other place nominated by the Company for its return).

11 Expenses

In addition to his salary hereunder the Executive shall be reimbursed the amount of all reasonable travelling hotel entertainment and other expenses properly and necessarily incurred and defrayed by him in the discharge of his duties hereunder. The Executive shall produce to the Company at its request all supporting vouchers and documents in respect of such expenses.

12 Pension and medical insurance expenses

During the Employment the Executive shall be entitled:

(i) to become and remain a member of the [*specify name of scheme*] Pension Scheme, full details of which shall be provided to the Executive; and

(ii) at the Company's expense become a full member of the Company's health scheme (or such other plan or scheme as the Board may decide as preferable).

13 Holidays

13.1 The Executive shall be entitled (in addition to public holidays) to [*specify number of days/weeks*] [weeks/months] holiday in every holiday year at such times as shall be convenient to the Company.

13.2 The holiday year is the calendar year from 1 January to 31 December and the Executive should take holiday during this period. The Executive will not be permitted to carry over unused holiday entitlement into a following holiday year except with the consent of the Company. Any holiday entitlement unutilised when permission has not been given for it to be carried forward will be forfeited.

13.3 For the holiday year during which the Executive's employment terminates the Executive is entitled to [*specify number of days*] working days holiday for each calendar month completed in the employment of the Company for that year.

14 Sickness or injury

14.1 The Executive is entitled to be paid his base salary during any period of absence from work due to sickness or injury, for a total of up to [*specify number of weeks*] in any one period of 12 months subject to the right of the Company to deduct from the remuneration of the Executive the amount of income benefit which he is entitled to claim in consequence of sickness or accident under any scheme for the time being in force of which by virtue of his employment by the Company he is a non-contributory member.

14.2 In the event that the Executive is incapable of performing his duties by reason of injury sustained wholly or partially as a result of action or negligence nuisance or breach of any statutory duty on the part of the any third party all payment made to the Executive by the Company by way of remuneration shall to the extent that compensation is recoverable from that third party constitute loans by the Company to the Executive (notwithstanding that as an interim measure income tax has been deducted from payments as if they were emoluments of employment) and shall be repaid when and to the extent that the Executive recovers compensation for loss of earnings from that third party by action or otherwise.

15 Confidentiality

The Executive shall not either during the Employment otherwise than in the proper course of his duties or thereafter without the consent in writing of the Company being first obtained divulge to any person firm or company and shall during the continuance of this Agreement use his best endeavours to prevent the publication or disclosure of any Confidential Information concerning the business accounts affairs or finances of the Company and the Group or any of their secret dealings or transactions which may have come or may come to his knowledge during the Employment or previously or otherwise.

16 Delivery of documents

Upon the termination of the Employment the Executive shall deliver up to the Company or its authorised representative all plans statistics documents records papers or property of whatsoever nature which may be in his possession or control and relate in any way to the business or affairs of the Company and its subsidiaries and no copies of documents shall be retained by him.

17 Summary termination

In any of the following cases the Company may terminate the Executive's Employment by written notice taking effect on the date of its service in which case the Executive shall not be entitled to any further payment from the Company except such sums as shall then have accrued due:

(*a*) If the Executive shall be guilty of gross dereliction of duty or non-observance of any of the provisions of this Agreement.

(*b*) The Executive shall be guilty of a criminal offence and sentence (except in a case not involving dishonesty) to a term of imprisonment.

(*c*) If the Executive shall lose his driving licence and be prohibited by law from driving his car.

18 Notices

Any notice given under this Agreement shall be deemed to have been duly given if despatched by either party hereto by registered post addressed to the other party as in the case of the Company's registered office for the time being and in the case of the Executive his last known address and such notice shall be deemed to have been given on the day on which in the ordinary course of post it would be delivered.

19 Prior agreements

This Agreement is in substitution for all previous contracts of employment express or implied between the Company or any Group Company and the Executive which shall be deemed to have been terminated by mutual consent as from the date on which the Employment commenced.

20 Post termination obligations

20.1 The Executive shall not during the period of one year after termination of the Employment (howsoever occasioned) solicit or endeavour to entice away from, or discourage from being employed by, the Company any salesman or any other employee in a support role to the sales staff who to his knowledge was an employee thereof at the date of such termination or whom to his knowledge it has at that date agreed to be engaged as an employee of the Company.

20.2 The Executive shall not for a period of [*specify period*] [months/years] after termination of the Employment (without the previous consent in writing of the Board and whether on his own account or for any other person, firm or company) solicit or endeavour to entice away from the Company any person, firm or company (i) who or which in the preceding [*specify period*] [months/years] shall have been a customer of or in the habit of dealing with the Company and (ii) with whom or which the Executive had contact during [the period of [*specify period*] [months/years] prior to the end of] the Employment

20.3 The Executive shall not for a period of [*specify period*] [months/years] after termination of the Employment (howsoever occasioned) [without the previous consent in writing of the Company] directly or indirectly do any business with or have any dealings with any person, firm or company who was a client customer supplier (agent or distributor) of the Company during the period of the Employment and with whom the Executive had contact during the period of [*specify number*] months prior to the end of the Employment provided that nothing contained in this sub-clause shall prohibit the Executive's activities which are not in direct or indirect competition with any business carried on by the Company at the date of the termination of this Agreement.

20.4 The Executive shall not for a period of [*specify period*] [months/years] after termination of the Employment (howsoever occasioned) (without the previous consent in writing of the Board) be engaged or interested (whether as principal, servant, agent, consultant or otherwise) in any trade or business which is situated within the Territory and any other territory where the Executive shall have served during the [*specify period*] years preceding the termination of the Employment and which is similar to or competing with any trade or business being carried on at the end of the Employment by the Company or any other Group Company with which the Executive shall have been directly connected during the preceding [*specify period*] [months/years].

20.5 The Exexecutive acknowledges:

(i) that each of the foregoing sub-clauses of this clause constitutes an entirely separate and independent restriction on him; and

(ii) whilst at the date of this Agreement the duration, extent and application of each of the restrictions are considered by the parties no greater than is necessary for the protection of the Company's interests and reasonable in all the circumstances it is acnkowledged that restrictions of such a nature may be invalid because of changing circumstances and accordingly if any of the restrictions shall be adjudged to be void or ineffective for whatever reason but would be adjudged to be valid and effective if part of the wording thereof were deleted or the periods thereof reduced or the area thereof reduced in some way shall apply with such modifications as may be necessary to make them valid and effective.

21 Disciplinary and grievance procedure

There are no fixed rules for the resolution of grievance or disciplinary problems. In the event of the Executive being dissatisfied with any decision taken against him, or have any grievance relating to the Employment he should apply in the first instance to the Managing Director who will either propose a solution or refer the matter to the Board of the Company for a final decision.

C—Research and Development Engineer

When drafting a service agreement for a research and development engineer, the first consideration will be to protect the employer's technical secrets. This agreement seeks to do so by not allowing the employee to take another job while working under it, and by expressly forbidding him to use or disclose secrets both during and after his employment. It deals expressly with the ownership of inventions.

This agreement is for a fixed term and the employer takes the opportunity to exclude the employee's statutory rights on the non-renewal of the agreement.

DATE:

PARTIES:

(1) [ ] [Limited] [plc] (registered number) having its registered office at [ ] ('the Company')

(2) [ ] of [ ] ('the Executive')

Operative Provisions

1 Definitions and interpretation

1.1 In this Agreement:

'The Board' means the Board of Directors of the Company and includes any committee of the Board duly convened by it.

'The Commencement Date' means the [ ] day of [ ] one thousand nine hundred and [ ].

'Group Company' means any company which for the time being is (i) a holding company (as defined in s 736 of the Companies Act 1985) of the Company, or (ii) a subsidiary (as defined by s 736 of the Companies Act 1985) of the Company.

'Confidential Information' means information relating to the business, products and affairs of the Company for the time being confidential to the Company or treated by the Company as such and trade secrets (including without limitation formula, processes, methods, inventions, technical data and know how) relating to the business of the Company.

'The Employment' means the Employment established by this Agreement.

'Intellectual Property' means (i) every invention discovery design or improvement, (ii) every work in which copyright may subsist, and (iii) moral rights as defined by s 77 and s 80 of the Copyright Design and Patent Act 1988.

'Termination Date' means the effective termination date of the Employment hereunder as defined by the Employment Protection (Consolidation) Act 1978.

1.2 The headings in this Agreement shall not affect its interpretation or construction.

1.3 Any reference in this Agreement to any statutory provision includes any statutory modification or re-enactment of it or the provision referred to.

2 Employment

The Company shall employ the Executive and the Executive agrees to serve the Company as a Research Engineer in the field of [*specify field of science or technology*] in accordance with the job description set out in Schedule I to this Agreement [*either attach detailed job description or set out in this agreement a full description of the duties the Executor will be required to undertake eg 'responsible for initiating supervising coordinating and conducting research and development intended to improve and supplement the manufacturing and finishing processes carried out by the Company and to apply them to other products and materials'*].

3 Period

3.1 The Executive's employment hereunder shall commence on the Commencement Date and shall (subject as hereinafter provided) continue for a fixed period of [*specify number*] [months/years] until the [ ] day of [ ] one thousand nine hundred and ninety [ ] and thereafter until terminated by either party giving to the other not less than [*specify number*] [weeks/months] notice expiring on or at any time after the said fixed term.

3.2 The Executive's previous employment with [*specify employer*] counts as part of the Executive's period of continuous employment with the Company.

4 Duties

The Executive shall well and faithfully serve the Company and use his utmost endeavours to promote the interest thereof further the Executive shall at all times comply with all the rules and regulations of the Company for the time being in force.

5 Devotion to duties

The Executive shall devote the whole of his time attention and abilities during normal business hours and at such other times as the Company or his duties may reasonably require to the business and affairs of the Company unless prevented by ill health from so doing and shall not during the term of this Agreement either on his own account or as the employer of others or otherwise be engaged or concerned in any business or engagement other than that of the Company or any Group Company except with the prior consent in writing of the Company but the Executive may nevertheless be or become a minority holder of any securities which are quoted on a recognised investment exchange.

6 Place of work

The Executive will initially work at the premises of the Company at [*specify place*] but the Executive shall if required to do so work in such place or places as the Company may reasonably require for the proper performance of his duties hereunder.

7 Hours of work

The Executive is required to work at such times and for such periods as the efficient and conscientious discharge of his duties hereunder requires. There are no fixed working hours for the Employment.

8 Remuneration

During the Employment the Executive shall receive as remuneration a salary at the rate of £[*specify amount*] per annum (or at such higher rate as the Company shall from time to time decide) to be paid by equal monthly instalments on the last day of each calendar month.

9 Car

9.1 The Company shall make available to the Executive for his use in performing his duties and shall replace from time to time as necessary a car of a type which it deems suitable and authorises the Executive to use it for his private purposes. The Company shall maintain, service, tax and comprehensively insure the car as appropriate and shall arrange for the supply of the Executive of petrol for his use in it. The Executive shall ensure that he has at all times a current valid licence to drive private motor cars.

9.2 Immediately upon the termination of the Employment howsoever arising the Executive shall return the car and its keys to the Company at its principal place of business (or any other place nominated by the Company for its return).

10 Expenses

In addition to his salary hereunder the Executive shall be reimbursed the amount of all reasonable travelling, hotel, entertainment and other expenses properly and necessarily incurred and defrayed by him in the discharge of his duties hereunder. The Executive shall produce to the Company at its request all supporting vouchers and documents in respect of such expenses.

11 Pension and medical insurance expenses

During the Employment the Executive shall be entitled:

(*a*) to become and remain a member of the [*specify nameof scheme*] Pension Scheme full details of which shall be provided to the Executive;

(*b*) at the Company's expense become a full member of the Company's health scheme (or such other plan or scheme as the Board may decide is preferable);

(*c*) participate in the Company's total disability/long term sickness benefit scheme subject always to the rules of the scheme.

12 Holidays

The Executive shall be entitled (in addition to public holidays) to [*specify number of days/weeks*] [weeks/months] holiday in each calender year at such times as shall be convenient to the Company and such additional holidays as the Board shall approve.

13 Sickness or injury

13.1 The Executive is entitled to be paid in full during any period of absence from work due to sickness or injury, for a total of up to [*specify number of weeks*] in any period of up to 12 months however to the provisions of clause 18 and also subject to the right of the Company to deduct from the remuneration of the Executive the amount of income benefit which he is entitled to claim in consequence of sickness or accident under any scheme for the time being in force of which by virtue of his employment by the Company he is a non-contributory member.

13.2 In the event that the Executive is incapable of performing his duties by reason of injury sustained wholly or partially as a result of actionable negligence nuisance or breach of any statutory duty on the part of any third party all payments made to the Executive by the Company by way of remuneration shall to the extent that compensation is recoverable from that third party constitute loans by the Company to the Executive (notwithstanding that as an interim measure income tax has been deducted from payments as if they were emoluments of employment) and shall be repaid when and to the extent that the Executive recovers compensation for loss of earnings from that third party by action or otherwise.

14 Confidentiality

The Executive shall not either during the Employment otherwise than in the proper course of his duties or thereafter without the consent in writing of the Board being first obtained divulge to any person firm or company and shall during the continuance of this Agreement use his best endeavours to prevent the publication or disclosure of any Confidential Information of the Company and its subsidiaries or any of their secrets dealings or transactions which have come or may come to his knowledge during the Employment or previously or otherwise.

15 Intellectual property

15.1 The Executive shall forthwith communicate to the Company in confidence all Intellectual Property which the Executive may make or originate either solely or jointly with another or others during the term of this Agreement.

15.2 In the case of such Intellectual Property as is made or originated hereunder wholly or substantially in the course of his normal duties or in the course of duties specifically assigned to him or which is relative to the affairs of the Company or any Group Company the following sub-clauses of this Clause shall apply.

15.3 Such Intellectual Property (or in the case of Intellectual Property made or originated by the Executive jointly with another or others to the full extent of the Executive's interest therein so far as the law allows) shall be and become the exclusive property of the Company and shall not be disclosed to any other person or company without the consent of the Company being previously obtained which if given may be subject to conditions.

15.4 The provisions of sub-clause *15.3* of this clause shall not entitle the Executive to any compensation beyond the salary hereinafter mentioned except that in the case of any invention on which a British Patent has been granted or assigned to the Company and the Company has derived outstanding benefit from such patent, the Executive may be entitled by virtue of s 40 of the Patents Act 1977 to claim additional compensation.

15.5 The Executive shall if and when required by the Company and at the expense of the Company do and/or combine with others in doing all acts and sign and execute all applications and other documents (including Powers of Attorney in favour of nominees of the Company) necessary or incidental to obtaining maintaining or extending patent or other forms of protection for such Intellectual Property in the United Kingdom or elsewhere or for transferring to or vesting in the Company or its nominees the Executive's entire right title and interest to and in such Intellectual Property or to and in any application, patent or other form of protection or copyright as the case may be including the right to file applications in the name of the Company or its nominees for patent or other forms of protection or for registration of copyright in any country claiming priority from the date of filing of any appli cation or other date from which priority may run in any other country.

15.6 If the Company does not wish to obtain patent or any other form of protection for such Intellectual Property in any country then the Company shall not unreasonably withhold its consent to the Executive so doing or participating in so doing provided always that in such case the Executive shall if the Company so requests grant to the Company or any Group Company and to take all reasonable steps to cause others to grant a free non-exclusive licence for all purposes under all patents or other forms of protection obtained in respect thereof together with the right to grant non-exclusive sub-licences thereunder on such terms as the Company may think fit.

15.7 Upon being indemnified by the Company against all costs and expenses involved the Executive or, if applicable, any person to whom the Executive's Moral Rights have passed (and the Executive hereby covenants that upon such rights passing he will procure the necessary consent from any such person) will if requested by the Company take such action as may be necessary to assent or enforce such Moral Rights. Further,

15.8 the Executive will not assert or seek to enforce Moral Rights (a) during the continuation of the Employment in connection with any work in which the Executive has Moral Rights; or (b) at any time after the determination in connection with any Work in which the Executive has Moral Rights acquired in the course of the Employment; against the Company, or anyone acting with the Company's prior or retroactive authority, without the prior written consent of the Company.

15.9 The provisions of this Clause shall remain in full force and effect notwithstanding that after the Executive has made or originated any such Intellectual Property his employment hereunder may have ceased or been determined for any reason whatsoever with the intention that the same shall bind the heirs of and or assigns of the Executive.

16 Delivery of documents

Upon the termination of the Employment the Executive shall deliver up to the Company or its authorised representative all plans, statistics, documents, records, papers or property of whatsoever nature which may be in his possession or control and relate in any way to the business or affairs of the Company and its subsidiaries and no copies of documents shall be retained by him.

17 Summary termination

In any of the following cases the Company may terminate the Executive's Employment by written notice taking effect on the date of its service in which case the Executive shall not be entitled to any further payment from the Company accept such sums as shall then have accrued due:

(*a*) if the Executive shall be guilty of gross dereliction of duty or non-observance of any of the provisions of this Agreement;

(*b*) if the Executive shall be guilty of a criminal offence and sentence (except in a case not involving dishonesty) to a term of imprisonment;

(*c*) if the Executive be adjudged bankrupt.

18 Short notice

If the Executive shall at any time become or be unable properly to perform his duties hereunder by reason of ill health accident or otherwise for a period or periods aggregating at least 180 days in any period of 12 consecutive calendar months the Company may by not less than three months notice in writing determine this Agreement.

19 Prior rights

The termination of the Employment shall be without prejudice to any right that the Company may have in respect of any breach of the Executive of any of the provisions of this Agreement which may have occurred prior to such determination.

20 Notices

Any notice given under this Agreement shall be deemed to have been duly given if despatched by either party hereto by registered post addressed to the other party as in the case of the Company its registered office for the time being and in the case that the Executive his last known address and such notice shall be deemed to have been given on the day on which in the ordinary course of post it would be delivered.

21 Prior agreements

This Agreement is in substitution for all previous contracts of employment express or implied between the Company or any Group Company and the Executive which shall be deemed to have been terminated by mutual consent as from the date on which the Employment commenced.

22 Post termination obligations

22.1 The Executive shall not during the period of two years after termination of the Employment (howsoever occasioned) solicit or endeavour to entice away from, or discourage from being employed by, the Company any employee reporting to the Executive or engaged on research work of any kind with which the Executive was engaged during his employment with the Company.

22.2 The Executive shall not for a period of [*specify period*] [months/years] after termination of the Employment (howsoever occasioned) without the previous consent in writing of the Company be engaged or interested (whether as principal, servant, agent, consultant or otherwise) in any trade or business and similar to or competing with any trade or business being carried on at the end of the Employment by the Company or any other Group Company with which the Executive shall have been directly connected during the preceding [*specify period*] [months/years] prior to the termination of the Employment.

22.3 The Executive acknowledges

(i) that each of the foregoing sub-clauses of this clause constitutes an entirely separate and independent restriction on him; and

(ii) whilst at the date of this Agreement the duration, extent and application of each of the restrictions are considered by the parties no greater than is necessary for the protection of the Company's interests and reasonable in all the circumstances it is acknowledged that restrictions of such a nature may be invalid because of changing circumstances and accordingly if any of the restrictions shall be adjudged to be void or ineffective for whatever reason but would be adjudged to be valid and effective if part of the wording thereof were deleted or the periods thereof reduced they shall apply with such modifications as may be necessary to make them valid and effective.

23 Disciplinary and grievance procedure

There are no fixed rules for the resolution of grievance or disciplinary problems. In the event of the Executive being dissatisfied with any decision taken against him, or have any grievance relating to the Employment, he should apply in the first instance, to the Managing Director who will either propose a solution or refer the matter to the Board of the Company for a final decision.

24 Reconstruction or amalgamation

If before the termination of this Agreement the Employment shall be determined by reason of the liquidation of the Company for the purpose of reconstruction or amalgamation and the Executive shall be offered employment with any concern or undertaking resulting from such reconstruction or amalgamation on terms and conditions no less favourable than the terms of this Agreement then the Executive shall have no claim against the Company in respect of the determination of the Employment.

25 Fixed term

Pursuant to s 142(1) and (2) of the Employment Protection (Consolidation) Act 1978 the Executive hereby agrees that no rights shall arise under ss 54 and 81 respectively of that Act in relation to this Agreement if the term of the Executive's Employment under it expires without being renewed.

D—Assistant Solicitor

This is an agreement for the employment of a solicitor by a partnership in private practice in the role of a salaried partner. It incorporates a special provision to ensure that the employment continues notwithstanding any change in the constitution of the employer firm. The agreement is effectively made conditional on the employee remaining entitled to practise as a solicitor.

On the employment coming to an end, three restrictions are imposed. First, the employee is not to solicit the employees of the firm; secondly, the employee is not to canvass the former clients of the firm; finally the employee is not to accept employment or act for former clients of the firm. It may be appropriate to add a provision to bar the employee from practicing in a certain area after leaving the employment of the firm. The latter restriction will only sometimes be appropriate and enforceable.

There is no provision for a pension as most solicitors; particularly those who are appointed salaried partners, will wish to make provision for their own pension.

DATE:

PARTIES:

(1) The Partners in the firm of [ ] having its office at [ ] acting by [ ] their agent for this purpose and

(2) [ ] of [ ] ('the Appointee').

Operative Provisions

1 Definitions and interpretation

1.1 In this Agreement:

'The Firm' shall mean the Firm of [*specify name of Firm*] and its successors for the time being.

'The Partners' shall mean the persons (exclusive for any person who is a salaried partner as defined below) who for the time being are and continue as Partners in the Firm under the terms of this Agreement.

'The Commencement Date' means the [ ] day of [ ] one thousand nine hundred and ninety [ ].

'Salaried Partner' shall mean any person who is held out as a Partner in the Firm but is in fact in the employment of the Partners (whether or not he is remunerated by a fixed salary) and who is entitled to be indemnified by the Partners against liabilities of the Firm other than liabilities arising from any act or default or negligence on his part in respect of which as an employee of the Firm he is under liability to the Partners.

'This Agreement' shall mean this document where the same shall be modified by agreement with the Partners then the same as so modified.

'The Senior Partner' shall mean the person holding at any time such position in the Firm.

'The Managing Partner' shall mean the person holding at any time such position in the Firm.

1.2 The heading in this Agreement shall not affect its interpretation or construction.

1.3 Throughout this Agreement where the context so requires or permits words which import only the masculine gender shall include the feminine gender and words which import only the singular number shall include the plural number and vice versa.

2 Employment

The Firm shall employ the Appointee and the Appointee agrees to act as a Salaried Partner in the Firm.

3 Period

3.1 The Appointee's employment hereunder shall commence on the Commencement Date and shall (subject to as hereinafter provided) continue until terminated by either party giving to the other not less than [*specify number*] calendar months notice.

3.2 The Appointee's previous employment with the Firm counts as part of the Appointee's continuous period of employment which began on [ ].

4 Duties

The Appointee shall:

(i) devote his whole professional time and attention during the customary hours of business exclusively to the Firm's practice;

(ii) faithfully and diligently perform those duties and exercise such powers consistent with them which are from time to time assigned to or vested in him save that he will have no right to participate in the management of the Firm except in such consultative role as may from time to time been granted by the Firm;

(iii) obey all lawful and reasonable directions of the Partners;

(iv) use his best endeavours to promote and expand the Firm's practice;

(v) not (without the Firm's prior written consent) be directly or indirectly engaged or interested in any capacity in any other business trade or occupation whatsoever and not hold offices as a director of any company or any public company or honorary office except with the consent of the Senior Partner;

(vi) not hold shares in companies which are major clients of the Firm and which are listed companies or companies where the Firm has access to price sensitive information concerning clients affairs.

5 Holding out

From the Commencement Date the Appointee will be shown as a Partner in the Firm's letterhead other business stationery, brochures and elsewhere where the Firm's Partners are listed and he will be accorded such treatment in relation to the Firm's staff, clientele, business associates and third parties generally as is appropriate to a Salaried Partner.

6 Indemnity

The Firm agrees to indemnify the Appointee from all liability for the losses debts and other obligations of the Firm during the continuance of this Agreement except liability arising from any wilful or malicious or negligent act or default of the Appointee for which as an employee he would be liable to the Firm.

7 Confidential information

The Appointee shall keep secret and shall not either during his employment or at any time after the termination of his employment without the consent in writing of the Firm being first obtained make use of or disclose for any reason whatsoever to any other person firm or corporation any private confidential or other information of any kind whatsoever obtained by the Appointee by the virtue of his employment with the Firm insofar as such information relates to the Firm or the Firm's clients its business matters trade secrets commercial private affairs clients or any other persons dealing with the Firm or the Firm's clients.

8 Delivery of documents

Upon the termination of the Appointee's employment he shall deliver up to the Firm or its authorised representative all plans statistics documents records papers or property of whatsoever nature which may be in his possession or control and relate in any way to the business or affairs of the Firm and its clients and no copies of documents shall be retained by him.

9 Remuneration

(i) During the employment the Appointee shall receive as remuneration a salary at the rate of £[*specify amount*] per annum (or at such higher rate as the Firm may from time to time decide) to be paid monthly by credit transfer to the Appointee's Bank account in arrears on the last day of each calendar month.

(ii) The Appointee obtains no right to share in the profits of the Firm nor rights to any of the assets of the Firm.

10 Professional fees

The Firm shall pay (a) the cost of obtaining the Appointee's practising certificate including any contribution due to the Law Society's compensation fund and any premium for compulsory professional indemnity insurance and (b) the Appointee's subscription to the Law Society.

11 Pension (and health insurance)

(*a*) There is no compulsory pension scheme applicable to the employment but the Appointee is expected to make provision for his pension by securing s 226 policies.

(*b*) The Appointee is entitled to be a non-contributory member of the [*specify name of private health cover scheme operated by the Firm*] full details of which will be supplied on request.

12 Holidays

The Appointee is entitled to the following paid holiday:

(i) Eight statutory holidays which are New Year's Day, Good Friday, Easter Monday, May Day, Spring Bank Holiday, Late Summer Bank Holiday, Christmas Day and Boxing Day.

(ii) [*specify number*] working days holiday in each holiday year which should be taken at times to be agreed with the Managing Director.

(iii) The holiday year is the calendar year from 1 January to 31 December and the Appointee should take holidays during this period. The Appointee will not be permitted to carry over unused holiday entitlement into a following holiday year except with the consent of the Managing Partner. Any holiday entitlement unutilised where permission has not been given for it to be carried forward will be forfeited.

(iv) For the holiday year during which the Appointee's employment terminates the Appointee is entitled to [*specify number*] working days holiday for each calendar month completed in the employment of the Firm for that year.

13 Incapacity

13.1 If the Appointee shall be prevented by illness (including mental disorder) accident or other incapacity from properly performing his duties hereunder he shall report or cause to be reported this fact forthwith to the Managing Partner and if the Appointee is so prevented for seven or more consecutive days he should provide a medical practitioner's statement on the eighth day and weekly thereafter. Immediately following his return to work after a period of absence the Appointee shall complete a self-certification form detailing the reason for his absence.

13.2 If the Appointee shall be absent from his duties hereunder due to illness accident or other incapacity duly certified in accordance with the provisions of sub-clause *13.1* hereof he shall be paid his full remuneration hereunder for up to [*specify number*] months absence in any period of 12 months and thereafter such remuneration if any as the Managing Partner shall in his discretion from time to time allow provided that there shall be deducted from or set off against such remuneration any Statutory Sick Pay to which the Appointee is entitled under the provisions of the Social Security and Housing Benefits Act 1982 and Social Security Sickness Benefit or other benefits recoverable by the Appointee (whether or not recovered).

13.3 For Statutory Sick Pay purposes the Appointee's qualifying days shall be his normal working days.

14 Termination of employment

The employment of the Appointee shall automatically terminate:

(i) on the Appointee reaching his 65th birthday;

(ii) if the Appointee ceases for any reason to be qualified or entitled to practice as a solicitor and to require the grant of a practising certificate as of right;

(iii) if the Appointee shall be guilty of gross dereliction of duty or non observance of the provisions of this Agreement;

(iv) if the Appointee shall be adjudged bankrupt.

15 Expenses

In addition to his salary hereunder the Appointee shall be reimbursed the amount of all reasonable travelling hotel entertainment and other expenses properly and necessarily incurred and defrayed by him in the discharge of his duties hereunder. The Appointee shall produce to the Firm at its request all supporting vouchers and documents in respect of such expenses.

16 Post termination obligations

16.1 The Appointee shall not for a period of two years after the termination of his Employment (howsoever occasioned) solicit or endeavour to entice away from, or discourage from being employed by the Firm any person who to his knowledge was employed by the Firm at the date of the termination of the Employment

16.2 The Appointee shall not for a period of two years after termination of the Employment (howsoever occasioned) (without the previous consent in writing of the Firm and whether on his own account or for any other person, firm or company) solicit or endeavour to entice away from the Firm any person, firm or company (i) who or which in the preceding five years shall have been a client of or in the habit of dealing with the Firm and (ii) with whom or which the Appointee had contact during the said period for the purposes of this provision client shall mean not only clients of the firm as constituted at the time when the Appointee ceased to be employed but also such firm or any constituent part thereof at any time previously constituted.

16.3 The Appointee shall not for a period of two years after the termination of the Employment howsoever occasioned (without the previous consent in writing of the Firm):

(i) accept employment in any capacity with any business concern which is a client of the Firm

(ii) accept instructions to act or act for any business concern person partnership firm company or other body who (*a*) shall have been a client of the Firm during the period of [*specify number*] years immediately preceding the termination of the Appointee's employment hereunder and (*b*) with whom the Appointee had contact during that period.

16.4 The Appointee acknowledges:

(i) that each of the foregoing sub-clauses of this clause constitutes an entirely separate and independent restriction on him; and

(ii) whilst at the date of this Agreement the duration extent and application of each of the restrictions are considered by the parties no greater than is necessary for the protection of the Firm's interest and reasonable in all the circumstances it is acknowledged that restrictions of such a nature may be invalid because of changing circumstances and accordingly if any of the restrictions shall be adjudged to be void or ineffective for whatever reason but would be adjudged to be valid and effective but part of the wording thereof were deleted or the periods thereof reduced or the area thereof reduced in scope they shall apply with such modifications as may be necessary to make them valid and effective.

17 Resignation of appointments

Upon termination of the Employment for whatever reason the Appointee shall at the request of the Firm forthwith in writing resign his position as a director of any company which is a client of the Firm and when that office is held by virtue of his employment as a Salaried Partner and shall sign all the necessary documents to transfer any shares held in his name as a nominee on behalf of any client of the Firm. Should the Appointee fail to comply with such requests the Firm is irrevocably authorised to appoint someone on his behalf to sign and do all documents and things necessary or requisite to give effect thereto.

18 Change in the Firm

The parties agree that a change in the Firm by reason of:

(i) any amalgamation of the Firm with another; or

(ii) the incorporation within the Firm of another practice; or

(iii) any other substantial change in the identity or composition of the Firm; shall not determine this Agreement and the Partners immediately before any change shall procure that the existence and terms of this Agreement are made known and assented to by all the Partners immediately after any change.

19 Prior agreements

This Agreement is in substitution for all previous contracts of employment between the Appointee and the Firm which shall be deemed to have been terminated by mutual consent as from the Commencement Date.

20 Disciplinary and grievance procedure

There are no fixed rules for the resolution of grievance or disciplinary problems. In the event of the Appointee being dissatisfied with any decision against him or have any grievance relating to his employment he should apply in the first instance to the Managing Partner who will either propose a solution or refer the matter to the Senior Partner for a final decision.

21 Notices

Any notice given under the provisions of this Agreement shall be duly served on the Firm if handed to any Partner in the Firm or left or sent addressed to the Firm by ordinary letter post to the Firm's office at [*specify address*] or on the Appointee if handed to him or left at or sent by ordinary letter post to his last known address and it shall be assumed that any notice sent by post shall be delivered on the day on which the letter would have been delivered in the ordinary course of post.

E—Overseas Expatriate Employment Agreement

Multi-national corporations will often want to send senior executives to carry out specific management functions for subsidiary companies overseas. The executive will be concerned that he will lose certain rights under his United Kingdom employment, and may find it difficult at the end of the term of the assignment to return to suitable employment in the United Kingdom within the company. Accordingly, great care has to be taken in the preparation of such agreements so that the executive is reassured as to the terms and conditions which will apply to the overseas appointment, and as to what will occur on his return. The vulnerability of the executive overseas can be alleviated by making provision for re-engagement or reinstatement on the executive's return and by incorporating a liquidated damages clause if suitable employment is not available when the executive is due to return to the United Kingdom.

The following agreement assumes that the employer is a local subsidiary company of a United Kingdom based parent company, the parent company currently being the employer of the executive. The parent company accordingly joins in the agreement as guarantor to give the executive greater security and reassurance as to the future.

DATE:

PARTIES:

(1) [ ] [Limited] [plc] a company [registered in] [incorporated under the laws of] (under registered number) having its [registered] [principal] office at [ ] ('the Company').

(2) [ ] [Limited] [plc] a company registered in Eng-

land (under registered number) having its registered office at [ ] ('the Parent Company').

(3) [ ] of [ ] ('the Executive').

Operative provisions

1 Definitions and interpretation

1.1 In this Agreement:

'Associated Company' means any company which for the time being is:

(i) a holding company (as defined in s 736 of the Companies Act 1985) of the Company; or

(ii) a subsidiary (as defined in s 736 of the Companies Act 1985) of any such holding company.

'The Board' means the Board of directors of the Company and includes any committee of the Board duly appointed by it.

'Confidential Information' means information relating to the business, products and affairs of the Company or the Parent Company (including without limitation marketing information) for the time being confidential to the Company and trade secrets (including without limitation formulae, processes, methods, inventions, technical data and know-how) relating to the business of the Company and the Parent Company.

'The Commencement Date' means [*specify the date of the commencement of the assignment*].

'The Employment' means the employment established by this Agreement.

'The Territory' means [*specify the country or region in which the Executive is to work*].

1.2 The headings in this Agreement are for convenience only and shall not affect its interpretation or construction.

1.3 Any reference in this Agreement to any act or delegated legislation includes any statutory modification or re-enactment of it or the provision referred to.

2 Appointment

The Company shall employ the Executive and the Executive agrees to act as [*specify the job title*] of the Company [to carry out the duties set out in the job description as specified in [ ] Schedule in connection with its operations in the Territory.

3 Duration

The Executive's employment hereunder shall commence on the Commencement Date and shall (subject as hereinafter provided) continue until the [ ] day of [ ] One thousand nine hundred and ninety[ ].

4 Duties

The Executive shall:

(i) Well and faithfully serve the Company and use his utmost endeavours to promote the interests thereof and to perform such duties and exercise such powers in relation to the conduct and management of the affairs of the Company and its subsidiaries (if any) that may from time to time be assigned to or vested in him by or at the direction of the Board and shall give to the Board such information concerning the affairs of the Company and its subsidiaries (if any) as the Board shall require and at all time shall conform to the reasonable directions of the Board.

(ii) At all times comply with the rules and regulations of the Company for the time being in force.

(iii) At all times comply with local laws and regulations and show respect for the local customs of the Territory.

(iv) On arrival in the Territory register his residence with his National Consulate and follow the Consul's advice in all matters related to his personal welfare and safety.

5 Devotion to duties

The Executive shall devote the whole of his time, attention and abilities during normal business hours and at such other times as the Company or his duties may reasonably require to the business and affairs of the Company and any Associated Company unless prevented by ill health from so doing and shall not during the term of this Agreement either on his own account or as the employee of others or otherwise be engaged or concerned in any business or engagement other than that of the Company or any Associated Company except with the prior consent in writing of the Company but the Executive may nevertheless become a minority holder of any securities which are quoted on a recognised investment exchange.

6 Remuneration

6.1 During the term of this Agreement the Executive shall receive a salary at the rate of [*specify amount*] pounds sterling a year to be paid by equal monthly payments on the last day of every month at the Company's local office in the Territory in local currency (the amount of each payment to be calculated at the rate of exchange ruling seven days before payment).

6.2 The Executive may at any time on giving one month's written notice to the Company and until further notice to have up to one half of his salary credited at his expense to any bank account in his name in any part of the world and in any currency (the payment being effected by the Company's bank and remitting at the rate of exchange then ruling) so long as it is lawful for the Company to make such payments.

7 Pension

The Executive shall be [or remain] a member of the [*specify scheme*] pension scheme while employed by the Company and shall make the contributions required by and be entitled to the benefits defined by the rules of that scheme.

8 Place of work

The Executive shall work at and from the Company's office in [*specify place*] and shall travel to such places (whether inside or outside the Territory) and in manner and on such occasion as the Company may from time to time direct.

9 Travel

9.1 The Company shall at its expense be responsible for arranging transportation for the Executive [and his immediate family] to the Territory at the commencement of the Employment and from the Territory promptly at the end of the Employment.

9.2 If there is any delay in such transport at the end of the Employment the Company shall continue to pay the Employee's salary until he [has] [and his immediate family have] been repatriated to the United Kingdom.

9.3 All air travel will be [*specify class*] class. The Executive [and his immediate family] shall [each] be entitled to an excess baggage allowance of [*specify number*] kilos in addition to the standard baggage allowance. This excess baggage allowance will apply only on the initial outward journey and the final return journey to the United Kingdom.

10 Accommodation

The Company shall provide the Executive with fully furnished and equipped air conditioned housing accommodation deemed suitable by the Company rent free in respect of which the Company will pay all local rates and taxes and the cost of fuel, lighting, water, drainage, repairs, decorations, maintenance, cleaning and telephone rental.

11 Car

The Company shall provide a car deemed suitable by the Company for the Executive's use both in the course of his duties and for private purposes in respect of which the Company will pay for all local licence duties and taxation, comprehensive insurance, repairs, maintenance, servicing and fuel.

12 Confidentiality

The Executive shall not either during the Employment (otherwise than in the performance of his duties hereunder) or thereafter without the consent in writing of the Board being first obtained divulge to any person, firm or company and shall during the continuance of this Agreement use his best endeavours to prevent the publication or disclosure of any Confidential Information concerning the business accounts, affairs or finances of the Company and its subsidiaries or any of their secrets, dealings or transactions which have or may come to his knowledge during the Employment or previously or otherwise.

13 Working hours

The Executive shall work for such hours and on such days as the local office in which the Executive is working normally works and such additional hours as are necessary to satisfactorily carry out the duties required by this Agreement.

14 Holidays

14.1 In every calendar year the Executive shall be entitled to three weeks paid holiday taken in the Territory.

14.2 In addition after every continuous period of [*specify period*] resident in the Territory during the term of the Employment or any extension of it the Executive shall be entitled to six weeks paid leave in the United Kingdom in respect of which the Company will also pay for [*specify class*] return air travel for the Executive [and his immediate family].

15 Medical examination

15.1 The Executive shall undergo periodic medical examinations by a doctor appointed by the Company and accept inoculations against endemic diseases as recommended by such doctor unless they are effected before his arrival in the Territory.

15.2 The Executive [and his immediate family] shall follow all advice from the doctor appointed by the Company as to reasonable medical and hygienic precautions to maintain fitness and good health.

16 Sickness

16.1 In the event of sickness rendering the Executive incapable of performing his duties he shall immediately inform the Company and shall within [*specify number of days*] of being absent send to the Company a certificate of disability signed by a doctor and during his continued absence the Executive shall send a further certificate each week.

16.2 The Executive shall be entitled to his full salary and other benefits notwithstanding his inability to perform his duties by reason of illness or accident for a total period of [*specify number*] [weeks/months].

16.3 If the Executive [or any member of his immediate family] is in need of medical or surgical attention which cannot be satisfactorily given in the Territory the Company shall promptly repatriate the Executive [or the member of family concerned and if so requested another member of the family to accompany that person to the United Kingdom].

17 Summary termination

17.1 If the Executive shall be guilty of any gross misconduct or any breach or non-observance of any of the provisions of this Agreement or shall neglect or fail (otherwise than by reason of accident or ill health) or shall refuse to carry out the duties required of him hereunder or shall commit any act of bankruptcy or shall take advantage of any statute for the time being in force offering relief for insolvent debtors then and immediately thereupon it shall be lawful for the Company by notice in writing to the Executive summarily to determine the Employment.

17.2 If the Executive shall at any time become or be unable properly to perform his duties hereunder by reason of ill health, accident or otherwise for a period or periods aggregating at least 180 days in any period of 12 consecutive calendar months the

Company may by not less than three months' notice in writing determine the Employment.

18 Notice

18.1 The Company shall have the right to terminate the Employment under the terms of this Agreement before the expiry of the term stated in clause 2 on giving to the Executive three months written notice and shall repatriate the Executive to the United Kingdom.

18.2 In such circumstances the Company or an Associated Company shall offer to the Executive alternative employment of equivalent status and comparable remuneration and benefits.

18.3 In the event that the Company or any Associated Company is unable to offer to the Executive such alternative employment as specified in clause 18(*b*) and the Executive's employment is terminated otherwise than in accordance with clause 17 the Company shall compensate the Executive by paying to him as liquidated damages in full settlement of any claims which he has against the Company by reason of the termination of the Employment a sum equal to 12 months base salary at the rate to which the Executive was entitled immediately prior to that termination.

19 Guarantee

The Parent Company undertakes to the Executive that the Company will at all times observe, perform and comply with its obligations as employer under and by virtue of this Agreement and agrees to indemnify the Executive against all loss, damage, costs and expenses suffered or arising as a result of any failure by the Company so to observe, perform or comply with its obligations with the intent that this undertaking shall be performed and may be enforced in England.

20 Notices

Any notice given under the provisions of this Agreement shall be duly served:

(i) On the Executive having handed it to him personally or left it or sent it by ordinary post to his last known address in the Territory or if he is known to be in the United Kingdom his last known address in the United Kingdom.

(ii) On the Company if left or sent by ordinary letter post to its registered office.

21 Jurisdiction

The parties to this Agreement shall submit to the exclusive jurisdiction of the English courts.

F—Preparation of a Service Agreement

1 Freedom of contract

Is the Executive free to take up employment without restriction?

2 Continuity of employment

Is the employment a continuation of current employment?

3 Standard terms

Are the Company's standard procedures, agreements and work rules to be incorporated or excluded?

4 Hours of work

Are there to be fixed hours of work?

5 Term of employment

Is the employment to be:
(a) for a fixed term
(b) terminable by notice
(c) a rolling term?

6 Consequences of termination

Is the Company and the Executive aware of the consequences of such provisions?

7 Companies Act

Does the company have the power under its memorandum and articles of association to enter into the service agreement? If the employment is to be a fixed term is the term contemplated permissible under the Companies Act—Yellow Book?

8 Duties

What is the Executive employed to do? Is there a job description? Any special duties? Is the Executive's authority to be limited?

9 Flexibility

Does the Company wish to reserve the right to require the Executive to work with other companies and to relocate if necessary?

10 Full-time employment

Is the Executive to devote the whole of his time to the Company's business?

11 Pay

What is the Executive to be paid:
(a) base salary
(b) directors fees
(c) bonus arrangements
(d) commission?

How and when do these benefits accrue to the Executive?

12 Pay review

When are the benefits reviewed? Is there to be a commitment to upward review of any of the benefits?

13 Pension

What pension arrangements are to be made for the Executive?

14 Benefits

What other benefits are the Executives to receive:
(a) share options
(b) medical expenses
(c) life assurance
(d) long term disability insurance
(e) accommodation
(f) club subscriptions
(g) professional subscriptions
(h) telephone/mobile telephone rental?

15 Car

Is the Executive to be given the use of a car? Are all expenses to be paid or only those relating to business use? Does the Company reserve the right to determine the type of car provided or is he subject to a company car policy? When is the car changed? Are there any restrictions on the use of the car eg no overseas driving?

16 Inventions

Is the Executive likely to invent, improve or create new processes? If so review the job description and incorporate a clause to ensure Company will retain rights insofar as it can of such works.

17 Holiday

How much holiday is the Executive to be given? Who authorises the taking of holidays? Is it to be linked to a holiday year and can holiday be carried forward? How does the holiday accrue?

18 Sickness

How long is the Executive to be paid if away from work due to illness? What reporting/certification requirements will the Executive be required to comply with? Is there to be a provision for the recovery of such pay when paid as a result of injury caused by accident?

19 Summary termination

In what circumstances is the employment to be terminated summarily:

(a) gross neglect
(b) non-observance of terms of engagement
(c) criminal offence
(d) bringing the Company into disrepute
(e) disqualification of Executive as director
(f) mental/physical incapacity
(g) loss of an important qualification?

20 Short notice

Are there any other circumstances where the fixed term or period of notice can be abridged eg sickness?

21 Amalgamation

Is it intended to ensure Executive's employment will be preserved despite amalgamation, liquidation or reconstruction of the Company?

22 Excluded rights

Where the Executive's employment is for a fixed term of one year or more is it intended to exclude statutory rights on termination of agreement by effluxion of time?

23 Confidentiality

What information will the Executive have access to? What protection does the Company need to secure its confidential information?

24 Restrictions

What additional restrictions does the Company need to incorporate to protect its business on the termination of the Executive's employment:

(a) non solicitation of employees
(b) non solicitation of customers
(c) non competition
(d) non dealing?

25 Survival of restrictions

If restrictions are required should the employer incorporate a provision to ensure their survival on summary termination without notice?

26 Directors fees

Is it intended for the director to receive directors fees in addition to remuneration?

27 Resignation as director

Should the Executive be required to resign his directorship immediately on termination of his employment?

28 Statutory particulars

Have all the particulars required by the Employment Protection (Consolidation) Act 1978 been covered?

29 Expenses

What expenses is the Executive entitled to recover? What supporting information is required to justify the claims?

30 Notices

Is it necessary to incorporate provisions as to service of notices?

G—Preparation of Restraint of Trade Clauses

1 The company's business

What is the general nature of the business of the Company which wishes to take the benefit of the restrictive covenants.

2 Group company

Check if the restrictive covenants are to cover not only the Company's business but also of the group of companies of which it is a subsidiary or associated company ('the Group').

3 Group business

If Group protection is required what is the nature of the roup's business.

4 Company/Group area of business

Identify precisely the geographical scope of the Company/Group business and how that business may develop in the future.

5 The Job

Clarify what the Executive does, his job title, his job description his pay and conditions.

6 Executive status

Clarify the status or seniority of the Executive and whether he will become the custodian of the Company's goodwill with its customers.

7 Objectives

Discuss in detail with the Company what they do not want the executive to do when he leaves and whether it is primarily concerned with protecting good will in which case a non-dealing or confidential information provision should be sufficient.

8 The Executive's access to information

Discuss with the Company the nature of the information that the Executive has access to within the business.

9 Nature of information

What sort of sales information will the Executive be given access to and is it treated as confidential by the Company?

10 Location

Discover where the Executive will work.

11 Sales area

Is the work carried out by the Executive related to a specific area?

12 Geographical perspective

Check the area on a map to establish if there are any problems that arise from the sales area or area specified by the Company and the area where the Executive is to be excluded from working.

13 How does the Company help the Executive

Enquire what steps the Company takes to ensure that the Executive builds up a good relationship with the Company's customers.

14 Replacement time

Clarify how long the Company anticipates it will take to re-establish its business contacts when the Executive has left.

15 Contact frequency

Determine how frequent the customer contact is (weekly/-monthly/quarterly).

16 Training

What training is the Executive to be given and how quickly can another employee be trained to replace the Executive should he leave.

17 Non solicitation of employees

Is it intended to protect other staff from poaching by the Executive on him leaving. Discover if the employees work in teams and whether there are key groups of employees who need to be protected.

18 Added protection

Is the Company prepared to pay for the protection by paying all or a proportion of salary during the restraint period after the termination of employment?

19 Return of company property

Check whether it is necessary to incorporate a clause for the return of Company documents and property and find out what sort of documents the Executive is likely to have at home or to take away with him that might be valuable.

20 Post termination payments

Check whether commission or other payments will be due to the Executive after the date of termination of the employment during the period of restraint.

21 Effect of restraint

Clarify what the effect of the restraint of trade provisions will be on the Executive if they are effective. Will they prevent him gaining employment elsewhere or will he be able to secure alternative employment without contravening the provisions?

Index